P9-BIY-746

Otto Rank [1884 – 1939]

Beyond Psychology

BY OTTO RANK

DOVER PUBLICATIONS, INC.
NEW YORK

Published in Canada by General Publishing Company, Ltd., 30 Lesmill Road, Don Mills, Toronto, Ontario.
Published in the United Kingdom by Constable and Company, Ltd.

This Dover edition, first published in 1958, is an unabridged and unaltered republication of the work which was originally privately printed in 1941 by E. Hauser, Philadelphia.

International Standard Book Number: 0-486-20485-5
Library of Congress Catalog Card Number: 58-14208

Manufactured in the United States of America
Dover Publications, Inc.
180 Varick Street
New York, N. Y. 10014

THE WORKS OF OTTO RANK

1884-1939

Der Künstler, 1907.

Der Mythus der Geburt des Heldens, 1909. English translation, The Myth of the Birth of the Hero, 1914.
Italian Translation, 1921.

Ein Traum der Selbst deutet, Jahrbuch für Psa II, 1910.

Die Lohengrin Sage, 1911.

Das Inzestmotiv in Dichtung und Sage, 1912. French translation, 1934.

Die Bedeutung der Psychoanalyse für die Geisteswissenschaften (with H. Sachs), 1913. English translation, 1915.

Psychoanalytische Beiträge zur Mythenforschung: Gesammelte Studien aus den Jahren 1912-14, 1919.

Der Doppelgänger, in Imago, 1914.

Homer: Psychologische Beiträge zur Entstehungsgeschichte des Volksepos, in Imago V, 1917.

Das Volksepos: Die dichterische Phantasiebildung, in Imago V, 1917.

Don Juan-Gestalt, in Imago VIII, 1922. In book form, 1924.

Eine Neurosenanalyse in Träumen, 1924.

Sexualität und Schuldgefühl, 1926.

Entwicklungsziele der Psychoanalyse (with S. Ferenczi), 1924.
English translation, The Development of Psychoanalysis, 1925.

Das Trauma der Geburt, 1924. French translation, 1928.
English translation, The Trauma of Birth, 1929.

Technik der Psychoanalyse. Vol. I, 1926. Vol. II, 1929. Vol. III, 1931.
English translation, Will Therapy, 1936.

Grundzüge einer genetischen Psychologie auf Grund der Psychoanalyse der Ich-Struktur. Vol. I, Genetische Psychologie, 1927. (Given in lecture form in English for the New York School of Social Work,

1926.) Vol. II, Gestaltung und Ausdruck der Persönlichkeit, 1928. (Given in lecture form for the New York School of Social Work and the Pennsylvania School of Social Work, 1927.) Vol. III, Wahrheit und Wirklichkeit, 1929. (Given in lecture form for the Pennsylvania School of Social Work, 1929.) English translation, Truth and Reality, 1936.

Seelenglaube und Psychologie, 1931.

Modern Education, 1931.

Art and Artist, 1932.

TO SANDRA

Contents

Foreword

This book, which the author had always intended to be his last, written as he once said "when I am old enough to write a social psychology," was complete, except for the final chapter, when death brought his work to an end. After a quarter of a century of continuous writing and publishing, he settled in the United States permanently and for six years confined his efforts to therapy and teaching. This "sabbatical leave," as he called it, was broken by the gradual emergence of "Beyond Psychology," his first book in English, which, while it contains the essence of his old-world scholarship, reveals the *beyond* of a new life that he found for himself in this country.

Preface

The idea of this book as expressed in the title was conceived of about ten years ago (1929/30) during a period when I was publishing three books which had already carried me beyond individual psychology to the appreciation of the influence ideologies exert upon human behaviour in determining the destinies of people. In those days when political ideologies were not yet in vogue, I tried to show how, in all systems of education as well as in the different styles of artistic creation, collective ideologies of the specific period of civilization determined the individual's efforts to develop beyond himself or to create something beyond his given natural self.[1] In the third of these volumes "Seelenglaube und Psychologie" (Vienna 1930), which has not been translated into English, I pointed out how individual psychology itself has been shaped, indeed determined, by collective ideologies which originated beyond the individual and did not spring from an understanding of the self.

Thus the idea of this book was not inspired by our present socio-political crisis, although these puzzling events which prove decisively the power of ideologies in the political realm of reality make this, my undertaking, so much more timely and perhaps intelligible. My main thesis which was derived from a crisis in psychology appears quite applicable to our present general bewilderment, inasmuch as it lays bare the irrational roots of human behavior which psychology tries to explain rationally in order to make it intelligible, that is, acceptable. When I first realized that people, though they may think and talk rationally—and even behave so—yet live irrationally, I thought that "beyond" individual psychology simply meant social or collective psychology until I discovered that this too is gen-

[1] Modern Education, N. Y., 1930. Art and Artist, N. Y., 1930.

erally conceived of in the same rational terms. Hence my recognition of the ideologies—including those determining our psychological theories—was not sufficient to complement our understanding of individual behaviour because they too were stated in terms of the rational aspect of human life. In fact these ideologies more than anything else seem to carry the whole rationalization which man needs in order to live irrationally. Paradoxically enough, the new collective ideologies of our time are not infrequently presented in an individualized form, seemingly with the idea of making them more intelligible. Not only the average journalist of our daily papers but even the intellectual interpreter of current political events easily succumbs to the temptation of writing idealised biographies of nations in terms of individual success-stories or of painting black pictures of "gangster"-nations,—thereby unwittingly emphasizing the irrational element in human behaviour instead of explaining it.

In this sense the "beyond" individual psychology meant not, as I first thought, a resorting to collective ideologies as the subject of social psychology; it actually meant the irrational basis of human nature which lies beyond any psychology, individual or collective. This realization, strongly confirmed by the socio-political movements of the last few years, allowed this book, originally conceived of as a challenge to individual and social psychology to grow into a creative experience of its own which ultimately crystallized into words—unfortunately, words which proved inadequate to express this very experience,—not because this is my first attempt to write in English but for the deeper reason that language, all language, is again a rational phenomenon meant to communicate thoughts and to explain actions in rational terms. Thus, what we need is an irrational language with a new vocabulary, something like what modern art is trying to find for the expression of the "sub-conscious."

In fact this linguistic inability to express the irrational verbally only reflects the deepest human problem, the clash between the two worlds in which man attempts to live simultaneously, the natural world and the man-made world. Man in his development of civilization has practically made over the universe, or at least the earth, in terms of his self only to fail, finally, in making this self over in terms of the world he has created. Therefore, we actually need two kinds of words for every thing in order to differentiate between the natural and the "Ersatz"-thing made by man. In struggling with the English orthography, it occurred to me that we might use a different spelling of the same word to designate the natural as against the man-made (i.e. control-natural and control-willful) ; meanwhile, not presuming to take the liberty of the artist, I have to be content if I succeed in using the available medium of communication to give a mere impression of the irrational which cannot be expressed directly save in a new kind of artistic creation. Even modern art in its various "isms" has not—in spite of all protestations of its theorists—succeeded in expressing the irrational directly. In their extremely conscious effort to reproduce what they call the "unconscious" modern painters and writers have followed modern psychology in attempting the impossible, namely to rationalize the irrational. This paradoxical state of affairs betrays itself in the basic axiom of psychoanalysis, a mechanistic theory of life according to which all mental processes and emotional reactions are determined by the Unconscious, that is, by something which in itself is unknown and undeterminable. Modern art has adopted this rational psychology of the irrational legitimately, because art itself, like psychology, has been from the beginning an attempt to master life rationally by interpreting it in terms of the current ideologies, that is, it has striven to re-create life in order to control it. The socio-political events of our day amply justify the need for something "beyond" our psychology which has proved inadequate to account for such strange happenings. How many times do we hear nowadays the expression "I cannot understand what is going on," indicating that our conception of the human being is insufficient to account for something which must be human after all, but which we have to consider "irrational" because it does not fit into our rational scheme of things. As we become increasingly aware that we have already gone "beyond psychology," I have realized more and more that, because of the inherent nature of the human being, man has always lived beyond psychology, in other words, irrationally. If we can grasp this paradoxical fact and accept it as the basis of our own living, then we shall be able to discover new values in place of the old ones which seem to be crumbling before our very eyes—vital human values, not mere psychological interpretations predetermined by our preferred ideologies.

These new values which have to be discovered and rediscovered every so often are in reality old values, the natural human values which in the course of time are lost in rationalizations of one kind or another. Yet, for such a re-discovery of the natural self of man, it is not sufficient to *see* the importance of the irrational element in human life and point it out in *rational* terms! On the contrary, it is necessary actually to live it and of this only a few individuals in every epoch seem to be capable. They represent the heroic type—as distinct from the creative—for the original hero was the one who dared live beyond the accepted "psychology" or ideology of his time. In this sense he is the prototype of the rebellious man of action who, through the revival of lost values which appear as new and irrational, preserves the eternal values of humanity. For the most part what we call "irrational" is just the natural; but our "rationale" has become so unnatural that we see everything natural as irrational. Hence our psychology as the climax of man's self-rationalization is inadequate to explain change because it can only justify the type representing the existing social order of which it is an expression.

Although this book is pleading for the recognition and the acceptance of the irrational element as the most vital part of human life, let it be understood that the rational structures which man has built up from time immemorial in religion and art, in philosophy and psychology are equally an essential part of human existence. It is merely a matter of the right proportion and a more balanced evaluation of the natural as against the artificial. That man so easily loses sight of his natural self and thus distorts reality to the point of madness is deeply rooted in his fear of natural forces threatening not only from without but even more from within, in his own nature. Above all, his fear of destruction by those elemental forces accounts for his need to build up a world and a life of his own in which he may feel secure. But there is a limit to all his efforts to control as long as death awaits the presumptuous conqueror of nature. That is why the fearless hero in defying death can utilize those elemental forces in himself to derive mankind's eternal values, yet in so doing, himself becomes the victim of his own heroic enterprise since the experiencing of those irrational forces must needs prove disastrous in one way or another.

The fear aroused by the destructive life forces which occasionally may be turned into the active expression of new values, excludes the ordinary man from more than vicarious participation; and that is all I expect at best from this effort to communicate my experience to others. I have not set out to convince or to convert, nor to divert anyone from his own pursuit of personal happiness. I have no panacea to offer, nor any solution to our human problems which seem to me to be part of man's life on this earth. We are born in pain, we die in pain and we should accept life-pain as unavoidable,—indeed a necessary part of earthly existence, not merely the price we have to pay for pleasure. This book is an attempt to picture human life, not only as I have studied it in many forms for more than a generation, but as I have achieved it for myself, in experience, beyond the compulsion to change it in accordance with any man-made ideology. Man is born beyond psychology and he dies beyond it but he can *live* beyond it only through vital experience of his own—in religious terms, through revelation, conversion or re-birth. My own life work is completed, the subjects of my former interest, the hero, the artist, the neurotic appear once more upon the stage, not only as participants in the eternal drama of life but after the curtain has gone down, unmasked, undressed, unpretentious, not as punctured illusions, but as human beings who require no interpreter.

Otto Rank

June 15, 1939.

I

Psychology and Social Change

THE RELATIVITY OF PSYCHOLOGICAL SYSTEMS

In the history of mankind we see two alternating principles of change in operation, which seem to present an eternal dilemma: the question as to whether a change in the people themselves or a change in their system of living is the better method for improving human conditions. In our own era of social distress, where the two principles of change seem actually to overlap, we are becoming increasingly aware of the two dynamic forces inherent in this human conflict of the individual striving against the social impact of the civilization into which he happens to have been born. This eternal conflict of humanity's striving for volitional control of uncontrollable circumstances is dramatically epitomized in our time by two opposite movements which clashed in the epoch called the World War: the heightened individualism of the pre-war period manifesting itself in the rise and development of individual psychology conceived of as an educational and therapeutic instrument, and the reaction following it of spontaneous mass-movements which found powerful expression in the social and political ideologies characteristic of our post-war era. While politicians, educators and psychologists are advocating their respective remedies for the most pressing symptoms of this conflict, unforeseen events, as so often in history, have taken matters out of their hands and are shaping systems, as well as people, far ahead of any expectations. The best we can do under these circumstances is to catch up with those spontaneous developments which occur about us and are affecting our own life, individually and socially. This catching up, though, to my mind, is not merely a realization of what is going on and an idea of what ought to be done about it, but an actual living in and with the flow of events, following its changing currents as we swim along fully aware of its dangerous under-currents.

Times of social crisis, such as we are now going through, do not permit of much reflection but call for quick action. The high tide of nineteenth century intellectualism, receding during the World War, has since given place to a period of hectic activity in which we are discovering, not without embarrassment, that our mind, despite its proverbial quickness, is failing to keep up with the torrent of onrushing events. Bound by the ideas of a better past gone by and a brighter future to come, we feel helpless in the present because we cannot even for a moment stop its movement so as to direct it more intelligently. We still have to learn, it seems, that life, in order to maintain itself, must revolt every so often against man's ceaseless attempts to master its irrational forces with his mind. No matter in what terms this presumptuous aim is attempted, sooner or later a reaction sets in, be it in the form of intellectual scepticism and pessimism—through which, for example, the Greeks perished—or in the actual rebellion of our frustrated human nature.

Whether we like to admit it or not, the fact remains that so far in history the most radical, that is, vital changes have been brought about through warfare and revolution, through an active change of order according to which the people changed, or rather, were forced to change. After a new order had been established through violence, education—conceived of in the broadest sense of the word—always was and still is the essential means of effecting the subsequent change of people. The strength, as well as the weakness, of any such indoctrination lies in its lack of flexibility; educational systems as representatives of political ideologies tend to become just as absolutistic as the religious systems which formerly provided the basic philosophy for education. Ever since Aristotle proclaimed it a necessity for the State to educate its youth in the spirit of its constitution, this principle has been the guiding rule of strong statesmanship throughout the ages up to the present time. At crucial points in modern history we find an increasing awareness of the political importance of education, as borne out by the German tradition that it was the "schoolmaster" who won the victory over Austria in 1866, just as in quite recent times it has been said that the Eton boys could not stand up against the drill of Hitler-youth discipline. As a matter of fact, the proverbial militaristic spirit of the German people seems to be nothing but a continuation into adult life of the classroom discipline. Even the Victorian English, despite their dislike of systems and theories, admitted that the battle of Waterloo was won at a school; and the individualistic French, after their defeat in 1870, drew the conclusion that the German "Gymnasium" must be superior to their own "Lycée."

In our times, however, modern educators, puzzled by the instability of our social order and the lack of generally accepted ideals, tried to replace the conforming philosophy of traditional education by a more individualistic one based on scientific psychology. Instead of adjusting the individual to a social order continuously shifting, hence, threatened in its foundation, progressive educators proclaimed the individual's capacity to change as the main goal of present-day education. They thereby tacitly declared the bankruptcy of traditional education, which, by its very nature, can only serve to indoctrinate and thus maintain collective ideologies but cannot foster the development of individual selfhood. Hence, the individualistic results of those psychological experiments carried out by a group of progressives proved contrary to the ideal of American mass-education. In fact, progressive education, or rather, certain progressive schools in this country, have been criticized for their anti-democratic catering to a "privileged" group who could afford a "child-centred" school for their offspring. While an educational strengthening of selfhood might be desirable for the individual in times of social upheaval, when he needs greater inner security to weather the threatening storms in his changing environment, it separates the individual from the social influences which, in one way or another, strive for uniformity. Yet it needed the threat of foreign ideologies to make progressive educators in this country aware of the danger, which I pointed out in *Modern Education*,[1] in 1930. The Detroit Conference of the Progressive Education Association, in 1939, found it necessary to re-define the ideal of individualism. Emphasis was laid, as against the "child-centred" school, on the "social-blueprint" theory of education orientated towards the fostering of democratic values.

At the same time, it is true that, just as traditional education aims at the establishment and perpetuation of the existing social order and the psychological type representing it, the individual's self-development tends towards difference, hence, makes for change. In this sense, educational philosophies, no matter how radical their origin, tend to become conservative if the social system which supports them is to endure. On the other hand, there operates, simultaneously with the traditional psychology of character which is taught, another more realistic one which has to be learned from spontaneous developments and applied to one's own change as well as to the changing of others. In all our educational efforts we have to recognize the decisive influence of living forces outside the established social order, in other words, the individual's education outside

[1] Alfred A. Knopf, N. Y.

the classroom. This state of affairs, commonly deplored as the unfortunate discrepancy between theory and practice, serves in reality the human need of balancing one extreme with its counterpart. Instead of striving for a one-sided, that is, absolute solution—which in practice would mean stagnation—we should realize that a dynamic dualism operates in the human being as a force of balance and not only as a source of conflict. In neglecting this basic dynamism in human nature, all education, especially that of our Western civilization, with its dependence on political ideologies, sooner or later fails to achieve uniformity, because it unwittingly fosters the growth and development of the opposite type from the one it set out to produce. We have seen how in Europe pre-war imperialism bred socialism, and how a democratic ideology in government and education led to fascism and communism. By the same token, the educational systems based upon those extreme political ideologies are in turn likely to precipitate individualistic reactions.

Be that as it may, we see at present, as far as the method of indoctrination and the result of uniformity are concerned, a strong comeback of traditional education, not only in the totalitarian states but also in this country which has yet to find the true democratic balance between individualistic liberty and the freedom of political equality. There remains, nevertheless, this essential difference between the democratic form of government and the educational philosophy of the totalitarian states: while the one practises the method of changing people, educating them to a better life, the other is adjusting the people to a change of system which promises an ultimate advantage to the individual. Here it becomes clear that the first method follows evolutionary principles, whereas the other is necessarily of a revolutionary nature. Both these principles are merely following, or rather, copying, the two natural processes seemingly necessary for the maintenance of life. Conceived of in this sense, evolution and revolution are not mutually exclusive ideologies which are played against each other as "natural" versus "man-made," but conceptions corresponding to the two antagonistic principles constituting life itself.

From this it follows that all the "either-or" controversies ending in a blind alley are, in the last analysis, due to man's inability or unwillingness to accept the simultaneous or alternate operation of the two principles which govern life and determine his destiny. Yet it is not merely the question of seeing the two sides or accepting them intellectually which seems to be so difficult, but an experiencing of them in actual living. For living consists of action, and action has to be one-sided, excluding any other alternative of behaviour. From this it follows that our insistence on a one-sided interpretation or solution of any given problem is the result of our transferring the main characteristic of action, its one-sidedness, to thought, which, on the contrary, consists of an alternate consideration of the two sides. That is to say, in our civilization thought has increasingly become the substitute for action, while we ourselves have become more and more inactive and increasingly talkative. This accounts for our reverting, in times when action is called for, to the dialectical interpretation of events instead of realizing the dynamic interplay of living forces behind this logical method of thinking. This predominance of thought finds expression in our designating the simultaneous operation of dynamic life forces as "irrational," while we conceive of the dialectical sequence of thesis, antithesis, and synthesis as a rational exposition. Because the will-ing side of human nature cannot allow for spontaneous happenings that are beyond its control, we falsify the whole outlook and meaning of life by conceiving of spontaneous natural developments as irrational and believing, contrary to all evidence, the will-ful to be the rational.

This paradoxical state of affairs is reflected in the conflicting struggle of different ideologies, be they political, educational or psychological. By emphasizing one aspect of the problem at the expense of the other, that is, the willful or the spontaneous, the rational or the irrational, in terms of evolution versus revolution, the different political creeds, educational systems and psychological schools are striving for a supremacy which cannot be established by any absolutistic dogmatism. Each of these ideologies, while claiming to have found the very truth, is actually only expressing temporary needs and desires of one side of human nature, thereby forcing the other frustrated side to assert itself alternately in violent reactions. Hence we have the eternal cycle of changing ideologies, in the face of which we still cling to the faith in an absolute solution.

The real problem seems to be our need for, or insistence on, the absolute—a general human problem that lies beyond psychology. Yet this, our "beyond psychology," does not mean a simple acceptance of the modern emphasis on other factors, such as economics, politics or technique, determining human behaviour. For that we have to go beyond individual and social psychology to group or mass psychology, because in the long run it is the masses who either create psychology or to whom it is forcibly applied. It means more psychology rather than less, but of a different kind. It is an emphasis upon the dynamic forces governing life and human behaviour, in a word, the irrational; whereas our present-day psychology is conceived of as a rational explanation of human behaviour, at best, a rationalization of the irrational but not an acceptance of it as an essential driving force. In fact, the tendency of our times to minimize the importance of all psychological explanation of human behaviour seems to me indicative of the failure of our rationalistic psychology to account for the increasing power of irrational forces operating in modern life. Hence, for the failing rationalistic psychology must be substituted other rational explanations of human conduct, among which the economic seems the most logical, although in reality it operates just as irrationally as every other rational principle carried into practice.

Let it be understood that by "irrational" forces we do not mean the blind biological impulses which have rationally been taken into account in analytical psychology. We mean rather certain powerful ideologies which have been accepted or interpreted as purely rational, when in reality they are emotional, while natural forces operating in the human being have been stigmatized as irrational because they seem uncontrollable. Thus we really have to reckon with two kinds of psychology: the one actually lived by the individual or the people, which, inasmuch as it consists of a simultaneous expression of two opposing principles, is "irrational"; the other, rational psychology, which as an explanatory science provides scientific methods for educational and therapeutic purposes. Whereas the irrational psychology automatically creates an attitude towards life which can find expression in action, the seemingly rational psychology easily develops into an ideology which, far from being an expression of life itself, is meant and used as a means by which to change life in terms of a certain social order. All attempts gradually to translate any such ideology into practice—be it educationally or politically—are likely to be overtaken by spontaneous developments of the irrational elements. Inasmuch as ideologies are created by the more sensitive type, who anticipates and crystallizes certain urgent needs and desires, they always remain somewhat untimely or out of step, either in their premature anticipation or in their belated application.

The rapid rise and sudden decline of our own psychological era provides a striking example of that fatal discrepancy in time and content between the immediate strivings of a certain epoch, their ideological expression or formulation by a creative personality and its systematic application. Individual psychology, which has failed us in the understanding and directing of present-day mass movements, was preceded by a cultural group-psychology inaugurated by Nietzsche, who, inspired by the Franco-Prussian War of 1870, analyzed the different reactions of opposed groups in their eternal struggle for supremacy. This dynamic conception of cultural types was followed, in an era of comparative stability, by Freud's medical approach to a scientific psychology of morbid individuals suffering in a seemingly healthy civilization. Particularly during its rapid development from the beginning of the century to the World War, therapeutic psychology seemed the long-sought panacea for all human evils. The humanistic ideal of the nineteenth century, which was to change the individual through rational methods of education and re-education, appeared to be practically fulfilled. Even straight psychotherapy, which was supposed to be concerned with the personal happiness of the individual, was only part of this idealistic educational scheme, in that its basic philosophy consisted of adjusting deviates to the accepted norm. The educational aim of psychoanalysis, however, was overshadowed from the very beginning by its more attractive aspect—the development of one's own personality. Accordingly, the individual's experience in the therapeutic process was elaborated into a general theory claimed to be a universal explanation of all human behaviour, regardless of time and place.

I realized the relativity of this psychology from my own experience before others became convinced by social events that modern psychology is far from being a generally valid, that is, absolute science. Spontaneous developments affecting large groups of the population have shaken considerably the social order from which those psychological theories sprang. War and post-war revolution, with their material and spiritual suffering, followed by social regimentation of one kind or another, radically change the ways of living before psychological methods had a chance to change the people. As a matter of fact, Freud himself discredited the whole psychoanalytic movement when he concluded his life-work with the pessimistic realization that he had not been dealing with neurotic individuals but with a morbid civilization. Such a statement, however frank, remains meaningless unless it is followed by the demand for a change of order, which again would have to be advocated in terms of a preconceived ideology, i.e. psychology. Besides, every civilization has its ills, its decline and decadence, and only by exaggerating our present suffering "neurotically," could Freud give it a therapeutic interpretation which was not a psychological one. For if our civilization is "neurotic," there is still hope of a "cure," and the evil is not fatal; whereas, actually, those crises are a part of life and have to be accepted as such. Ailments of that kind, in any case, cannot be cured in a consulting room but are taken care of by spontaneous reactions on the part of the people themselves. Such unwelcome reactions, coupled with Freud's disappointment in his therapeutic results, led him to diagnose our civilization as morbid—a conclusion which Nietzsche drew half a century before in his *"Kultur-Psychologie,"* where he dealt with the resentment in the suppressed and the will-to-power in the ruling classes.

In the midst of one of those eternal struggles, we find scientific psychology, with its claim to be an absolute criterion for human behaviour, inadequate in regard to both its aspects, the explanation and the education of the existing type of man. What we actually find in practice is a variety of psychological theories sponsored by different leaders who accuse each other of not being scientific without realizing that their psychologies, as they have been interpreted and used in practice, are in reality ideologies representative of certain classes and types. Their "unscientific" aspect I believe to be their real value, inasmuch as they express vital needs and desires of a certain type or class within a certain period of time and a special environment. They outlived their significance when things changed, but they were useful in their time and place.

Instead of trying to reconcile these different schools of psychological thought in the name of objective science, we should learn from recurring events that realistic psychology, as a living expression of the people, is changing as everything else is, and, furthermore, that it has to change in order to keep alive. Such a living psychology—which is not the one we study in the laboratory and learn from textbooks, but the one we ourselves have and practice in our daily life—can never be strictly scientific, that is, mechanistic; hence, can never be the absolute criterion for which it was taken and which we still seem to look for. It not only changes in time and place, but varies within one and the same civilization. Human psychology is constantly being influenced by all the forces that are building and molding the particular civilization of which it is an outgrowth. Every system of psychology is just as much an expression of the existing social order and the type representing it as it is an interpretation of the same. Psychology, in other words, is not an objective instrument, like a telescope or microscope, which can be applied for purposes of observation to the reactions of individuals or groups of people; it is not a science beyond or above the civilization it presumes to explain. On the contrary, these psychological theories themselves have to be explained as a part of the whole social system and understood as an expression of a certain type representing one particular layer of it. This makes intelligible the different schools of psychology we find, simultaneously, within one and the same cultural strata. Each of these contradictory systems claims to present the absolute truth, whereas in reality they represent different types, groups and classes, and register the shifting of human conditions along the lines of change. In that sense, theories of psychology change, one might almost say, like fashions, and are perforce compelled to change in order to express, as well as make intelligible, the existing type of man in his dynamic struggle for maintenance and perpetuation.

THE IRRATIONAL BASIS OF MODERN PSYCHOLOGIES

To focus the social implications of our psychological controversies, we merely have to put in juxtaposition the most disputed theories of modern psychology. About half a century ago, psychoanalysis started as a purely individual method of therapy and as such was helpful to a certain type of patient. The more Freud and his followers developed their therapeutic experience into a general psychological system, the more evident became the cleavage between this presumably universal theory of psychological facts and its therapeutic use for the interpretation of the behaviour of a certain type in terms of a specific social ideology. Hence, any deviation from the theoretically prescribed "norm" was soon called "neurotic," even when it was not an outspoken illness but merely a matter of difference in temperament, character or social standards. True, the scientific basis of psychoanalysis was evolutionary biology applied to the individual's personal development, but this naturalistic theory was put into the service of an educational philosophy expressing the needs and desires of what might be called the "bourgeois" type or upper middle class. Freud, that is to say, automatically interpreted certain fundamental drives in the human being in terms of a therapeutic ideology which justified the psychology of a then successful type with its social and moral standards. The seeming revolutionary tendency of which professional conservatives first accused psychoanalysis was contradicted by its own therapeutic aim of adjusting the deviating individual to the prevailing social order. In such an educational conception I can see the living value of a practical psychology—so long as this is not proclaimed an absolute system applicable to all types differing from the standardized norm. That Freud's psychology, being an interpretation rather than an explanation of human nature, was not valid for all races, Jung pointed out; that it did not apply to different social environments, Adler emphasized; but that it did not even permit individuals of the same race and social background to deviate from the accepted type led me *beyond these differences in psychologies to a psychology of difference.*

As it happens, these spontaneous reactions within the psychoanalytic movement itself provide an excellent illustration for that development. Freud's tendency to absolutize his psychology was counteracted at an early date (before the World War) by two diametrically opposed reactions: Adler's antithesis and Jung's synthesis, fulfilling, as it were, the dialectical completion of the whole system, thereby bringing the movement to a standstill. Freud, as is only too well-known, pronounced the sexual instinct the driving force in the individual, whereas Adler stressed the individual's ego-drive for power, dominance and supremacy. We do not mean to explain their difference in view-point by assuming that each of them saw only one side of human nature; it is more important for us to realize why each shows the special emphasis characteristic of his thought. It does not seem to me irrelevant that Adler, before he became interested in psychoanalysis, was a general practitioner in the poorer sections of Vienna and politically belonged to the Socialist Party. That all his patients suffered from an "inferiority complex," whereas Freud's cases seemed to be full of guilt, might very well have resulted from the fact that their respective clientèle came from different classes. Be that as it may, the suffering from inferiority and the striving for dominance is unquestionably the psychology of a suppressed type, or under-dog. Freud's conception of neurosis as a result of biological repression, on the other hand, virtually expresses the psychology of the "arrivist," that is, the type who has used up his instinctual forces in order to gain power and maintain position. Jung, though realizing that both Freud and Adler dealt only with one particular type, did not recognize the social implications in the dynamic struggle of those opposing forces. He tried to reconcile the dispute between the two psychologists by developing his theory of two "psychological types," the introvert and the extrovert. Those static types, the product of abstraction, are of little practical value, because in real life the suppressed type may explode into action, that is, tend to become extrovert, whereas the successful type is likely to develop a guilty conscience and on that basis become introspective.

What we have disclosed by this social analysis of these contradictory theories is a psychological dualism which runs through the history of mankind. Nietzsche was the first to formulate it by contrasting the psychology of the ruler with that of the ruled. This duofold psychology applies not only to the strivings of groups, classes or nations against one another but to individual relationships, such as those between leader and followers, master and pupil, therapist and patient, parent and child, and, as Nietzsche saw it, man and woman. In neglecting the human value of such realistic psychology of difference, Freud revived Rousseau's sentimental conception of natural man's fundamental likeness, a humanistic ideology which has set the pace for social experimentation since the French Revolution. The basic fallacy of this political theory of equality lies in the psychological presupposition that we are also born alike. As a matter of fact, the very act of parturition, as I pointed out in *The Trauma of Birth*,[1] varies to such a degree with different individuals that this in itself, regardless of hereditary factors and environmental influences, would account for a variety of temperament and behaviour. Yet, on the assumption of a fundamental likeness in man, all our educational systems rest, and all the inconsistencies of modern psycho-therapy can be explained by our dual attempt to strengthen both the individual difference in given personalities and, at the same time, the social likeness to the preferred type. Supported by a seemingly universal psychology of human behaviour, politicians and educators felt justified in molding and shaping the undefined masses according to their own purposes or ideals instead of frankly acknowledging and respecting their *equal rights and chances* as citizens. Since men are not alike and cannot actually be equal, psychology could at least explain them as alike with the more or less open purpose of making them alike—be it through an indoctrination of educational, therapeutic or political ideologies. In this bold enterprise, the duofold—or rather, three-fold aspect of psychology serves as a "utility tool"; as an expression of the mentality of a certain type it perpetuates this very type, hence, can finally be conveniently used to explain it. Yet opposing this "inspirational" psychology, which aims at influencing people, there operates another realistic psychology as a spontaneous expression of the people; not the psychology we create by which to change, but the one which creates change—in others as well as in ourselves—spontaneously.

This overlapping of the two kinds of psychologies, the spontaneous and the deliberate, the irrational and the rational, reflects the deeper struggle between the evolutionary and revolutionary principle of life as interpreted by man. Our concept of "evolution" signifies the denial of the age-old belief in the immutability of species expressed

[1] Harcourt, Brace and Co., New York, 1929.

in the dogma that God created all living things as they now exist. By supplanting this doctrine of creation with the doctrine of progressive evolution, Darwin established a mechanical conception of organic life that suited the machine age, and led far beyond biology to a new conception of education and government. Yet what seemed to him and others so revolutionary an idea was in effect an admission that man is not his own creator and an acceptance of uncontrollable happenings which determine our destiny. Thus, with Darwin, man accepted a natural development of which he is not the creator but the creature, not the master but the victim. The well-known fact that the scientist published his epoch-making work only after twenty years of doubtful hesitation is not explained by his fear of shocking the world, but by his inner resistance to renouncing man's creativity while he himself was creating his own man-made universe. Likewise, the lifelong frailty which prevented him from working more than three hours a day, and which has been blamed for this delay, seems rather to have been a result of his inner conflict. Be that as it may, a person whom the slightest excitement, such as a visit with friends, sends to bed with a "shivering fit and nervous vomiting," certainly contradicts his theory of "the survival of the fittest," in the biological sense of the word. What enabled Darwin not only to survive but finally to triumph over physical obstacles and inner resistances was his creative urge and social position. The former he denied in his theory of "natural selection," which merely explains why forms have become extinct but tells nothing about the mystery of new creation. The latter, his social position and class-consciousness, he affirmed positively in his theory, which has been taken to justify the success of the victorious class in the industrial revolution—its meaning, not that the fittest survive but that those who survive ought to be considered the fittest.

While it is true that Darwin's theory has been used to bolster the doctrine of laissez-faire and thus defend competitive capitalism, it is equally true that he himself, not unlike Nietzsche, compensated in his theory for his physical weakness and, at the same time, justified his privileged position through creation. The same holds good for the great social theorist of his time, Karl Marx, in whose battle-cry against capitalism the victims of the industrial revolution found expression. This propagator of a classless state grew up as an individualistic bourgeois in a liberal Germany where the humanitarian effects of the French Revolution had begun to make themselves felt. Especially must the emancipation of the Jew, whom Napoleon had included in his liberation campaign, have stimulated Marx, the son of a successfully assimilated Jew, to revive the century-old aspiration of his race to gain equal civic rights. Although there was some justification in the Germany of those days for such a hope, Marx, like most other great theorists, was not content with any simple "realities," but had to advocate a perfect egalitarian state on earth. He thereby "did nothing other than to reconstruct the particularities of the economic age into the general elements of the history of mankind."[1] It seems that all epoch-making theories, whether they deal with biological, sociological or psychological phenomena, owe their popular appeal to their ideological conception of universality. For this reason, in that they reach beyond scientific predictability into the realm of dogmatic certainty, they easily become substitutes for religious beliefs. Not unlike the Prophets in their apocalytic visions, those intellectual leaders seem to know exactly how the future will work out. By interpreting the past and predicting the future in terms of their secular "religion," they project specific conditions of a certain time

[1] Sombart, Werner. *A New Social Philosophy,* Princeton University Press,

and age—which to be sure brought to light different aspects of human life—into a timeless and placeless universe.

Darwin and Marx, dealing respectively with the hereditary and environmental conditions for survival and self-preservation, are both concerned with the individual's different equipment in his struggle for survival. Freud, being psychologically as deterministic as Darwin was biologically and Marx economically, made the less excusable error. By applying both Darwin's biological and Marx's social determinism to the personality itself, he deprived it of the very qualities which make man's life human; autonomy, responsibility and conscience. The latter he had to explain in true Old Testament fashion as the result of a past guilt—equivalent to original sin—instead of realizing in man's consciousness the dynamic struggle of those human characteristics against any kind of determinism. For if determinism can be applied to biological and even economic influences, it certainly can never be the psychological answer to the human problem, because it denies the human phenomenon par excellence, the individual will. Even if human nature and man's behaviour are absolutely determined, man's belief in his free will, ability to choose and individual responsibility would still be his "psychology" and the real object of human psychology. But such "unrealistic" notions were relegated by Freud to the realm of ethical controversy and theological speculation, without his realizing that for centuries, long before "scientific" psychology had reduced man to a purely rational puppet, religion and philosophy had represented the real psychology of people and individuals. As it is, this mechanistic theory of the "psyche," if applied to the creative building-up of the personality, must necessarily, like religion, produce guilt. It will do so for the simple reason that it not only conceives of the individual will as something opposed to the deterministic "will of God" but, as an inspirational psychology, expects the individual to live up to this unrealistic picture of human nature. In this respect it does not make much difference whether the individual is judged by a religious, social or even a self-ideal; in any case he "makes out" bad, be it in terms of sin, guilt or inferiority. But while religion still offers the acceptance of sin, that is, human nature, as a constructive remedy, psychoanalysis, despite its naturalistic terminology, does not accept human nature, because it is based on a social ideology aiming at the individual's conformity to the prevailing standards of goodness.

Modern psychologists thought to raise their philosophy above this biological struggle for survival and social striving for supremacy by re-emphasizing man's fundamental likeness, only to find how much they differed among themselves. While Freud states that we are all alike in our unconscious—conceived of as instinctual—Jung says that there is where we differ. In this sense Jung's "racial unconscious"—which for Freud is universally human—appears to be the psychological equivalent of Freud's "super-ego," inasmuch as this represents the environmental influence shaping the individual personality and determining its behaviour. Thus the one puts the essential difference on top, the other at the bottom, of the personality structure. Here we realize that their difference of interpretation reduces itself to a mere shift of emphasis with regard to the fundamental problem of likeness and difference. Whereas Freud conceives of all people as fundamentally alike, for Jung they are different (though racially alike); while Adler maintains that though their behaviour is different it ought to be alike. Although Adler's therapeutic aim is the development of "social feeling," he terms his system, "Individual Psychology," thereby betraying the Janus-faced tendency of all modern psychology which in theory proves psychological inequality but at the same time preaches the dogma of equality through therapy and education. Thus what

Adler described in his studies of human behaviour as "neurotic character" is actually individual psychology, because excessive individualism for him is bound to cause "neurotic" reactions in our civilization.

In his remedy, the developing of "social feeling" in the individual, Adler was striving for a kind of equalization from within, whereas Freud's "adjustment" aims at external uniformity. Jung, the son of a minister, less realistically concerned with the individual's environment, approaches more nearly a subjective psychology of the individual than do either Freud or Adler. His early experiences with psychotic types, whose main characteristic is their complete withdrawal from reality and the building-up of an inner world of their own, led him to believe that the individual's fundamental problem lies in the feeling of isolation, regardless of what his environment may be. Consequently, he did not look for the individual's salvation in his relation to reality either through rebellion or submission but in a sublimation of those inner forces which were frustrated. In this psychological process of sublimation, the individual, according to Jung, makes use of the symbolism in his racial unconscious, thus achieving as it were a kind of collectivity within his own self. Such a striving towards an almost mystical union between the self and its racial background is supposed to link the isolated individual with a bigger whole of which he can feel an essential part. Sex, then, for Jung, is but one approach to this cosmic union, whereas Adler conceives of it as a struggle for power and Freud sees in it a general outlet for all sorts of suppressed emotions. In their different attempts to work out a psychology of the individual, all three seem to have reached a similar conclusion, namely, that the evil from which our personality suffers is over-individualization; hence, they agree in the remedy consisting of an emotional unity with something beyond the Self. Freud sees it in sex, Adler in social fellowship and Jung in racial collectivity. In this sense, psychology is searching for a substitute for the cosmic unity which the man of Antiquity enjoyed in life and expressed in his religion, but which modern man has lost—a loss which accounts for the development of the neurotic type.

In this respect it is interesting to note that all those psychological systems, from Nietzsche onward, are either directly advocating or at least picturing a psychology of superiority. Through a rational utilization of suppressed energies they promise strength and power, in a word, manly qualities. In this sense, psychology is not only man-made, as is civilization in general, but *masculine* in its mentality. Hence, it explains woman also in terms of man. The different psychologies which, by the very fact of their existence, prove that man did not even succeed in explaining all men alike, seem to agree in their attempt to explain woman as merely lacking in, or having qualities differing from, masculine characteristics. Adler's "masculine protest" and Freud's "castration-complex" are attitudes indicative of that masculinized psychology which puts all difference on a sexual basis. These two express rebellion in terms of sexual inequality; Freud's famous "Oedipus-complex," designating the child's supposed desire to kill his father and sleep with his mother, symbolizes the boy's natural rebellion against the restrictions of custom and convention. Jung, who has no definite sexual psychology, places the difference in the unconscious, thereby defining it as essentially racial. In our attempt to carry the discussion beyond the controversy of different psychologies to "a psychology of difference," we have to allow for the individual as well as for social and racial differences, and furthermore to consider woman—the child, for that matter, too—as another important group in need of a psychology of its own. At present, to define what is meant by "masculine" or "feminine," respectively, is bound to lead to hopeless confusion, as we see in the cultural school of anthropology, unless it is conceived of on a broader basis than that given by biological facts, psychological interpretations or even cultural patterns of specific civilizations. It is, in the last analysis, as in all problems of difference, a question of two different world-views, two opposite attitudes towards life, springing from the prevalence of either the rational or irrational tendencies in the human being.

A PSYCHOLOGY OF DIFFERENCE

Nietzsche was the first to recognize, from a cultural study, the human value of irrational forces in the suppressed self, which Freud in his rationalistic system could only see as the cause for neurosis. Hence, the cure psychoanalysis had to offer the individual could not be the creative expression of those energies. Freud's therapeutic method aims at making the individual merely conscious of his irrational self, thereby convincing him that it had been rightly suppressed and should now be rationally condemned. Thus originated the famous theory of the "unconscious," a term designating the most vital force of human behaviour as a mere absence of consciousness. Such a negative conception at the basis of the whole psychoanalytic system betrays not only Freud's purely rationalistic approach but also his moralistic philosophy. Originally conceived of as the receptacle of the individual's "badness," the unconscious became a kind of private hell which housed the evil self. Only after Jung had extended its content beyond the repressed material in the individual was it christened with the broader but quite neutral term, "id"—unfittingly borrowed from Nietzsche's intuitive philosophy of self-expression ("id thinks, in me," as opposed to the psychological notion, "I think."). Although with this new name some positive recognition was given the unconscious, Freud's conception remains an unsuccessful attempt to rationalize the irrational.

Freud did not discover the unconscious, as has been erroneously claimed by his followers; he merely rationalized this nebulous conception typical of German romantic philosophy. Those philosophical romanticists of post-Napoleonic Germany conceived of the Unconscious as the irrational element in human nature manifested in racial folk-tradition. Freud, on the other hand, by comparing his achievement to the drainage of the Zuider Zee as a piece of progressive engineering, prided himself on having made it "psychological," that is, of having brought it, so to speak, under the individual's control. He believed he had saved this wasted human area for "civilization" by interpreting the very life-force of the irrational self in biological terms of the ego. Jung, not satisfied with such individualization of an extra-individual force, saw in it the sum of racial inheritance as expressed in religious traditions, whereas Adler replaced both those racial notions by the social- or group-feeling, likewise an extra-individual conception. Thus, while all three psychologists admitted the extra-individual quality of the unconscious, they all rationalized it in terms of their respective individual psychology, thereby missing its real meaning, namely, that this increasingly denied side of human nature always was and will be potent—and if frustrated breaks through in neurotic or anti-social, i.e. irrational behaviour.

In our attitude towards those deviations, however, is again shown the conforming drive which is the undercurrent in our psychology, as the result of the same force which is striving for the maintenance of the existing social order. While we excuse emotional maladjustment as "neurotic," and are willing to help the individual towards a normal adjustment, we condemn and punish anti-social behaviour as "criminal." Our recent attempts to "cure" the criminal psychologically do not seem to change the behaviour of a dissatisfied type who asserts his difference in social action instead of taking it out on himself "neurotically." Are not all our attempts, then, towards adjusting, helping, curing, in the last analysis, born of a deep-seated fear that our security may be upset by a rebellion of people who cannot or do not want to adjust to our social system? Such a conception implies more than a struggle of classes for material power and political supremacy; it is basically, like all the eternal fighting of mankind, a struggle for self-perpetuation. In man, however, this elemental struggle is lifted from its purely biological basis, which he knows to be limited by death, to some kind of spiritual perpetuation, be it in a certain type, group, class or nation.

Herein I see the origin and meaning of warfare and revolutionary struggle, which so far have precipitated the most decisive social changes in history. This dynamic force of change springs from the eternal conflict between man's desire for personal immortality as against biological survival, which is anti-individualistic and can only be attained by a more or less homogeneous group of people. Man's immortality, being naturally universal, that is, the survival of mankind on earth, has been individualized from time immemorial in order that he might maintain his belief in personal immortality. Since this always remains uncertain, man resorted to a collective immortality originally embracing small units, such as the clan or tribe, and eventually extending to the conception of a nation. Hence, nationalism already represents a form of individualized immortality as compared to the survival of mankind in general. All antagonism between neighboring clans and feuds among related tribes resolve themselves, in the last analysis, into a competitive struggle not merely for biological survival but for eternal survival, i.e. immortality. The question of who is the "chosen people" to survive all others accounts for the perpetual struggle between the striving for likeness—in order to be included in the privilege of an eternal life of the group—and the emphasis on individualistic difference, be it personal or racial, in order to exclude the different ones from the blessings of eternity.

All warfare and revolution, no matter how well rationalized, historically, have their origin in those irrational ideologies of immortality, that is, in the man-made conception of survival; hence, are bound to fail in their attempt to establish supernatural conditions in this world of reality. At least to channel those irrational forces by rationalizing them in terms of an intelligible ideology is the special gift of the leader. He literally operates as the head of the forceful body under his control and the masses follow him because he is one of them, a leader emerged from the people themselves, for whom revolution is simply an expression of their irrational selves with a none-too-definite goal. The dissatisfied masses of the under-privileged groups, suffering from unbearable social difference, are likely to over-react towards an impossible equalization which can only lead to newly accentuated differences. In this sense, revolution always fails, because it resolves itself into a mere change of power from one class or party-group to another. In striving politically or economically towards an egalitarian society, all great revolutions in the history of our Western civilization—from the highly spiritualized Christian movement and the bloody slaughter of the French Revolution to the "cold" revolution in present-day Germany—decisively prove the impossibility of establishing on this earth man-made ideologies pertaining to a better beyond. The spiritual principle of equality, which forms the basis of Christian faith and which still forms the ideological basis for our methods of government and education, cannot be translated into realistic terms of political equality and economic freedom. Equality does not flourish under natural conditions of freedom, as Rousseau, the father of the French Revolution, wanted to believe; real natural conditions rather foster inequality and the reign of competition as Darwin saw it in nature. Hence, what has been sensationally termed "the betrayal of all great revolutions" reveals itself as the inherent paradox in our ideological interpretation of spontaneous developments.

Revolution, therefore, unavoidably leads to the Thermidorcycle, that is, the giving way of original revolutionists who provided the ideology for the dissatisfied groups to compromising politicians who are able to catch the rebellious movement on its rebound to more balanced conditions. This was the rôle of Napoleon, who, a typical bourgeois himself, paved the way for the victory of the upper bourgeoisie. Such a "betrayal" on the part of the leader who liquidates the revolutionary movement still seems to be the fate of his modern successors. Having themselves emerged from the middle-class, they eventually strengthen that average layer of the population. This is not only necessary, because that very group forms the economic backbone of modern society, but finds its deeper reason in the fact that its members represent a well-balanced psychological type whose ideology comprises a livable political and social order. For this reason, all revolutions and counter-revolutions, to the Left or to the Right, show one common principle—one which rationally one would least expect in them: the moral principle of good and evil which invariably emerges as the final symbol of difference between the opposing groups, no matter what their political creed. This process is known to historians as the alternate reign of terror and virtue, best documented from the French Revolution, but inherent in all revolutionary movements, be they as different in their background and result as was the American from the French and English Revolution, or in recent times the Russian from the German.[1] Ultimately,

[1] Brinton, Crane. *The Anatomy of Revolution,* W. W. Norton & Co., N. Y., 1938.

the two fighting groups, after having indulged in the typical atrocities of the revolutionary scheme, are divided into the bad and good ones, the latter naturally being the victors in the final battle on whose side God is fighting and who thus get their blessing of immortality. By making good themselves, the successful leaders become automatically virtuous; by virtue of this moral achievement they take it upon themselves to make the citizens virtuous, that is, good citizens of the new regime. They achieve this goal by denouncing loose living as a capital crime against the State. But just as little as the reign of terror can last can the reign of virtue be maintained, because such division between good and bad is too artificial; the human being cannot live up to either extreme for any length of time.

In this sense, revolutions are not only organized terror but subsequently become organized virtue or order; hence, really do not destroy but rather restitute the general civil order after having provided a temporary outlet for the dissatisfied element, a kind of purge of badness in human nature undertaken finally by the State which takes it out of the hands of individuals or groups. Revolutions, therefore, automatically lead back to a natural division of society based on the inherent inequality in human beings. These differences exist regardless of economic realities or political ideologies as psychological types, whom Leonardo da Vinci described as "those who do not see, those who see when they are shown, and those who see by themselves." The latter, the creative type, will always become a leader in one way or another, if not by actually ruling, then by propagating some powerful ideology which creates a new type, thereby precipitating social change. There is always the large group which will join the leader in order vicariously to share his power, and the still larger group which wants to be led. Revolutionary movements, it follows, never can fulfil any of their extreme programs either politically or socially, and so far have only taught through repeated experience the same lesson, namely, that on account of psychological differences a certain hierarchy in social organization is not only unavoidable but necessary for a livable compromise between the rational and irrational forces in human nature.

In the eternal conflict between these two elements in mankind is to be found the dynamic source of human behaviour and also the explanation of psychology itself as man's final attempt to control nature—within himself. Primitive man, on the contrary, was primarily concerned, as is borne out by his magic beliefs and practices, with the control of forces outside himself, the so-called supernatural. This practical aspect, that is, the tendency to control and direct other people's actions, psychology has never lost. In modern times, it is rehabilitated through psycho-therapy as a kind of "white magic," promising to "cure" everything in the other which we dislike. Here our therapeutic psychology of the neurotic betrays its deceptive character by making all psychology appear "teachable," like Socrates' virtues. On a large scale, however, such "education" can only be attempted by violence whereby the opposing groups—whatever they may represent—accuse each other of being irrational, while their leaders pretend to have rationalized their needs and demands. At a point when this whole conflict was internalized and stated in psychological, instead of religious or political terms, the individual himself became the object of self-observation and at the same time the subject of introspective self-therapy. Then the sophisticated rationalism of the late Greeks was revived in a new interpretation of the old slogan, "Know Thyself." This new knowledge of oneself was, however, not, as with Socrates, the beginning of a self-conscious era in the history of mankind, but was conceived of as man's final conquering of nature in himself, the crowning of his evolutionary development.

In this sense, modern psychologies are not only an expression of a certain type or class within a given civilization, but psychology itself, as a "Weltanschauung," is the outgrowth of a specific mentality which flourished during the latter part of the past century. A conceited intellectual type emerged at that time, priding himself on having revealed the secret of nature and thus being able to master her. In replacing his former belief in God by a worship of the new Goddess of science, pure reason, modern man followed in the wake of the French Revolution which had furnished the political ideology for the self-sufficient bourgeois type. This type represents psychologically the nuclear element of the democratic ideal, which was originally the characteristic of one homogeneous class, the lower middle class, whose members were actually very much alike. As soon as the democratic ideal of equality derived from this psychological likeness was adopted as a general principle of government, as happened in America, a great deal of regimentation became necessary to make up for the actually existing inequality in human nature and social conditions. It almost seems as if the fathers of the American constitution stressed the equal right of all human beings to life, liberty and the pursuit of happiness (not "property," as in the original political treatise of Locke) in order to check the too rugged individualism of the ruthless colonists who could reconcile their newly won liberty with the slavery of others.

The idea of self-government on which the democratic state is supposed to function has been derived from the philosophic ideology of self-determination as promoted by Kant. By idealizing and ideologizing the victorious type of the French Revolution, this German philosopher envisioned a new type of ruler who set out to determine himself and be himself. It was this cultural pattern of self-discipline, resulting from the "cold revolution" of the German thinker, which became a German virtue, whereas political self-government is not. This latter, through Jefferson's educational application, became the foundation of American civilization. Thus democracy was first of all an ethical absolute—not a political creed—which gives practical expression to the famous categorical imperative of Kant: "So act as to treat humanity, whether in thine own person or in that of any other, as an end withal, never as a means only." Yet in actual practice the striving towards self-autonomy in the liberated individual was counteracted by his adherence to the political creed of equality, and thus failed in the test. A science of the Self was needed to support the autonomy of the ego, and thus developed individual psychology as a "Weltanschauung," supplementing and justifying the democratic ideal of self-determination.

It cannot be denied that modern psychology offers a possibility for self-realization to the individual who can make use of it for his own self-liberation outside the realm of education. But where are the limits of all the numerous and subtle educational influences, and how is the individual to draw the line between his own psychology and that of his environment which has become a part of himself? The only light to be shed on this intricate problem comes from our experience with individuals who definitely do not fit into the prevalent educational scheme. Psychology to them offered a special sort of education or re-education. This therapeutic psychology, though it promises to the individual self-fulfilment and autonomy, actually aims at his adjustment or re-adjustment to his so-called reality, which, however, is not the reality of life. As a matter of fact, such re-adjustment to "reality," i.e. environment, and not to life, is the social philosophy to which the various professions dealing with human problems of behaviour are bound by their community standards. This environmental coercion, under the pretence of individual liberation, as we see it operating in psychological therapy and in modern education, is as dangerous as it is ineffective. Self-development and adjustment rarely go together, and to educate deviating types to the prevailing ideas and ideals remains unsuccessful unless we allow a dynamic interplay of spontaneous forces. The more potentialities the individual has for developing a strong personality of his own, the more forcefully will he express it in new and different forms, given the opportunity. The educator's concern as to whether an individual differing from the average is to become a genius, a fool or an outcast can only be answered by life itself, that is, by taking chances, and not by psychological experimentation and controlled tests. In this sense, I conceive of human help for the individual not as a planned method of psycho-therapeutic techniques with respect to a control of his stimuli and responses but as his experiencing of the irrational forces within himself which he has not heretofore dared to express spontaneously. Such a conception, however, does not mean giving free range to the hidden desires of the ego, but rather permits the individual to accept his inner limitations or outer restrictions in his own terms and on his free volition.

It was on this vital issue of philosophies underlying individual therapy that I definitely deviated from Freud and his mechanistic conception of the ego as a mere product and puppet of the extra-individual forces, the "id" and the "super-ego," commonly known as hereditary and environmental determinants. Such deterministic interpretation of behaviour may serve to justify neurotic attitudes but leaves little room for any constructive development of self-autonomy and responsibility. The whole question of psychological therapy resolves itself, in the last analysis, to the philosophical problem of a deterministic versus a vitalistic point of view. But even if psychology could be conceived of scientifically in terms of strict determinism, psycho-therapy as a living process of personality development can never be based on a deterministic point of view. In trying to establish what the individual is, and not what has happened to him, constructive therapy does not aim at adjustment but strives to develop autonomy in the individual, thereby liberating his creativity. Neurosis is neither the result of social inhibitions which the majority seem able to accept nor is it caused by the subsequent repression of impulses, but appears as the result of an excessive control on the part of the individual's will over his own nature. In brief, neurosis is the result of willing the spontaneous, which, in other words, amounts to an attempt to solve the conflict between determinism and freedom in actual life instead of on paper. In this sense, the neurotic type of our time appears to be the caricature of our own over-rationalized psychology; that is to say, in him is reached the climax of rational self-control (control of the natural self) at the breaking-point where the irrational forces get the upper hand.

In the light of this, the whole conception of neurosis has to be revaluated in terms of what we consider rational or irrational, for what we call "neurotic" appears so only from our rational point of view which denies to the irrational any right to exist. Thus the whole problem of behaviour, neurotic or not, betrays itself as the age-old conflict of the human versus the natural. The individual will is either asserted in creation or lost in neurosis, depending upon the individual's attitude towards this dilemma. The neurotic does not feel free, being so to speak a victim of our deterministic world-view; yet through excessive willing he wills himself unfree—as manifested in his self-inhibiting symptoms. Thus, willing as it were his whole self instead of simply being it, his total personality becomes perverted; for he not only tries, as we all do, to give life a meaning but is forced by his fear of his natural self to create a private life of his own, thereby perverting the life-force itself into its own denial.

While, on the one hand, the development of neurosis on a large scale indicates that man has over-reached himself in his attempt to control his nature, the neurotic type, at the same time, rebels against becoming a victim of over-rationalization. The dual rôle which his conflict forces him to play makes the neurotic personality appear irrational to himself and to others. To "understand" him, as psychoanalysis rationally attempts to do, is merely to mis-interpret him, because his whole being rebels against the over-rationalization of which psychology represents our last futile attempt. Not unlike the fool at the courts of medieval rulers, the neurotic of our time reflects our own foolishness under the guise of his symptoms. The only difference is that he really suffers from his foolishness, which is considered an illness, although it indicates just as much the cure for our own ills, namely, the need for legitimate foolishness, that is, creative expression of the natural self which we condemn as irrational. In this sense, psychoanalysis as the psychology of the neurotic type—but not the cure for it—is in itself a sign of a decadent civilization. Hence the psychoanalyst who undertakes the task of curing the neurotic rationally becomes necessarily a representative of the existing order—no matter how bad he thinks it is. He has to conceive of "therapy" in terms of his own social philosophy as expressed in his psychological theory. By supporting the individual striving for self-realization, I freed the therapeutic process from the fetters of ideological prejudices and permitted it to be a growth process in terms of the personality instead of an educational training towards conformity. In respecting emotional expression as a positive will manifestation without condemning it as "resistance," I shifted the emphasis from the individual's past to his present self, thereby allowing it a much more active rôle than that of merely being an object upon which the therapist operates.

This dynamic conception makes room for the developing and functioning of the individual's own will as the most constructive factor in the therapeutic movement. By will, I do not mean will-to-power as conceived by Nietzsche and Adler, or "wish" in the Freudian sense, though it might include both these aspects. I mean rather an autonomous organizing force in the individual which does not represent any particular biological impulse or social drive but constitutes the creative expression of the total personality and distinguishes one individual from another. This individual will, as the united and balancing force between impulses and inhibition, is the decisive psychological factor in human behaviour. Its duofold functioning, as an impulsive and likewise inhibiting force, accounts for the paradox that the will can manifest itself creatively or destructively, depending upon the individual's attitude towards himself and life in general. Since it seems to be a lack of balance in his will-organization which compels the neurotic to deny instead of affirm his individuality, I derived from this dynamic growth of the total personality a new conception of the neurotic type. Instead of stigmatizing all failure in normalcy as "neurotic," I saw in a certain neurotic type—which the French call "artist manqué"—a failure in creativity. This type is characterized by the same vivid imagination, which, thwarted as it is, takes on morbid forms. In other words, it is the destructive aspect of the will which produces neurotic symptoms, whereas the creative type through a strong will-organization is able to objectify his self-creation in work. Both types, alike deviating from the average, encounter similar difficulties in trying to adjust themselves to the prevailing standards of normalcy. Thus, in all our educational and therapeutic attempts to "adjust" such deviates, we find the forces of spontaneous growth and creative urge rejecting the acceptance of the environment and resisting acceptance of the Self. Hence, psycho-therapy can only be based on an individualistic psychology, that is, should strive to adjust the individual to himself, which means enable him to accept himself. Such self-acceptance, regardless of the "milieu," does not imply resignation; it rather signifies a new start, making it possible for the individual to do the best with himself in and with his environment.

All social experimentation, on the other hand, no matter on how big a scale, amounts, in the last analysis, to an attempt at improving human conditions by change of environment after educational methods have proved insufficient to change the individual from within. Both methods, however—the change of system as well as the change of people—are not aiming at the individual's "optimum" in contributing to and receiving from his environment but are used by the group in power as means by which to gain its own ends. Psychology, in tracing these two social methods for the fulfilling of this ambition to its biological correlate, that is, the influence of hereditary versus environmental factors in the individual, did not escape ideological prejudices. In the changing evaluation of those two fundamental factors, we recognize once more the influence of scientific fashions upon the trend of social developments. Psychoanalysis, in this respect, appears as ambiguous as it does otherwise. In its practical aspect, it naturally had to emphasize environmental factors in order to justify any therapeutic endeavor, whereas the development of its theoretical structure brought out the importance of constitutional factors which conveniently served to justify its failures. This practical justification for the shift of emphasis seems to coincide with social motivations of a larger order. At a time of comparative stability, when psychoanalysis was flourishing, the individual was blamed for his own unfitness, whereas nowadays, in the face of social crisis, its therapeutic importance is justified by blaming a "morbid civilization" for individual suffering.

It is then a matter of convenience when progressive analysts stress what they call the "cultural factor" in neuroses. Such acute awareness of the ever-present influence of the "milieu" smacks too much of an excuse for therapeutic failure, unless it is carried to its practical conclusion, which means, to a change in the social order. In advocating psychological mass-education instead of individual therapy for the prevention of misfits, those social evolutionists are putting the cart before the horse. For education is always an expression of the existing order and remains a willing instrument in the hands of the prevailing type by means of which he imposes his own psychology on the masses. Radical social movements, on the other hand, are not primarily concerned with individual difficulties. Social improvements following in their wake affect only one group favorably, while harming others. When a new regime suppresses dissatisfied individuals and groups, in one way or another, that does not mean that it has abolished all social evils; it merely amounts to a change in form and conception of mal-adjustment, including neurosis and crime. Be that as it may, the neurotic type will feel and appear mal-adjusted in any environment, regardless of whether a defeatist attitude is considered a private matter or a public menace.

Having thus disposed of any social panacea for the abolishment of neurosis, mal-adjustment, and crime, we find no consolation in the theories of evolutionary science. The biological problem as to whether the evolutionary process is determined by the inheritance of acquired characteristics, or comes as the result of natural, i.e. environmental selection, seems to be irrelevant for the behaviour of man, who has created his own environment. This controversy between hereditary versus environmental causation of human behaviour is only a game of hide and seek played by our wishful thinking. A realistic philosophy has always acknowledged—at least tacitly—the individual personality as the practical causation of human behaviour. This implies, however, that the individual will, using impulse and environment alike for the fulfilment of personal desires and social needs, creates an inner causality of its own. Such creative exercise of impulse upon environment automatically leads beyond a mechanistic causality, which separates the individual from his culture, to a dynamic causality of the will, determining the personality as well as its specific culture. Almost all contradictions and controversies of the psychoanalytic schools are due to this confusion between mechanistic causality on which theory has to be based and dynamic causality on which therapy rests. That means, explanatory psychology has to trace the causal links beyond the individual to its social and collective sources in the remote past, where the basic conceptions of human culture and personality originated. Therapy, on the contrary, has to be based on the individual's will as an autonomous force operating beyond and above heredity and environment. Causal explanation, in other words, only acts backwards; we can explain how something has happened—for that matter, in various ways—but we cannot build up life, that is, effect therapy on that basis. We cannot, and what is more, should not try to predict human behaviour to the point of control, inasmuch as we permit and desire growth and development of the self. The human will, moreover, produces not only creative values, but also undesirable reactions equally unpredictable.

Collective therapy manifested in spontaneous reactions of the people seems to follow the same tendency of automatically liberating frustrated forces in the human being. In this sense, revolutions, conceived of as therapeutic mass-movements, provide a paradoxical parallel to individual neurosis. I am not referring here to the superficial disposal of revolutionary behaviour by calling it "neurotic," but to a creative significance of a social behaviour in the light of mass-movements. Each neurosis, on the other hand, is a kind of revolution on the individual's part; a revolution not only against his environment and heredity, but also against the self representing both, and in this sense also a revolution against psychology as the basis of education. Nietzsche, in one of his revealing flashes of insight, puts to psychiatrists the bold question: are there no "neuroses of health"? Are there, that is, spontaneous reactions on the part of frustrated individuals towards a positive liberation of their blocked energies? Every neurosis seems to me to betray that tendency of a rebellion directed, however, not, as in the more active type of revolutionary behaviour, against the environment but against another part of the Self. Whenever this internal struggle becomes too intense, it is externalized by some kind of clash, be it between individuals, groups, classes or nations on the basis of physical, mental or spiritual difference. Such forceful assertion of difference is not to be confused with a constructive tendency towards differentiation inherent in every individual as a life-principle.

Modern psychology, as the last scientific rationalization of the spiritual need for likeness, is only forcing the frustrated expression of natural difference in the direction of hostility and hatred. Thus develops the vicious circle of increasing antagonism—be it between individuals or groups—in which hatred has to be bred as a means of continuous self-assertion, the "neurotic" substitutes for real selfhood. As the believing victim of the democratic ideal of equality, the self-sufficient type of our times is forced to fight his battle of difference within himself. Hence all the reactions of fear and guilt following unavoidable differentiation are condemned as selfish if they cannot be excused as "neurotic." Prevented through his ego-centricity from accepting any kind of difference, either within or without, he feels compelled to change others according to himself. Such craving for likeness in the face of all the multiform differences—individual, social and racial—originates in man's need to counteract the negative aspect of individualization, in the last analysis, death, by the most primitive and elemental idea of perpetuation: namely, the immortalization of one's own self in another resembling it as much as possible.

Whether this universal need for immortalization is expressed in religious, political or psychological terms, it is bound to enhance individual difference and thus create hostility. The democratic ideal of Liberty, Equality and Fraternity is to be understood, from that point of view, as a safeguard against excessive difference—a normal amount of which is necessary for the continuation of any kind of life. In recent times, democracy has been accused of preventing, instead of fostering, individualization, as it is presumed to do. In particular, it has been said that its two basic conceptions, equality and liberty, are entirely antagonistic and irreconcilable. Even a man as liberal as Madariaga frankly states that "liberty and equality seldom go together in actual life. Inequality is the inevitable consequence of liberty."[1] His plea for inequality is, however, not meant in an economic or political sense but rather as a frank recognition of the inherent inequalities in human beings in the sense of our own thesis. As a matter of fact, the idea of liberty in the great democracies of our times has developed in varying degrees from an economic reality of free competition into a psychological unreality of self-expression which the democratic type needs in order to survive. Not unlike the Catholic confession and the therapeutic catharsis, the political freedom of public opinion in speech and print serves as a safety valve against the explosion of resentment

[1] Madariaga, Salvador de. *Anarchy or Hierarchy,* The Macmillan Co., N. Y., 1937.

and hostility in dissatisfied individuals. Such dramatization of personal freedom has little effect on the real politics of the ruling class as long as it is in power. In England, for example, which has been governed for more than three hundred years by an oligarchy of an "aristocratic" type, "there no longer exists a free press," according to Hilaire Belloc.[1] This is not because the press is gagged by law but merely because it is restricted by custom. The idea of personal liberty, however, is still held up and any soap-box orator in Hyde Park is free to *talk* his head off, which would be *taken* off by his listeners in a less psychologically minded country. Hence, our modern revolutionists, having established themselves as communistic and fascistic dictators, rejected this "bourgeois" psychology, although in its duofold aspect it embraces both their ideologies. The behavioristic presupposition that all men are alike psychologically is carried to its socio-economic extreme in Communism, whereas the individualistic extreme of differentiating Psychologism found expression in nationalistic Fascism whose leaders glorify Nietzsche's superman.

Whatever one's attitude may be toward those extreme collectivist movements, it seems necessary to face the fact that they represent cancerous outgrowths of basic democratic principles. The ideal of equality not practically realized in any of the democracies has been carried to its realistic extreme in Communism. On the other hand, the democratic principle of self-determination—extended from individual psychology to whole nations—could serve as the basis for undemocratic totalitarianism. The same holds good for the paradoxical confusion around the other principle of democracy, liberty. In striving for the absolute freedom of the beyond on earth, man becomes more and more unfree—not unlike the neurotic caught in his own

[1] *Essay on the Nature of Contemporary England,* The Macmillan Co., N. Y., 1937.

rebellion against himself. Consequently, the ideal of liberty is used to justify the "laissez-faire" principle in economics, and at the same time allows for economic slavery to carry it through. Besides, the belief that the individual can only express himself fully in his creative power when he is or at least feels entirely free, is a psychological fallacy. Proof of this, to cite only one example here, is the obvious fact that most of the great masterpieces in literature have been created in protest against denied liberty—many of them having been written in prison or exile—but rarely in celebration of achieved freedom.

In order to understand and reconcile such contradictory paradoxes we have to go beyond the absolutistic ideals expressed in those theories of government to the dynamic conception of changing values. Inasmuch as democratic principles are working against individualism and for uniformity, they are at the same time counteracted by automatic reactions on the part of certain individuals or groups, be it in political, economic or psychological terms. In other words, there are always spontaneous reactions working against governmental collectivity, with the important difference that they are willed by individuals and not planned by society.

In the last analysis, all these misunderstandings of the dynamic principle leading to our confusion go back to the difference between ideal conceptions which man needs as something not so much to strive for as by which to justify his realistic mode of living. Equality, as stated, is obviously an ideal never achieved in reality, but seemingly held up as a check against rugged individualism; yet it is conceived of and dealt with as if it were a fact. True, law, with its institutionalization in government, stands as a symbol of equality, but only in the most general sense by which all individuals are alike before God. Equality, in fact, is originally a religious conception introduced or fully expressed by Christianity and promising primarily immortality to everybody, the dispossessed as well as the privileged, in the life beyond. Hence, in our day, where we are faced with the complete breakdown of all those irrational ideologies—including psychology—the few remaining humanists are reverting to Christianity as the only chance democracy has in its struggle against the secular religions of Fascism and Communism. Yet the failure of political democracy to fulfil the true Christian ideology is responsible for the success of the two totalitarian ideologies, which can dispense with Christianity because they come closer to fulfilling the hope of the dispossessed than does democratic Christianity, especially in its Protestant adaptation to industrial capitalism. As a matter of fact, our present crisis, as Drucker points out in his excellent treatise, *The End of Economic Man*,[1] is due to the failure of Western civilization to translate the spiritual conception of equality into a reality. The attempt towards economic equality signifies only the last of these failures; it having been preceded by the failure to establish political equality. In this sense, Marxism, particularly in its present interpretation as Communism, failed to achieve rationally what Christianity could not maintain spiritually, namely, to translate the supernatural into the natural, i.e., to make it realistic. It is an attempt to do the impossible, because the political and economic values of rational man, equality and liberty, are at bottom irrational ideologies aiming to achieve on earth a "perfection" which is only to be found in the beyond. Psychology, in this development, signifies its climax but also its end, for it betrays the final over-reaching of rational man beyond his legitimate control of nature to the very denial of the vital life-force itself.

All our human problems, with their intolerable sufferings, arise from man's ceaseless attempts to make this natural

[1] Drucker, Peter F. John Day Co., Inc., N. Y., 1939.

world into a man-made reality, thereby hopelessly confusing the values of both spheres. In this sense, all human values no matter how real they seem to us—as, for example, money—are unreal, which paradoxically enough does not mean irrational. The rational and the irrational both being human values are not equivalent to the real and unreal representing natural values. The result of this confusion manifests itself in the paradox that the reality in which we live is determined by unreality which we believe to be real because it is rational. All this once more illuminates the importance of my main thesis, namely, that ideologies much more than realities influence, indeed, determine, the behaviour of the individual and subsequently the fate of people. The mere fact that they all eat, sleep and reproduce can only serve as the basis for a general psychology so long as the basic spiritual values expressed in their different mentalities are thought of as being merely of secondary importance in the lives of individuals and the destinies of nations. Hence, in our day, political theories have to appeal to the same need for absolutistic universalities as do the religious and psychological ideologies they fight. Yet what the opposing camps have in common is the fundamental need for immortalization of the self (of their type); the only difference, that one group attempts it in terms of likeness, the other in terms of difference, that is, collectively or individualistically.

In the light of the sweeping social movements of our time, modern psychology appears as a desperate attempt to achieve internally, in the individual self, what those extreme political ideologies are trying to bring about by a change of social system. The temporary compromise achieved in and by our psychological type of the democratic ideal has once more been split up into its two extreme components, manifesting themselves in the struggle between two world-views stated in terms of antagonistic political philosophies. The educational ideal of shaping people according to a uniform type has been replaced by the shaping of a new type of society into which people are forcibly born alike though not equal. Uniformity forced upon the individual from without, however, lacks the personal satisfaction which he seemingly finds in his internal struggle for likeness. Hence, we see the recent systems based on equality, far from being acclaimed as the fulfilment of man's striving for likeness, are counteracted by a heightened sensitivity with regard to social and racial differences.

From this it follows that the present struggle is no longer one for *equal* rights of individuals and nations, but for the right of these to be themselves, that is, just different. In spite of all appearances of a mass-movement in which suppressed and persecuted minorities of various kinds are resisting and succumbing to their exploiters, this world-wide revolution has a highly individualistic keynote. It is neither a fight for equality nor for supremacy, although the two extreme political movements are sailing under those respective flags. It is the age-old strife for self-maintenance extended from the individual to his nation, whose ideology—be it racial, political or intellectual—once more guarantees a spiritual perpetuation of the self in an eternalized type. This struggle of Western man for equality or likeness, as a religious conception, against the realism of individual, social and racial difference, is only one manifestation of man's basic problem of eternalizing his earthly existence by living on a supernatural plan. Human history provides ample proof of man's struggle not so much against the reality of nature as for the unreality of his belief in an eternal soul. In this sense, psychology, by its very nature, is ambiguous in explaining all men as fundamentally alike and yet stressing their differences as personalities. As an explanatory science, psychology shows every individual to be a unique entity in and by himself, whereas the ideology represented by every psychological theory assures the individual of his fundamental likeness to his fellowmen, thereby guaranteeing self-perpetuation regardless of social and political differences. In this sense, too, as I have shown in my book "Seelenglaube und Psychologie," psychology is the last and youngest offspring of religion, more specifically of the age-old belief in the Soul. Yet, just as our political and economic ideologies of equality and liberty could not fulfill their early promises, neither could it replace religion; because in order to appear rational, psychology had to deny the very existence of its parent, the belief in the soul, and rationalize man's desire for immortality in terms of a psychological equality or likeness, which in turn precipitated the willful assertion of difference, economically, politically and racially, from which we are suffering now.

2

The Double as Immortal Self

OUR VIEW of human behaviour as extending beyond individual psychology to a broader conception of personality indicates that civilized man does not act only upon the rational guidance of his intellectual ego nor is he driven blindly by the mere elemental forces of his instinctual self. Mankind's civilization, and with it the various types of personality representing and expressing it, has emerged from the perpetual operation of a third principle, which combines the rational and irrational elements in a world-view based on the conception of the supernatural. This not only holds good for primitive group-life carried forward on a magical world-view, but is still borne out in our highly mechanized civilization by the vital need for spiritual values. Man, no matter under how primitive conditions, never did live on a purely biological, that is, on a simple natural basis. The most primitive people known to us show strange and complicated modes of living which become intelligible only from their supernatural meaning.

Although this has been recognized by modern anthropologists, most of them—not unlike the psychologists—look down on this supernatural world-view as an interesting relic of the primitive's belief in magic which we discarded long ago as superstition. Sir James Frazer, in the last volume of his encyclopedic history of magic, *The Golden Bough*, considers it "a dark chronicle of human error and folly, of fruitless endeavor, wasted time and blighted hopes."[1] Freud, for his part, in comparing primitive superstition with

[1] *Aftermath*, The Macmillan Co., N. Y., 1937.

neurotic behaviour merely brought to light the survival of irrational forces in modern man[1] and thereby proved the inadequacy of rational psychology to explain primitive man's world-view. It signifies little when some advanced writers, in thrusting aside those scientific classifications, seem ready to admit that we ourselves are just as superstitious as the primitive; in fact, are still primitive beneath the surface. Such an admission smacks too much of reform, hence, seems to have a frightening rather than a liberating effect. The fear of this "primitiveness" within ourselves is obviously the result of an unsuccessful attempt to deny it. Be that as it may, this primitivity, which we are able to admit so readily, is to a large extent the product of our own imagination. That is to say, what we really have in common with our remote ancestors is a *spiritual*, not a primitive self, and this we cannot afford to admit because we pride ourselves on living on a purely rational plane. In consequence, we reject those irrational life forces as belonging to our primitive past instead of recognizing them in our present spiritual needs. In this sense is to be understood my earlier conception of the supernatural as the really human element, in contradistinction to the biological life which is *natural* (homo naturalis). My human interpretation conceives of the supernatural as basically identical with what we call "culture," which is after all made up of things non-existent in nature. I mean by that not only all spiritual values of mankind, from the early soul belief to religion, philosophy and its latest offspring psychology, but also social institutions. These too were originally built up to maintain man's supernatural plan of living, that is, were meant to guarantee his self-perpetuation as a social type.

Thus we distinguish in the development of culture and the simultaneous creation of the civilized self three layers: the supernatural, the social and the psychological. The

[1] *Totem and Tabu,* Moffat Yard, N. Y., 1913.

biological self of natural procreation is denied from the beginning, since it implies the acceptance of death. In this sense, the earliest magical world-view was for primitive man not a consoling illusion in his difficult struggle for biological survival but an assurance of *eternal* survival for his self. This man-made supernatural world-view forms the basis of culture, since man had to support himself increasingly with more and more concrete symbols of his need for immortalization. The most powerful instrument for the creation of his own cultural world was religion as expressed in cult ("culture"), from which spring the fine arts, as well as architecture, drama and literature; in a word, the sum of what survives the short span of one personal life-time. Specialists in the fields of archeology, anthropology and sociology are re-constructing from relics of bygone civilizations the characteristic patterns of various culture periods. Here we are not interested in any specific civilization nor do we intend to draw conclusions by comparing material pertaining to different civilizations. On the contrary, we have in mind an approach which I like to call "algebraic," because it deals with the general problem of why and how the human being built up civilization at all and with it a civilized self. That is to say, by re-discovering in our own life lost or disguised spiritual values, which still have to give meaning to our biological and social existence, we intend to show how both the individual personality and his culture emerge from the same need for immortalization.

Man creates culture by changing natural conditions in order to maintain his spiritual self. On the other hand, culture and cultural patterns are instrumental in shaping this self into various personality types. This simultaneous growth and mutual development of personality and culture is not merely valid for the understanding of man's past history, the culture we inherited, but is a living process underlying the creation as well as the maintenance of any given civilization. In this sense, our presentation differs from the approach of the humanistic sciences in that it does not separate the individual from his culture, but conceives of both the personal and cultural development as one inseparable unit. The different sciences dealing with these developments have to split up this unity not merely through the necessity of their specialization but for the deeper reason of their causal ideology, which actually sets us apart from our past by disposing of it—"historically." While one scientist, pointing to our past, proudly states: "That's where we came from," another disapprovingly adds: "that's where we still are." This need to detach ourselves from our past while we are still living on its spiritual value creates all the human problems and social difficulties which the humanistic sciences cannot solve because they themselves are victims of this "historization," due to man's gift—or curse—of memory. By making memory alive, that is, in being fully ourselves instead of thinking about it, we can acknowledge our spiritual needs without having to condemn them as primitive.

In order to show how culture develops, neither geographically nor anthropologically but from that inner spiritual need, we will confront in the following pages the dynamic personality of modern man with its remotest but still living ancestor, the spiritual self of primitive man. This primitive material we are introducing not in an historical or explanatory sense but merely as illustrative of survivals in modern man, who, having created civilization and with it an over-civilized ego, disintegrates by splitting up the latter into two opposing selves. Those two aspects of the self which in modern man are opposing and fighting each other provide, to be sure, the original raw material for his personality makeup. Yet it makes all the difference whether they are united in the expression of a total personality or driven by conflicting strivings between the two selves, manifested as the antimony of acting or "thinking and feeling." Such dichotomy of conflict, interfering with full living and functioning, is not to be confused with the basic dualism between the natural and spiritual self which was dynamically balanced in the magic world-view. The primitive and modern material concerning the Double, which we are confronting in this chapter, will show how a positive evaluation of the Double as the immortal soul leads to the building-up of the prototype of personality from the self; whereas the negative interpretation of the Double as a symbol of death is symptomatic of the disintegration of the modern personality type. Such a complete reversal, as is borne out by our juxtaposition of folk-loristic and literary tradition, betrays a fundamental change in man's attitude towards life from a naïve belief in supernatural forces which he was certain could be influenced by magic to a "neurotic" fear of them, which he had to rationalize psychologically.

As early as 1914, before the emotional shock of the World War upset the foundations of an over-rationalized civilization, I published an essay on the literary motif of the Double,[1] the structural analysis of which laid bare the irrational roots of human psychology in primitive magic. Such development of a respectable science from earlier superstitious beliefs cannot be surprising or embarrassing when we remind ourselves that from time immemorial man was forced to protect himself against the unknown forces of nature by pretending to be able to control them in one form or another. Centuries before our Western science of astronomy was established, the high priests of Oriental religion practised astrology in order to foresee and thus direct the destiny of their people; this very science, in fact,

[1] "Der Doppelgaenger," "Imago," 1914. Reprinted, Internationaler psychoanalytischer Verlag, Vienna, 1925. French translation under the title, "Don Juan, Une étude sur le Double," Paris, 1932.

was made possible by an objective observation of planets, which, in the ancient civilizations of the East, emerged from such subjective interpretation of the firmament. Likewise, our science of chemistry was developed from the mysterious experiments of medieval alchemists, determined to outdo nature by producing gold, indeed, creating life itself in their cauldrons. Whether or not these scientific children of a later age are willing to acknowledge their uneducated parents, we should not hesitate to trace their ancestry and their heritage, especially with such a problem child as we have found psychology to be.

As a student, having fallen under the spell of the new scientific psychology, I became aware in its early days of the inadequacy of rational psychology—even that of the unconscious—to explain the unchanging effect of an age-old theme throughout the centuries. More than twenty-five years ago, I happened to see a moving-picture which revived the theme of the Double—famous since the days of Greek mythology and drama—in a more phantastic realism than has ever been possible on the stage. The popularity of this eternal tragi-comedy of errors caused by man's encounter with his double has, however, as is the case with many renowned literary motifs, been periodic. Just as the subject of antagonism between brothers was typical for the literary epoch at the end of the eighteenth century, and the motif of incestuous love between brother and sister characteristic for the Elizabethan age, so it was in the era of German Romanticism that the theme of the Double was in vogue. The renewed interest shown then in the old "Double" of stage-fame, whose humorous entanglements with himself had become subjected to a psychological scrutiny by introspective novelists, cannot be sufficiently accounted for by their eccentric personalities alone. Similar currents in German philosophy at that time suggest that a deeper reason is to be found in the mentality of a whole period once more questioning the identity of the Self. After Kant —"the Philosopher of the Revolution"—had systematized the mentality of the bourgeois type, the underlying principle of self-determination was carried to its individualistic extreme by the romantic philosophers. Disappointed at the actual results of the French Revolution, the romantics outdid Kant, who had taught that the laws of nature had been legislated by the mind. This idealistic conception they applied to the whole pattern of historical development which they conceived of as identical with the growth of self-consciousness. Hence, the true object of knowledge could only be self-knowledge. On that basis they justified personal, class and national aspirations as being evolved from the development of the Self, construed by Fichte as ethical, by Hegel, as logical and by Schelling as aesthetical.

It is not surprising to find that this philosophic self-centredness of the Romantic epoch appears reflected in its contemporary literature. In fact we find these romantic authors interpreting the theme of the Double as a problem of the Self, that is to say, they first looked at it from a psychological point of view. Their choice of the *subject* of dual personality for the probing into the depth of the human Self, resulted undoubtedly from their own inner split personality, characteristic of the romantic type—hence the conflicting and frustrated emotions of the romantic, a paradoxical type shaped by the repercussions of the French Revolution and glorifying Napoleon, who emerged victorious after it, as the ideal super-man. Once more man had become aware of the irrational forces within himself, the artistic expression of which he had to justify intellectually by subscribing to a new philosophy of the Self.

While this preoccupation with the Self accounts for the romantic's obsession with the *subject* of the Double, the explanation for the typical *form* in which this motif persistently appears from Antiquity to the present day has to be derived—beyond the psychology of the individual—from ancient traditions and primitive folk beliefs. Since the plot of the above-mentioned film, "The Student of Prague," drawn from the well-known "Story of the Lost Reflection" by the famous romanticist, E. T. A. Hoffman, combined practically all the old motifs inherent in the subject, I choose to perform what might be called an autopsy on this generalized literary motif. The hero, a reckless libertine, in one of his desperate moods sells his own reflection to a human impersonation of the Devil, only to realize too late the vital importance of his seemingly useless image in the mirror. This, to his bewilderment, takes on an independent life of its own; it follows its former owner, interfering with his social ambitions and his amorous affairs until it becomes a real persecutor driving its victim to suicide. The gruesome death of the hero is brought about through his final attempt to end this terrifying persecution by killing his alter-ego, thereby destroying his own self. Those phantastic happenings take on an uncanny feature with the appearance of the double—played in the film by the same actor as the youthful image of the hero, who himself is aging and has adopted moral standards contrary to those of his former self. The encounters of these conflicting selves at crucial moments in the hero's life provide the necessary complications for a plot, the moral of which seems to imply: a man's past—represented in the film by the hero's own youthful image—is so intimately bound to his vital being that misfortune befalls him if he tries to detach himself too completely from it.

While some writers, like Robert Louis Stevenson in his *Strange Case of Dr. Jekyll and Mr. Hyde*, dramatized this moral aspect of the subject in a hero possessed by an evil self, others, like Dostoievski, in his early story "The Double" (1846) elaborated its psychological intricacies to a point reaching the clinical exactness of a study in paranoic persecution and megalomania. In such psychological and moralistic presentations of the Double, their authors are dealing with illusions in a more or less split personality, whereas in other stories the double appears concretely personified by an identical protagonist, as in Edgar Allan Poe's tale, "William Wilson," where the hero's namesake acts as his guardian angel. In German romanticism, however, this same motif, namely, two figures appearing in identical form like twins has been elaborated upon in a truly morbid fashion. Jean Paul, the father of romantic fiction, especially, dwells in his complicated plots on pathological types whose identify becomes confused with that of their doubles. In his most noted work, *Titan,* he is said to have derided Fichte's philosophy of the Self by carrying his transcendental idealism ad absurdum. One of the most pathological figures in this novel cannot look at any part of his body without being seized by the dread of his double, a fact which drives him into such a rage that he breaks all the mirrors reflecting his despised self; no wonder he dies insane—with Fichte's phrase of identity on his lips.

Compared to such extravagancies in vogue during the Romantic period, other presentations in which the hero sells his reflection to the Devil or loses his shadow, as in the famous story of Peter Schlemihl (known to English readers from Howitt's translation), appear, despite the hero's tragic fate, naive, not to say, fairy-tale like. There seems inherent in the subject itself a dual aspect which permits its treatment in different forms, varying from the naive comedy of errors enacted between identical twins to the tragic, almost pathological loss of one's real self through a superimposed one. Bearing in mind these duofold potentialities of our subject, we turn to the constant symbolism which this theme—no matter how greatly elaborated upon—has preserved throughout the ages: namely, the presentation of the second self by one's own shadow or reflection. This motif I have traced back, in my essay on the Double referred to, to ancient traditions and folk beliefs which may be considered man's first conception of the soul. Numerous superstitions regarding one's shadow or image still prevalent in all parts of our civilized world correspond to widespread tabus of primitives who see in this natural image of the self the human soul.

This belief explains both the reverence shown the shadow and the corresponding tabus based on the conception that any harm done the shadow affects its owner. Primitive people are not only afraid to let their shadow fall on certain objects, especially food, but also dread the accidental falling upon them of the shadows of other people—above all those of pregnant women and mothers-in-law. They are careful that no person shall ever cross their shadow and take special care that their shadows do not fall on the dead, or on a coffin, or a tomb—one reason, it is supposed, why their burials often taken place at night. Their greatest fear, however, concerns the intentional injury of their shadow by means of magic, since according to a common belief an enemy can be killed by the wounding of his shadow. Many other folk traditions of a similar kind clearly indicate that primitive man considers the shadow his mysterious double, a spiritual yet real being.

Still another dual aspect of the double itself is one of the most puzzling features of this seemingly naive conception of a primitive soul and accounts for the confusion on the subject in anthropological literature. It seems inconceivable for modern man, brought up with the idea of a unified personality and trained in rational thinking, that a contradictory meaning should be simultaneously given to one and the same phenomenon. Yet the double in its most primitive form, the shadow, represents both the living and the dead person. Accordingly, the shadow is protected from injury like the real self, the death of which, however, does not affect the shadow surviving it. Strangely enough, the latter seems to have been endowed not only with an independent life of its own but is considered the most vital element of the human being, the soul. Illness and health among the primitives are diagnosed by the appearance of the shadow: one which is small or faint indicates that the owner will fall ill; a strong shadow predicts health; and the absence of one altogether signifies death. According to some authors, the fact that a corpse lying on the ground could not cast a shadow also proved that the shadow had departed with the soul. Even in our present day, among certain primitives, the sick are brought into the sunlight in order that their shadow may be recalled and with it the departing soul. In this connection it is of human interest to report a story about Chamisso, the creator of Peter Schlemihl, the man who lost his shadow. Just what this strange motif signifies was a question much disputed at the time. A number of interpretations were suggested, none of them satisfactory, least of all to the author himself. He always remained sceptical of those explanations of the shadow, but a remark he made to a friend a few weeks before his death touches precisely upon its essential meaning. "People," he said, "have often asked me in the past what I think the shadow signifies. If they were to ask me this now, I would answer: 'It is the health which I lack. The absence of my shadow is my illness.' " The waxing and waning of the shadow—treated in a charming poem of Stevenson's, "My Shadow"—as an indication of good or ill health is actually made a criterion for immortality by the Zulus who believe that the large shadow of a man will some day join his ancestors, whereas the short one will remain with the dead.

Although anthropologists agree that primitive man regards the shadow as the equivalent of his soul, their explanation of this belief is based on our rational conception of a unified personality which they ascribe to him and which denies the essentially dualistic nature of man. Recent investigations on the subject, particularly from a linguistic point of view, have clearly shown that Tylor's conception of an "animistic" soul as the condition of life constituting the unity of all the spiritual faculties[1] by no means applies to the belief of all primitive peoples. Far more widespread is a dualistic or an even still further differentiated idea of the soul. Many peoples designate the soul of the living man—as the vehicle of vital and often of the conscious life —and the soul which survives, the spirit of the dead, by quite different names and regard them as two distinct entities. Sometimes the division goes even further; a number of souls are thought of as surviving, while on the other hand there are several life-souls for the vital functions in the conscious life. Although some primitives use the same word for shadow and spirit or soul, the most primitive people known to us distinguish verbally and conceptually between two different souls in man. The inhabitants of Northern Melanesia, who have remained at a very primitive stage, have for "shadow" and "soul" two words, though derived from the same root. According to Frazer, certain natives of Australia distinguish between a soul located in the heart and another intimately bound to the shadow. The natives of the Fiji Islands, who picture the soul as a miniature human being, believe that every man has two souls: a dark soul which dwells in his shadow and eventually perishes, and a light one which is seen in his reflection in water or a mirror and remains with him when he dies. Similarly, the inhabitants of Greenland and the Algonquins believe in the existence of two souls, even as the Tamais who live in New Guinea distinguish between a long soul

[1] Tylor, Sir Edward Burnett. *Primitive Culture,* 2 vols. J. Murray, London, 1871.

that moves—identified with the shadow—and a short one that leaves the body at the moment of death.

How man came to see the soul in his shadow may be explained by the assumption that he first saw his own image in it, inseparable from himself and yet not only changing its form but also disappearing at night. It seems to me that this observation of the human shadow disappearing with the fertilizing sun to reappear with its return made it a perfect symbol for the idea of an immortal soul. According to a universal conception of mankind, the sun disappeared each day into the underworld and gave to the souls who continued to live there their shadow-life, that is, the possibility of survival and return to earth. It is then, in my opinion, not so much the resemblance of the shadow to the self as its appearance and disappearance, its regular return to life, as it were, which made the shadow a symbol of the returning soul still surviving in our spiritual belief in immortality. In the original duality of the soul concept, I am inclined to see the root of man's two endeavors to preserve his self and to maintain the belief in its immortality: religion and psychology. From the belief in a soul of the dead in one form or another sprang all religion; from the belief in the soul of the living, psychology eventually developed.

This development was initiated in ancient Greece, where out of the religious idea of the soul the first rational psychology was formulated. The connecting link is to be found in philosophic speculation, especially in Plato's philosophy of the soul, the material aspect of which his pupil Aristotle systematized into a psycho-physiology. The development of Greek views on the soul, first outlined in Erwin Rohde's fundamental work, *Psyche,*[1] and since amended by modern scholars from more recent studies of the primitives, is of basic importance for the understanding of the whole Chris-

[1] Leipzig, 1893.

tion mentality of our Western world. Homer, who preserved for us the oldest and best evidence of Greek folk-views on the subject, had no idea of it as unified, any more than do the primitives who distinguish the soul of the dead from the mental functions of the living. "According to Homer," Rohde states, "man has a dualistic existence, the one in his visible appearance, the other in his invisible image which becomes free only after death—this, and no other, is his soul. In animate man there dwells as a strange guest a more feeble Double—his other Self in the form of his Psyche—whose kingdom is the world of dreams. When the conscious Self sleeps, the Double works and watches. Such an image (*ειδωλον*), reflecting the visible Self and constituting a second Self, is, with the Romans, the Genius; with the Persians, the Fravauli; with the Egyptians, the Ka."

"Psyche" in Homer, according to the latest interpretations, denotes only the soul of the dead, whereas the various functions of the living (reason, emotion, etc.) are ascribed to vital organs of the body (like the diaphragm or the heart), any injury to which results in death. Thus the Homeric idea of the soul corresponds in essence to that of primitive man, there being in both a conception of dualism between the soul of the living and the soul of dead which only later came to be united in a single concept of the soul, the Psyche. This word itself originally denoted only the soul which survives after death, the spirit of the dead, the duplicate soul, and did not comprise the multiplicity of living functions. The conception of a Psyche which assumed the soul of the dead also to exist in the living, appears thus as a late product of philosophic speculation.

In confronting those ancient conceptions of the dual soul with its modern manifestation in the literature of the Double, we realize a decisive change of emphasis, amounting to a moralistic interpretation of the old soul belief.

Originally conceived of as a guardian angel, assuring immortal survival to the self, the double eventually appears as precisely the opposite, a reminder of the individual's mortality, indeed, the announcer of death itself. Thus, from a symbol of eternal life in the primitive, the double developed into an omen of death in the self-conscious individual of modern civilization. This revaluation, however, is not merely due to the fact that death no longer could be denied as the end of the individual existence but was prompted by the permeation of the whole subject of immortality with the idea of evil. For the double whom we meet after the completion of this developmental cycle appears as a "bad," threatening self and no longer as a consoling one. This change was brought about by the Christian doctrine of immortality as interpreted by the church, which presumed the right to bestow its immortality on the good ones and exclude the bad ones. At a certain period during the Middle Ages this fear of being doomed on Judgment Day—that is, of not participating in the eternal life of the good—became epidemic in the cult of the Devil, who in essence is nothing but a personification of the moralized double. His origin in the old soul belief is still shown in numerous stories where the hero sells his shadow or reflection to an impersonation of the Devil in order to gain worldly pleasures. This common folk-belief of a soulless Devil eager to secure a good man's immortal soul by seducing him to evil has been immortalized in Goethe's "Faust." The artist took the traditional folk-tale and lifted it from its superstitious entanglements into a human struggle for self-immortalization through work, that is, self-realization.

Similar revaluations in the history of famous literary subjects[1] point to a social function of the artist who humanizes traditional folk-beliefs by animating them with his own spiritual struggle for immortality. What enables the crea-

[1] See my book, *Don Juan, Une Étude sur le Double,* Paris, 1932.

tive writer to express his inner dualism—Goethe through Faust speaks directly of the two souls in his bosom—without being too much thwarted by its conflicting struggle, is not, as modern psychology suggests, simply a matter of degree.[1] Though both the artist and the neurotic are beset by similar conflicts, it does not mean much to explain the one type by the other. The irrational forces which are operating in both types are striving for some kind of rationalized, that is, accepted form of expression. The neurotic fails in that attempt inasmuch as his productions remain irrational, whereas the artist is able and permitted to present his creation in an acceptable form justifying the survival of the irrational in the midst of our over-rationalized civilization. This cultural function, which I have always considered the main distinction of the artist,[2] is borne out in the treatment of the Double-motif as it was developed in the works of prominent authors. There can be no doubt that it is the same exaggerated fear of death threatening the destruction of the Self which the artist has in common with the neurotic. Yet the creative type, in dealing with this fundamental problem of the Self, achieves his personal justification by performing his cultural function—to revive the spiritual values of irrational forces for his generation and thus promote their continuity. Hence, the astounding limitation of literary inventiveness and the seeming monotony of ever-recurring plots. We have to turn from the content of literature to its function in order to appreciate that the artist's imaginative faculty is shown not so much in the invention of new motifs as in recapturing the true spirit of popular tradition to which his irrational self is sensitive.

It is for this reason that we find the most popular stories of the Double based on current folk-belief. At the same

[1] My differing viewpoint is fully documented in *Art and Artist,* Alfred A. Knopf, Inc., N. Y., 1932.

[2] *Der Kuenstler, Internationaler* psychoanalytischer Verlag, Wien, 1907.

time, it is not surprising to find pathological elements, such as the hero's persecution by his double, introduced by modern authors whose creative sensibility responds likewise in morbid moods to the threat of irrational elements. It is almost as if the primitive curse of overstepping the tabus, which protected the double, has struck the artist daring to gain immortality by creating a profane image of his spiritual self. Some of these authors while writing their stories felt death, as it were, on their heels. Stevenson was severely ill from a hemorrhage when, in a dream, he conceived the essential scenes of his *Strange Case of Dr. Jekyll and Mr. Hyde.* This first draft, however, he burned as unsatisfactory and hastened to re-write the whole story, a feat which he accomplished in three days, presumably not to lose it again but actually for fear of his failing health. "I drive on with Jekyll," he wrote in a letter, "bankruptcy at my heels."[1] Guy de Maupassant wrote his gruesome account of a spectre, "Le Horla," seemingly at the beginning of his fatal illness. The common assumption that the author was already insane when he wrote this story has recently been refuted by his former valet Francois.[2] Francois, who at the age of seventy-eight still refers to his late master as "Monsieur," said that Maupassant was perfectly lucid at the time he wrote the book, in August, 1887. When he sent the novel to the publisher, he told Francois that before a week had elapsed all Paris would be saying he was crazy. Actually, it was not until 1891, four years later, that Maupassant began to feel insanity coming on; when he realized he could no longer retain his right state of mind, he attempted suicide by cutting his throat. This typical outcome of persecution by the double, although precipitated by the author's illness, was by no means caused by it. Through-

[1] Balfour, Sir Graham. *The Life of Robert Louis Stevenson,* Charles Scribner's Sons, N. Y., 1901.

[2] In an interview with "Paris Soir," July 3, 1933.

out his life Maupassant had been struggling against the "Intimate Enemy," which he had long recognized as a double personality in himself. Like Poe and Hoffman, he also suffered from hallucinations which he described in his work.

There exists one account of an actual experience of this sort which Maupassant had in 1889 and which he related that same evening to a friend. He was sitting at his desk in his study, having given strict orders that no one was to be admitted. Suddenly he had the impression that someone had opened the door. He turned around and to his great astonishment saw his own self enter and sit down in front of him, resting his head on his hand. All that Maupassant wrote on this occasion was dictated to him by his double. Having finished, he rose and the phantom vanished. This account[1] sounds like a scene from his *Le Horla* which, however, must be considered an intuition rather than a recording of another such actual experience. Of Poe, it is well known that he died at the early age of thirty-seven in a fit of delirium tremens. His story, "William Wilson," is generally regarded as a confession, since it pictures the fate of a man ruined by gambling and drinking, who finally, despite the efforts of his better self to save him, kills himself. Many years before his end, Poe also suffered from various obsessions and nameless apprehensions; he was troubled by a persecution mania and had delusions of grandeur. In his recent book, *Edgar Allan Poe; a Study in Genius,*[2] Joseph Wood Krutch considers the famous stories and poems not as works of artifice but as more or less disguised expressions of queer realities in Poe's life, particularly since it is known that many of his ideas came to him in visions and hallucinations.

Of all the authors who introspectively recognized an

[1] Quoted from Sollier, *Les phénomènes d'Autoscopie,* Paris, 1913.
[2] Alfred A. Knopf, N. Y., 1926.

early split in their personality, no one probably was more driven by the fear of death than was Dostoievski. While still a student at the Polytechnic, he suffered from slight fits, probably epileptic, and was afraid of being buried alive, as was Poe, likewise a victim of epilepsy. In many passages of his works, Dostoievski has described his later "grand mal" in masterly fashion. Before going into the aura, he was able to catch a glimpse of the "happiness that could not be experienced in ordinary life and of which no other man could have an idea. . . . This sensation is so powerful, so agreeable, that one would give ten years for a few seconds of such felicity, and perhaps even one's life." After each fit, however, he was terribly depressed and felt himself a criminal. During the last days of his life to Petrograd, he wrote: "I have had an attack lasting ten days and for five days since I have been prostrated. I am a lost man—my reason has really suffered and that is the truth—I know it. My nervous confusion has often brought me near to madness." He not only experienced these states of unconsciousness frequently but having been condemned to death as a revolutionist and graced only at the last minute, he actually died, so to speak, a living death, described in *The Idiot*. His feeling of being constantly persecuted by death, which even seems to account for the expressionism of his hectic style,[1] cannot be explained as the result of those abnormal experiences alone, but is the most fundamental feature of his personality make-up. According to Merejkovsky, the theme of the Double was for Dostoievski his main personal problem: "Thus all his tragic and struggling pairs of real people who appear to themselves as complete entities are

[1] "In these rapidly sketched, mobile, fluctuating descriptions of Dostoievski's, one feels the hurried impressionism and abnormal clarity of a consciousness already anticipating the approach of insensibility. In his descriptions we find a completely unique form of realism of an epileptic, and one who has suffered the death sentence." (Grossman, L., in his recent edition of Dostoievski's works in Russian.)

presented as two halves of a third divided personality—halves which, like the doubles, seek themselves and pursue themselves." This is carried out in the most grandiose manner in his last and greatest novel, *The Brothers Karamazov,* where Smerjakov is pictured as the double of his brother Ivan, the two not only usually appearing together and discussing the same subjects but being inseparably united by a favorite motif of Dostoievski's, the idea of the potential criminal. This double (says Ivan) "is only a personification of myself, in fact only a part of myself . . . of my lowest and stupidest thoughts and feelings." In some of the omitted passages of *The Possessed*, Stavrogin, still trying to convince himself that his hallucination of the double is subjective and not the Devil, says: "I don't believe in him, do not yet believe. I know that this is only myself in different manifestations, splitting myself and talking to myself. But he is determined to become an independent Devil, so that I have to believe in his existence." In this last work of Dostoievski, the hero Ivan propounds the author's moral philosophy in a poetic vision of the Devil, who is presented as a creation of man in his own image. Before Ivan becomes insane, the Devil appears to him and declares himself his double; Ivan, however, refuses to recognize the reality of the apparition. "You are an illusion, a malady, a deception, but I do not know how to destroy you. You are an hallucination, you are only a manifestation of myself, that is to say, of my thoughts and of my most abominable thoughts at that. All that has been long since dead, all the opinions that I uttered long ago, you bring up here as if they were new."

Here we find ourselves again confronted with the meaning of the double, as a representative of the individual's past. Originally, the double was an identical self (shadow, reflection), promising personal survival in the *future*; later, the double retained together with the individual's life his personal *past*; ultimately, he became an opposing self, appearing in the form of evil which represents the perishable and mortal part of the personality repudiated by the social self. Those three essential stages in the development of the ideas on the double we find epitomized in the successive treatment of this theme in three of Dostoievski's masterpieces: his early story, "The Double," his most fascinating study, *The Possessed,* and his last and maturest work, *The Brothers Karamazov.* Dostoievski himself has confessed that Goliadkin, the paranoiac hero of his early novel, was the mouthpiece of his own feelings. The author had planned to rewrite this too-revealing account but evidently felt compelled to treat the same subject in a more objective manner. In this, his second story of a double, called "The Youth," the hero is definitely characterized as a case of split personality who describes himself in the following words: "You know, I seem to duplicate myself, to divide myself into two parts—actually double myself and I'm terrified of this doubling. I feel as if my double were standing next to me; one is oneself sober and sensible and the double absolutely wants to do something silly, sometimes something very funny; and then one suddenly realizes that one actually wants to do this oneself. God knows why, one wants it somehow involuntarily, one resists it and yet one wants it with all one's will power." Interestingly enough, Dostoievski closes his description of Versilov's split by a self-conscious remark which indicates that the author has familiarized himself with the current literature on psychopathology: "What is the double really?" he asks. "He is—at least according to a medical book of an expert that I consulted lately on this subject—nothing but the first stage of insanity which may end in disaster, a dualism between feeling and willing." Following the above-sketched development of the idea of the double in three successive characters of Dostoievski's main works, Professor D. Tschizewskij, exiled in Prague after the revolution, concludes in his philosophical interpretation of *The Double in Dostojevskij*[1] that they represent the artist's protest against nineteenth-century rationalism, according to which man only exists in the material world and in a material sense. The double breaking through as he does in Dostoievski's characters is evidence of the uncertainty an individual feels when confronted with a more real existence opened up in the face of unknown forces. The first witness, Goliadkin, appears as a more passive victim of this principle, in that the rational forces are crushing him from without, whereas Stavrogin and his fully developed successor, Ivan Karamazov, are consumed by their rationalism from within.

This literary development of the Double-motif shows how its moralistic revaluation of folk-tradition is accompanied by an intellectual interpretation in literature aimed to counteract its threatening irrational power. In giving the main folk-belief a tragic form, the artist not only disposes of his irrational self in his work but at the same time enables the public to detach itself from both the writer and his creation. Such artistic transformation of a primitive motif differs, however, from the historical detachment of scientific classification in that it appears as a living expression of powerful personalities still under the spell of those irrational forces. In giving them form, that is, rational expression, the artist enables the public to feel sufficiently removed from the irrational elements to dare vicariously to participate in them. This dual rôle of the public explains the fascination great tragedies have for us, in that we not only take part in the hero's human suffering but by the same token participate in the super-human greatness for which he suffers. Our form of tragedy as the offspring of early Greek cult and ritual still performs the same spiritual function as did those religious ceremonies: that of temporarily

[1] Reichenberg, 1933.

uniting the "commoner" with irrational life-forces from which the average man in his daily existence had to be protected by all sorts of strict tabus. On certain festive occasions, however, when those tabus were lifted, the priests and kings permanently endowed with the sacred duty of preserving that essential life-force communicated it to the people. It is from such seasonal renewal of the irrational self in the spiritual ceremonies of magic participation that culture developed. Culture is derived from "cult," not only linguistically but also functionally, that is, as a continuous translation of supernatural conceptions into rational terms. Culture, then, is conceived of here as an expression of the irrational self seeking material immortalization in lasting achievements. In this sense, culture serves a dual function: it preserves the old spiritual life-values in a more permanent form, independent of the seasonal re-creation, and at the same time provides a more direct and permanent participation of the average group member in the creation and maintenance of its symbols.

This dual aspect of culture as a rationalized concretization of spiritual values is epitomized in the earliest personification of the Double-soul, namely, the *twin*, a symbol of greatest importance in the building-up of human civilization. Among primitives we find an ambivalent attitude towards the unusual phenomenon of twins who—similarly to the shadow—were at the same time tabued and venerated, feared and worshipped. Although these folk-traditions have been known to anthropologists, they were merely considered another example of curious superstitions representing primitive man's ignorance. It was not until recent times that a scholar in the field of religion convincingly showed that an early cult of twins was a decisive factor not only in the formation of religion but in the origin of all human civilization. In his learned book called, with reference to the Biblical theme, *Boanerges,*[1] Rendel Harris has impressed upon us the cultural significance of a subject which has been known to us only through its human appeal in literary presentation.

Yet while the theme of the Double as a symbol of modern man's split personality found expression in the tragic fate of the hero, the subject of the twin has been familiar to us throughout centuries in its humorous treatment. Everyone knows the famous twin-comedies which for more than 2000 years provided the theatre of our Western world with never-failing entertainment. From the original Greek of Plautus ("Menaechmi"), numerous variations and imitations of this humorous entanglement between two identical heroes have been drawn. We mention only Shakeseare's "Comedy of Errors" (recently revived on Broadway as "The Boys from Syracuse"), Molière's version of the Greek "Amphitryon" (where the valet's name "Sosie" became the French synonym for "double") and in more recent times Gilbert and Sullivan's "The Gondoliers" and Tristan Bernard's "Les Jumeaux de Brighton" (lately adapted to the screen by Laurel and Hardy in "Our Relations"). Of all the humorists who revived this immortal motif to expose the all-too-human fallacies of their fellowmen, there was only one, Mark Twain, who recaptured its underlying depth and thus gave back to the sophisticated motif its true human value. Fascinated by this curious subject, which was so deeply rooted in his personality that it even determined his choice of a pen-name, he brought out its uncanny aspect previously buried by farcical depreciation. Besides the well-known stories in which Mark Twain used the symbol of twinship to present the conflict in man's dual nature—in *The Prince and the Pauper*, for example, or more directly in his explanatory appendix to *Pudd'nhead Wilson*—there exists a less-known personalized story presumably record-

[1] London, 1913.

ing his interview with a reporter. There Mark Twain bemoans a fictitious twin-brother who, as he says, died as a baby. In response to the reporter's surprise that this forgotten incident should still move him to tears, Mark Twain goes on to explain the circumstances of the accident: he and his twin-brother looked as much alike as two peas, so that even their mother could not tell them apart. One morning, when they were taking their bath together, his little brother drowned; then, after some time, while everyone was mourning him, it was discovered that it was not his brother, after all, but he himself who had drowned.

In the survey that follows of the most primitive and ancient twin-traditions we shall find this motif of interchangeable twins—one of them, as it were, dying for the other—of the utmost importance in the development of the heroic type and his creation: human civilization. In the early folk-traditions concerning twins and twinship, among practically all primitive peoples there exists a rigorous *tabu* of twins; the religious cult of twins appears only at a later stage in civilization. From this, Rendel Harris concluded that the transition from primitivism to civilization was accomplished through a gradual mitigation of the barbarous custom of killing the mother and her twins to a mere expulsion of the tabued infants from the community. To assume such an origin of the cult of twins from a civilized moderation of their tabu seems to be putting the cart before the horse, since this explanation presupposes an automatic progress of civilization without explaining through what dynamic struggle people became civilized. This common fault of most anthropological studies is due to the false perspective civilized man has towards primitive life. Primitive man with his supernatural world-view maintained his life-pattern unchanged throughout the ages not because he cannot change—which would only mean because he is "primitive"—but because he *does not want to change*. Comparable to Alois Riegl's epoch-making discovery in the realm of aesthetic expression, the style of life is just as much "willed" as is the style of art. The Egyptians, for example, did not produce an art inferior to that of the Greeks because their paintings lacked perspective; they simply produced the kind of art they wanted to produce as an expression of their whole civilization (Riegl's "Kunstwille"). By the same token, civilized man starts and continues his cultural development through a will to change in order to differentiate himself more and more from other groups of people. Primitive culture, on the other hand, is based on a will to permanency as expressed in the seasonal rituals which have to be performed exactly in the traditional manner handed down through generations. In liberating himself from this eternal cycle of seasonal revival, civilized man had to find another expression for his need of permanency, which is manifested in the different forms of creative achievement called culture.

In order to appreciate primitive tradition as a different and not inferior order of culture, we have to take into account the dualistic tendencies simultaneously striving towards permanency and change, in psychological terms, towards likeness and difference, respectively.

In one of the first-hand reports from which Harris drew his evidence, the twin-tabu is explained on the basis of that dualistic aspect. Count Goblet d'Alviella, in his report on the Belgian excavations in Court St. Etienne, says: "Amongst most of the non-civilized the birth of twins has always been regarded as, or at least suspected of being a supernatural occurrence, a sorcery, which involves the immolation of the children, and frequently that of the mother; whereas, among other advanced races, they are content with tabu, that is, expulsion or quarantine, in order to prevent their contaminating the rest of the population. But, among the non-civilized, the supernatural is easily confused with ideas of good and bad, lucky and unlucky. It is not surprising, therefore, that our predecessors at one time immolated and venerated certain of their new born twins together with their mothers." Similar beliefs, stating even more positively the divine gifts possessed by twins, were reported verbatim by the Catholic missionary, J. H. Cessou, from the West African (Liberian) tribes: "Twins have indeed the singular gift of learning many things from dreams. This may be because they see the spirits of the dead whose life in the other world is the replica of the earthly life." Here we clearly see the connection between the cult of twins and the belief in the soul. This belief exists among primitives in the form of the totem. Among one certain group of these, the Golahs, the principal tabu forbids the eating of a certain animal, the "bush-goat," which represents a man, or rather, the spirit of a dead man. The name "bush-goat" is, consequently, sometimes given to twins, and continuing his quotation, Cessou writes: "Why then, may not twins eat the bush-goat? Certain twins long ago, the old people told us, saw, it appears, in their dreams that the spirits of dead men take the bodies of bush-goats. They saw some bush-goats which were not animals but men. If you see a bush-goat protecting himself in a certain manner, he is not an animal, but a spirit. Twins, knowing then, from having seen it in a dream that certain bush-goats are men, 'they know them to be man,' cannot eat them; this would be wrong and also if they were to eat them, they would lose their privileges, 'they could not get good heads again, and they no fit see again the things they fit see otherwise.' "

Combined with traces of the ancient cult of animals, we find the cult of twins also among more civilized peoples whose belief in the soul has developed beyond totemism. In ancient Greece, the Dioscures twins, Castor and Pollux, as well as their sister Helen, are venerated as the children of

Leda and the swan. In the history of ancient Rome, the she-wolf (in some versions the woodpecker) is venerated as the foster-mother of the exposed twins, Romulus and Remus. The history of civilization shows that the cult of twins is connected with the domestication of certain animals, such as the horse and bull, and with their use in the service of man, as exemplified by the Açvins—a name signifying "rider twins"—otherwise known as the Heavenly Twins, who played an important part in ancient Hindu religion. On account of an early belief which credits the Açvins with being descended from a horse, they were honored as tamers of the horse, and above all for having invented the yoke, as drivers of chariots. It is not easy to think of the twin-cult being extended to the idea of the harnessing of a team of horses under the same yoke; yet when we meet with the same idea with reference to a team of oxen drawing a plough, or a pair of horses pulling simultaneously, all doubt concerning the cultic origin of pairing or teaming should disappear. Whatever one's opinion on this subject may be, it is certain that the Heavenly Twins were honored not only as heroes who to lighten labor had forced the bull under the yoke but also as inventors of the yoke and even of the plough—briefly, as artisans who laid the foundation for culture.

Among primitive people we find only one of these culture-fostering functions of twins: that of the founding of towns. The first traces can be detected in certain parts of Africa where the following custom is in usage. There exists a form of sanctuary to which a mother must go with her tabued twins to live for a certain time, or even permanently, if she wishes to escape death. Any man wanting to live with her despite her tabu must also go and live in this town of twins, which, situated on an island or in an isolated spot in the forest, gradually becomes the habitat of all the tabued. If we compare this primitive custom with ancient traditions concerning the founding of cities, we find there also the twins playing a most important but quite different part. The story of Romulus and Remus, the founders of Rome, the "eternal city," of Amphion and Zethod, the builders of ancient Thebes, and other similar legends relate how the twin brothers began quarrelling over a place and how one murdered the other in order to become the founder of the city. In a distorted form, this motif appears in Genesis where Cain, after having killed Abel—in some traditions referred to as his twin brother—was driven from his home and through his son Enoch founded the first city of that name.

We cannot here go into the interesting history of twins as founders of cities which, according to Harris, existed in great numbers at a certain period in Europe and are still to be found in the "twin-cities" of America. What we are concerned with here is the changing rôle of twins in the founding of a city, the essential symbol of civilized stability. Among primitives, the isle of salvation (the sanctuary) is founded by the *mother*, who is banished with her twins; whereas among civilized peoples, the city is built by one of the adult brothers after the killing of his twin. The mother, herself, in the latter case, appears only in a minor function as foster-mother, not infrequently in the form of an animal.

This gradual elimination of the mother from her original protective function implies a symbolic significance bearing on the belief in an immortal soul. Prehistoric burial rites clearly indicate that the most primitive idea of a tomb for the dead was a housing for his soul—a replica of the maternal womb from which he was to be reborn. As the primitive conception of the soul—formerly attributed only to the dead—was extended to the living person, the original idea of the grave as the house of the soul was ascribed to the human body itself, as the "housing" of the soul. This development, as I have shown elsewhere,[1] signified a further step towards self-realization impelling the individual to immortalize himself increasingly in personal creation of his own. The twin-traditions are particularly important as the transitional link between the primitive conception of the Double as immortal self and its creative self-expression in works of art. For the twins through their unusual birth have evinced in a concrete manner the dualistic conception of the soul and thereby given proof of the immortality of certain individuals singled out by destiny.

Among such specially endowed individuals, really deviates, the twin stands out as one who was capable of bringing with him into earthly existence his living double and thus had no need to procreate himself in any other form. By the same token, twins were considered self-created, not revived from the spirit of the dead, but generated through their own magic power, independent even of the mother. In the totemistic system, the mother was at least accepted as the instrument through which the spirits of the dead effected re-birth, although no fatherhood was acknowledged. The twins have dispensed with the mother, too, and are dependent only upon each other. In the Egyptian tale of "The Brothers," the earliest known literary record of this motif, dating back to 2000 B.C., the two brothers Anup and Batu, although not designated "twins," were united by a magic bond which made them inseparable throughout life and death. Whatever one experienced the other felt simultaneously; they came to each other's aid in any danger. It appears that in the beginning the twins could only carry out their heroic deeds together, because it was precisely the magic significance of their twinship which assured them invincibility. This seems to be evinced by corresponding South American traditions (especially the epic *Popul Wuh*) in which their disagreement started only after they had ful-

[1] *Art and Artist,* Alfred A. Knopf, Inc., N. Y., 1932.

filled their mission. The killing of one of the twins occasioned by the building of a city has been explained as a propitiatory sacrifice to assure to the dwelling (house or city) long, even eternal life. This cruel custom still practised in medieval times by burying a living child in a new building is, however, the offshoot of a belief among primitives which justifies the killing of one of the twins by explaining that were this not done both would have to die. In our modern conception of the Double, the killing of the alter-ego invariably leads to the death of the hero himself, that is, suicide; at earlier stages, on the contrary, the sacrifice of one of the twins was the condition for the survival of the other. Hence, in twin-mythology the typical motif of fratricide turns out to be a symbolic gesture on the part of the immortal self by which it rids itself of the mortal ego.

This motif contains the nucleus of a conception highly important for the development of human culture. I believe that the heroic type emerged from the cult of twins and the self-creative tendency symbolized in the magic meaning of twinship. As the twins appear to have created themselves independently of natural procreation, so they were believed to be able to create things which formerly did not exist in nature—that is, what is called culture. By working a charm they could make plants grow, without waiting for that growth to occur spontaneously. Not so much by reason of the miraculous fertility which twinship implies as through inherent creative power, they were considered the originators of agriculture. Because they also are totemistic animals, having made themselves independent of sexual procreation, they could tame the bull and, by castration, harness his sexual power. This idea of self-creation seems to be substantiated by the belief that twins of opposite sex can accomplish the sexual act in the womb before they are born, thereby transgressing the severe tabu of exogamy, for which one of them was usually killed after birth.

This idea of the self-creative principle symbolized in twinship leads to the conception of the hero as the type who combines in one person the mortal and immortal self. The birth of the hero from the spirit of twinship can be detected in a tradition common to all civilized people, glorifying the extraordinary lives and deeds of their earlier national heroes. Since those legendary biographies were chiefly concerned with the supernatural origin of the hero, I deduced from them the pattern of "The Myth of the Birth of the Hero,"[1] with typical almost standardized motifs. The most naïve form it takes is found in a Babylonian inscription dating back approximately to 2500 B.C., in which the founder of the first dynasty cryptically states that his father was unknown and his mother exposed him in a basket on the water which carried him down to the city where he eventually became king. The reader will instantly recall the well-known story of Moses in the bulrushes without, however, realizing that he has struck upon the veritable hornet's nest in anthropological discussions, namely, the problem of diffusion of culture. The issue in question is whether those typical motifs are found widely diffused because they have wandered all over the world, as the mythological school maintains, or because they are genuine products of the human mind, as the more psychologically oriented anthropologists are inclined to believe. In my early work on this subject, I applied Freud's observation of individual foundling-phantasies ("success-stories")[2] to the understanding of those mythical biographies which, although representing the nation's early history, appear to be written from the point of view of the hero. Their similarity all over the world, I explained, however, from Adolf Bastian's theory of "elementary ideas" as a cultural phenomenon which seems to develop unfailingly wherever man lives. Whether

[1] In my book of that name, 1908. English translation, N. Y., 1914.
[2] Confirming statistics concerning the frequency of those phantasies.

or not these mythical traditions also wandered from one country to another seems to me less important than that they invariably relate that the *hero* has wandered from one country where he was a commoner to another where he became a leader. This universal illustration of the old saying that no one is a prophet in his own country seems to reflect the typical experience that the hero, saviour or leader of a people is usually of foreign origin. Even when he has successfully established himself as the legitimate ruler starting a dynasty of his own, sooner or later another foreigner emerges in times of crisis to turn the people to a new allegiance. Since history records such epoch-making events in the advent of Jesus, the Jew, who became the founder of Christianity, or Napoleon, the Corsican, who made himself the master of a foreign country, indeed, of a continent, we can assume that mythical traditions, abounding with such "success-stories," must reflect some truth. Whether this is always an historical truth or sometimes but a mythical one seems to me irrelevant, since these legendary traditions appear to transmit the spiritual pattern according to which the hero is supposed to live and act, that is, to make history. From Sargon, the fatherless gardener, who came down the river to found the dynasty of the rulers of Akkad, and Moses, the Egyptian child, who became the national leader of the Jewish people—through the whole series of foreign-born national heroes enumerated in my earlier work—down to the medieval knight with the swan, Lohengrin, who was sent from no-man's land as a saviour to again disappear into the unknown, we can trace the records.

What we see in these traditions concerning the life-story of a hero is the recurrence of a few motifs within the framework of a more or less elaborate national history. The standardized pattern applied to the various national heroes rectifies as it were the hero's life by making it true to form; a form which seems to be the mythical replica of a stereotyped rite carried through as a symbol of immortality. One of those typical motifs which invariably opens the life of the hero, namely, "exposure in water," clearly betrays its cultic origin. Whether or not this tradition reflects the cruel custom of exposing an unwanted child, practised among others besides primitives, it can convincingly be shown from our material that the original motivation for such an act was not a practical, but a magical one. It is reported that certain primitives whose custom it was to kill one of the twins used to expose them both in a small basket on the water to see which would survive. In other words, the exposure of the child was not dictated by economic necessity, but was performed as a rite with the idea of "sink or swim." If the child was going to be a strong man, a future hero, he should be able to save himself. More or less elaborate rationalizations of this motif are to be found in later traditions of the hero's life, among the Greeks, which form the plot for their most impressive tragedies. There, as for example in the famous "King Oedipus," the child is exposed because his father has been warned by an oracle before its birth that his son is to become a mighty hero who will dispossess and murder him. How the hero is saved from an early doom by the substitution of another child who is killed in his stead is a common feature of all those stories and leads us back to the twins.

It seems that in the development of the cultural conception of the hero, as we have said, his semi-mortal twin had to die to assure immortality to the other. The killing of another infant simultaneously born with the hero and replacing his twin became in the final tradition a true earmark of the heroic type. Mythologically, he is constituted by a fusion of the two separate selves, the mortal and immortal, in one and the same personality; he has, so to speak, absorbed his original double, be it shadow or twin, into a doubled self which has, as it were, two lives to spare. This process of absorption is clearly shown in some classical traditions where the hero's twin-bother leads only a shadowy existence, whereas among the South American Indians the double is realistically buried with the after-birth, which is considered to contain the hero's soul. Here we find the lost twin dying a natural death in parturition, instead of being killed later as a symbolic sacrifice assuring the hero's immortality. It seems then that the hero's life-story had to be equipped with the mythical requirements for his immortal deeds to follow by carrying along the original twin in the rudimentary form of the twin-motif. Not infrequently a twin was brought in by proxy, thus giving the future hero's life the indispensable sanctity—at least in retrospect. We know of many instances of such manufactured twinship—Rendel Harris could even detect one in the life-story of Jesus—yet, whatever form the motif takes, the idea of a doubled self, which the hero inherited from his two parents, is the essential characteristic of the genuine heroic type.

The idea prevalent in the traditions of civilized peoples that one of the twins is immortal emerged from the earlier belief in the double, since the twin appeared as a concrete personification of the soul resembling the body like a double, in other words, as the soul in person. This not only makes him independent and invincible but also the fearless revolutionist who dares all mortal men and even the immortal Gods. It is this utter independence which makes the twin the prototype of the hero. In this sense, the traditions of the birth of the hero whose life is saved by the death of a twin are not merely mythical biographies of these individuals, but in their totality they epitomize the birth of the heroic type as such from the magical conception of twinship. At the same time, the form in which they appear reflects the self-creative principle carried to perfection in the heroic type. The autobiographical character of these "success-stories" glorifying the hero's self-elevation—

indeed, self-creation—is clearly shown in the oldest and most genuine tradition of the kind—that of Sargon, king of Akka, who presents the brief summary of his life-career in the first person. Thus, the mythical record of the hero's independent self-creation presents itself at the same time as his first and most lasting creation: the creation of his very type which from a deviate, the twin, became divine, an immortal self.

This conception of the hero, deeply rooted in primitive soul belief—as I have shown in the aforementioned book, *Art and Artist*—crystallized into a type in early Greek civilization and forms the basis for its unsurpassed spiritual achievements. The Greek artist took all his inspirations from commonly known episodes in the lives of the nation's heroes, thereby expressing artistically his own creative self shaped after the heroic type of action. In this sense, the true artist type may be thought of as the hero's spiritual double, who told in immortal works of art what the other had done and thus preserved the memory of it and himself for posterity. It seems that in the development of the Greek artist one form of the double—hitherto referred to only as a variation of the shadow—took on a creative importance. It is man's reflection in a mirror (originally water) which provides a more life-like image of the self than the dark featureless shadow. In Greek mythology, we find traditions bearing out this creative significance of the mirrored image for artistic inspiration. One of the most primitive deities in prehistoric Greece, Dionysos, known through his mysterious cults, was said to have been conceived by his mother Persephone as she admired herself in a mirror. He himself, according to Proclues' account, created the world of things after his miraculous re-birth in the following manner: one day Dionysos gazed at himself in a mirror, the work of the mythical artisan Hephaistos, and, seduced by the reflection, created the external world in his own image.

This self-centred conception of the world's creation has its parallel in Hindu cosmogony, according to which the reflection of the first Being was the cause of the material world. The Neo-Platonists and the Gnostics reversed this theory when they maintained that Adam had lost his celestial nature because he fell in love with his own image.

The latter pessimistic interpretation is deeply rooted in a Greek tradition familiar to us through the well-known story of Narcissus. In its poetic form related by Ovid, the famous seer Tiresias, when asked at the birth of Narcissus whether the boy would have a long life, replied: "Yes, if he never sees himself." Narcissus, equally cold towards youths and maidens, saw his own reflection in the pool and became so enamoured of the beautiful image that he fell ill from love, and, according to tradition, finally committed suicide; even in the Underworld he was said to have continually gazed at himself in the Styx. In a subsequent version related by Pausanius, Narcissus became inconsolable after the death of his twin-sister, who, except for the difference of sex, was his duplicate in every respect. The story goes that eventually he took solace in his own image.

This lyrical tradition of decadent Greece, in which some modern psychologists claim to have found a symbolization of their self-love principle, appears to me as an anti-climax to the self-creative hero and his human representative, the artist-type. The latter's emergence was only possible by the renunciation of the egotistic principle of self-perpetuation in one's own image and the substitution for it of the perpetuation of the self in work reflecting one's personality. In this sense, the sad story of the beautiful youth's early death seems to convey a warning to the individual not to cling to the easy belief in an immortal double by indulging in mere self-admiration. For even in the epoch of Greek tradition, a new religion of immortality had come into being, the deification of the hero, who, being himself immortal, successfully competed with the Gods. This idea of a self-creative power attributed to certain individuals signified a decisive step beyond the naive belief in an automatic survival of one's own double, in that it impressed upon man the conviction that he has to work for his immortality by creating lasting achievements. In this sense, the great Alberti, in the early fifteenth century, could say that when Narcissus saw his reflection in the water and trembled at the beauty of his own face he was the real inventor of painting.

In order fully to appreciate the complete change in world-view implied in this new creative immortalization of a certain type, we have to revert once more to the primitive's ambiguous attitude towards his double. This conflict manifests itself in the perpetual association and rivalry of two groups of ideas regarding the belief in an immortal soul: the one, the notion of a life after death in the same form as that familiar to the living (like the Indians going to their old hunting ground); the other, that of a return to life on earth in a new form which varies according to the cultural pattern. This second idea, in the course of time, has over-shadowed the more primitive one, as borne out in the totemistic belief that the soul of the father or grandfather lives again in the new-born child. The original belief, however, is still apparent in the father's fear that if the child bears too great resemblance to him he is doomed to die; the idea being that it has taken from him his image or shadow, that is to say, his soul.

This fear of a real double—often carried into a phobia of hononymy, as depicted in Poe's "William Wilson"—brings to us man's eternal conflict with himself and others, the struggle between his need for likeness and his desire for difference. Torn between those two opposing tendencies within himself, he creates a spiritual double in his own image only to repudiate his natural double in the physical resemblance of his son. This fight against biological procreation in favor of self-perpetuation received its everlasting impetus from the constant threat of death which overshadows man's life and accounts for all his fearful tabus carried in one form or another into our present day.

While the cult of the dead even among prehistoric man called for some crude image of the deceased, and the later custom of embalming sought to preserve the entire form like a statue, most primitive people show distinct fear of a too life-like image. The horror of having a portrait or photograph made is, according to Frazer, to be found all over the world. Explorers have reported it as true of the Eskimos, the American Indians, and the inhabitants of Central Africa, Asia, and the East Indies. On the basis of their soul-belief those people are afraid that a stranger getting hold of their image might expose them to some evil, possibly death. Some primitives actually fear that they will die as a result of having their pictures taken, and among certain natives of Africa the same fear extends to plastic reproduction in general. Echoes of this primitive fear of likeness are still alive in our Western civilizations, not only in the Balkans but even in parts of Germany, England and Scotland.

Such survival in the highly differentiated personality of our times indicates the eternal conflict between the two essential forms of self-perpetuation. In the artist-ideology of aesthetics a striving for "likeness" has gradually been replaced by an emphasis on difference as the true expression of personality. This development, which we owe to the Greeks, carries the struggle between likeness and difference from the personal plane to a cultural one, where the two opposing aspects appear as the struggle of permanency against change. From that point of view we get an impression of the powerful forces against which the first artist had to struggle, not only to make his work acceptable to others but also in himself to create the artist-type. The first products of these strivings of the artist as a type we still venerate in the heritage of Greek culture. To give the image of a deceased personality the life-like quality resembling his vivid reflection became the highest ambition of the sculptor who in his portraits was striving not for mere likeness but for the recapture of the individual's essential features, that is, his soul.

Simultaneously, in his work the artist could immortalize his own creative ambition as a reflection of his personality. While the average type had to contend with his survival in his image, be it that of his living child or his animated picture, the artist's creativity sprang from the more primitive spirit of self-perpetuation as objectified in the work. At the same time, this true expression of the creative self which first and foremost created the artist-type carries the danger of becoming merely the self-expression of an egocentric personality. The difference is that the real artist as the successor of the heroic type finds his subject in the heroic life, whereas the artisan as a ready-made type finds his sole subject in himself: the one creates because he is an artist; the other has to produce in order to prove that he is one. While his prototype, the hero, through his self-generating activity, had given rise to a new belief in the immortality of creation, the artist-type became more and more self-conscious of his individual difference, and consequently, losing his original creativity, became an artificial type himself, a mere artisan of technical skill. Finally, we see this whole heroic ideology of Greek culture perish under the sophisticated scrutiny of its philosophers, who paved the way for the rational scientists of the Western world. The immortal soul became a mere subject of philosophic speculation and the narcissistic attraction to one's image ended in psychological self-analysis.

3

The Emergence of the Social Self

IN THE preceding chapter we followed the development from the immortal double—which might be called the magic self—to the independent creative self immortalized in the hero. We now follow the formation of the social self as it emerges from primitive group-life. There, no "social self" as a type existed in our sense, because the group itself and group-life with its joint activities carried the social self outside the individual. Personally, every individual was assured his immortality by his alter-ego, the double. The two selves, the mortal and immortal, were naively unified in the magic self and again creatively harmonized in the heroic self after the simple belief in the immortality of the physical self had been replaced by a creative perpetuation of the social self.

The first social organization—as contrasted with simple group life—we encounter in totemism, a highly complicated system, which, as the first form of religion (to uphold this supernatural world-view regarding man's survival on earth and his eternal destiny), established a kind of collective immortality in the re-birth of the souls of the dead through the totem of the clan. With its strict clan organization and the sharply circumscribed function of its different members, the totemistic system clearly shows the origin of social organization in the spiritual needs of the individuals.

Although it may seem to us that primitive men resemble each other more than do civilized people, they not only differ as much from one another (even in speech) as we do, but they are really more individualistic—a fact borne out by their firm belief in personal survival. We, too, it should be noted, have to emphasize our individual difference more conspicuously with all sorts of class and caste distinction (custom, conventions, uniforms, etc.). On the other hand, their social self was carried by the common group activities of their standardized social life, the essence and climax of which was religious cult and ceremony. In and through religion, primitive men became alike because they wanted to be alike, inasmuch as they thereby gained a new kind of collective immortality. This was guaranteed by their special clan-totem, which—functioning as a kind of immortalizer for the entire group—was a primitive fore-runner of civilized man's God and his earthly representatives, the hero, the saviour, the king.

We see how the passive participation in religious cult, whereby the members of the group willingly renounce their individuality in favor of a collective ideology, precedes the development of the social self. Thus, with religion—in its primitive form—starts the first class distinction between some supreme immortal beings guaranteeing eternal survival and the rest of the population vicariously gaining self-perpetuation by participating in this supernatural power. Totemistic religion, with its animal worship, paved the way for the creation of the heroic type, who being himself double—mortal and immortal—collectively replaces each individual's double. Thus, immortality was shifted from each single individual to one symbolic figure representing the individuals taken collectively. This development found its climax in the creation of a god-like figure emerging from both a personification of the totem and a glorification of the hero. In such development I see the second stem of all human religion, namely, a collective personification of heroic qualities which I called the "will-god."[1] This "will-god" of the more civilized peoples gradually overshadowed

[1] *Seelenglaube und Psychologie,* F. Deuticke, Leipzig, 1930.

the originally individualistic "soul-god" of the primitives without ever completely replacing it. In both religious systems, however, the common man gave up his personal immortality which he could no longer maintain individually but could regain collectively through some kind of active or passive participation. Such a social participation—the collective counterpart of psychological identification—not only is the essential feature of all religious creed and ritual but plays a most decisive rôle in all social development and the customs, conventions, laws expressing and maintaining it.

KINGSHIP AND MAGIC PARTICIPATION

One of those early social institutions, which—springing from magic ritual—became so important that it can be said actually to have made the history of mankind, is the institution of kingship. In it I see the final development of what might be called socialized hero-worship. In this sense, the institution of kingship epitomizes the transition from the immortalized heroic type to the social self of the commoner. The history of kingship, as Frazer reconstructed it anthropologically, although it was practised more among civilized peoples, as for example in ancient Rome, begins with the widespread custom among primitives of the killing of the divine king. It was, in fact, the mysterious rule of the priesthood of Diana of Nemi, obliging every priest—the King of the Wood, as he was called—to be slain in single combat by his successor in office, which started Frazer on a worldwide search into the primitive custom of regicide. We cannot be surprised to find this cruel custom among the high priesthood of ancient Rome, in the legendary history of which the famous twins and the killing of one by the other was depicted as the basis of civilization. Thus, we easily recognize in the killing of the divine king by his successor a historization of the original twin murder. The divine king, like the twin, is regarded as having power over the works of nature, and just as the twin was venerated as the inventor of agriculture—and culture in general—so the divine king's primary function was to secure for his people plentiful harvest and general prosperity and well-being. Among primitives in Africa, where the custom has been preserved into our own times, the term of the king's office is usually limited to two years. When that period expires he is killed, usually by strangulation—a sacred duty performed by two executioners. In former times, two slaves were killed in front of the royal tomb. It seems to me that the number two running through this ritual like a "*leitmotif*" is reminiscent of the twin origin still preserved in the two lictors or consuls of historic Rome.

This magic ritual of regicide, varying somewhat in detail according to time and place, is found in such widely separated parts of the world and different cultures represented in them as Africa, Babylonia and ancient Mexico. There are two main participants: one of them is sacrificed; the other is anointed king (with the blood of the first one), thus, through the assimilation of his vital life force, conserving the remarkable qualities of the sacrificial victim (which he in turn passes on to his successor). For the descent of kingship did not go from the reigning king to his son, but to any offspring of any deceased king provided he could kill the reigning king in combat. The killing was a ritual execution performed on magical or religious grounds, sometimes by the brother of the king, who, in any case, inherited his brother's wives even if someone else became the king's successor. These primitive customs and ancient traditions, however, later appear confused with elements from other cultural stages, since this magical transmission of outstanding qualities remained in force long after the legitimate heritage of the king's palace had been established.

Thus we find in Central Europe a survival of this primitive custom enacted as a mimic play at the beginning of spring. It is known as the sacred marriage ceremony of the King and Queen of May, a magical rite celebrating the re-awakening of nature. This spring festival differs from the primitive custom in that it merely represents a playful celebration of the same new beginning which in more primitive times was intended to promote the continuation of life by the actual slaying of the king. Furthermore, there is added to the ceremony a queen; whereas in the original custom there were only two male participants, and the succession of the new king was independent of sexual procreation. The secondary rôle of the woman in this ritual is not only borne out by early and primitive traditions, where the queen had no place, but also by actual examples from antiquity of such sacred marriages (still performed in India) in which living women were wedded to the Gods, but then secluded in chastity as priests of a temple or actually sacrificed.

Thus we find two different forms of this strange seasonal succession-rite surviving into present times. The one more primitive as still practised among many tribes in Africa is simply regicide, whereby the successor has to prove his equal or superior strength by killing the reigning king. The second form, the sacred marriage of the May-king in which the woman is given her rôle in the process of succession, has become known among civilized peoples the world over as the carnival. This pagan festival, inaugurating the arrival of early spring and the conquering of winter, is characteristic for sea-bordering countries and probably had its origin on the Mediterranean shores of Europe. In the south of France it is supposed to antedate the arrival of Julius Caesar and certainly that of the Christian church. The name "carnival" itself signifies the boat (navel) carried along on land, in which there arrives—from nowhere—the May-king or spring hero whose task it is to kill and replace for the term of a new season the old white king: winter.

Interestingly enough, we find in the French settlement in the South of this country the European carnival side by side with its more primitive form, especially as enacted by the Negro population of New Orleans. From the vivid description of those two carnivals, the black and the white, by Lyle Saxson,[1] as seen through a boy's eyes, we get a dramatic picture of the playful survival of an ancient ritual.

"Now there are a great many people who have been born in New Orleans and who have lived there all their lives, but who have never seen the arrival of the Zulu king; and I feel sorry for them, for surely there is no more characteristic sight to be seen in the South. This custom has continued for many years—a sort of burlesque of the grander Mardi Gras of the white people, and it provides the note of humor which is lacking in the great parades."

. . . "The Zulu king and his faithful henchmen were approaching slowly, the barge propelled by a tiny puffing motor-boat. The barge itself looked as if it had been rather hurriedly decorated with whatever scraps happened to be at hand. The canopy over the throne was made of sacking, and was supported by rough poles. A bunch of paper flowers adorned its top, and beneath it, in a tattered Morris chair, the king sat. He represented a savage chieftain, but whether from modesty or from fear of cold, the Zulu king wore, instead of his own black skin, a suit of black knitted underwear. There were bunches of dried grass at throat, ankles, and wrists, and a sort of grass skirt such as hula-hula dancers wear, and he wore a fuzzy black wig surmounted by a tin crown. In his hand he carried a sceptre—a broomstick—upon which was mounted a stuffed white rooster. There were some tattered artificial palm-trees at the four corners of the royal barge, and a strip of red

[1] *Fabulous New Orleans*, N. Y., Century, 1928.

cloth was draped from palm to palm. Four henchmen, dressed almost exactly like the king—save that they wore no crowns—were capering about beside him. Some red and purple flags were about here and there. And as the barge approached us, the king opened a bottle of beer and drank a toast from the bottle; while negro men and women on the bank produced flasks from their pockets and drank their own."

. . . "When they were quite near us, I saw the king and his followers had improved upon Nature's handiwork by blackening their faces and by putting stripes of red and green paint liberally upon their cheeks and upon their black union suits. These things I noticed as the barge was tying up at the end of the canal quite near me and while flasks on shore were passing from hand to hand.

"A delegation of Negro men wearing evening clothes and having red and purple scarves draped from shoulder to waist, waited upon the bank, and they kept calling out greetings to His Majesty:

" 'Wha' de Queen?'

" 'Ain't yo' brought us no Queen?'

" 'Ain't you' lonesome all by yo'self?'

"And to these gibes, the king answered grandly, 'Ef I has a Queen she goin' tuh be a man—'cause I'm through wid wimmen!'

"This was considered magnificently humorous, for a cry of joy went up from those who lined the bank."

. . . "And now came the disembarking. With difficulty the Negroes in evening dress opened a way through the crowd and a wagon drawn by mules was brought close to the barge. The wagon was a large, almost square vehicle without sides; only a flat door over the wheels. At the moment it was bare. But not for long. The king rose, picked up his Morris chair and climbed aboard. The henchmen followed, each bearing a potted palm. The bunting was stripped from the barge and was nailed into place around the edge of the wagon—and the flags and flowers were distributed about. And, with the king and his four followers, it moved along and another wagon took its place."

In the fourth chapter, entitled "Hail, Rex!," the author gives a vivid description of the white man's carnival—after the Zulu king and his royal court had entered a negro "barrel house" for refreshments.

"There before me, stretched out as far as I could see, was a mass of maskers, and beyond them a series of glittering mountains were moving toward me. . . The Carnival King was coming.

"First came the mounted policemen who cleared the way, and behind them were masked courtiers riding black horses; they wore gold plumes on their hats, and their purple velvet cloaks trailed out behind them over the flanks of the horses; they wore doublets and hose, and they carried gleaming swords in their hands. There were perhaps twelve of these outriders, gaily dressed except for the fact that they wore black masks which gave a sinister effect. Two negroes carried between them a large placard emblazoned with one word, 'Rex.'

"And now the parade was actually upon us. The first float in the procession seemed to me the most wonderful thing that I had ever seen. It was a mass of blue sky and white clouds surmounted by a glittering rainbow, and under the rainbow's bridge were masked figures in fluttering silk, men and women who held uplifted golden goblets. It was the title car and upon its side was written the subject of the parade—a subject which I have forgotten wholly today, but which dealt with some phase of Greek mythology. The glittering float towered as high as the balconies which overhung the street from the second stories of the houses, and as this gay-colored mountain came gliding past me I was impressed with the fact that the car was swaying and that it seemed fragile for all its monumental size. It was almost as though the whole were on springs. The car was drawn by eight horses covered in white and with cowls over their heads.

"A blaring band followed the title car, then more outriders, dressed this time in green and gold and wearing purple masks; and then behind them came a car which was even larger than the first. It was like a gigantic frosted wedding cake and at the top on a golden throne was seated Rex, King of the Carnival. Such a perfect king he was, with his fat legs encased in white silk tights, a round fat stomach under shimmering satin, long golden hair and a magnificent curled yellow beard! His face was covered with a simpering mask, benign and jovial. On his head he wore the very grandest crown I had ever seen, all gold and jewels which sparkled in the sun; and he carried a diamond sceptre in his hand which he waved good-naturedly at the cheering crowd. Behind him a gold-embroidered robe swept down behind the throne, cascaded over the sloping back of the float and trailed almost to the ground, its golden fringe shaking with the movement of the car."

. . . "The King's back was turned toward me now, but I could see that he was greeting some one upon a balcony opposite . . . There in the first row of seats on the balcony was a beautiful girl wearing a big floppy pink hat. She stood with both hands outstretched toward Rex as he sat before her on his throne. They were separated by a distance of perhaps twenty feet, but his high throne was almost level with her, and both of them were far above the heads of the crowd in the street below. They were exchanging greetings. And then from somewhere came a man with a step-ladder which was set up in the street. Up the ladder a man ran nimbly, bearing a tray with a white napkin over it. He presented the tray to the king. Suddenly a bottle was opened with a loud pop, and I saw champagne poured out into a thin wine glass, champagne which spilled over the edge of the goblet and ran down into the street below. Rex, King of the Carnival, was toasting his queen. Years afterward, I heard the story of this, why it was done and how old the custom was, but then the small boy who looked upon it saw only another fantastic happening in that dream of Mardi Gras."

This dramatic description of the carnival starts with a burlesque version of the inauguration of the Zulu king, whose arrival and reception are supposed to caricature the white man's carnival, but, on the contrary, represent a modernized form of the primitive regicide. Whereas the Zulu king, according to primitive tradition, has no queen to accompany or complement him, the white man's king of carnival is courting the most beautiful girl in order to make her his queen, and, when he does, brings about the climax of the festive ceremony which—like its primitive forerunner—culminates in sexual promiscuity. The customary masks and disguises worn by men and women on that occasion are not merely meant to conceal their identity, but in their superhuman size and magical appearance symbolize the elevation of the self, which every individual in magic participation shares with the king. This elevation of the self into another world of magic, irrationality and immortality is as little to be confused with our sophisticated escape from the ego as the magic participation in the ritual is to be explained by "psychological identification" with another person.

In looking "beyond the psychology" of those primitive survivals in the midst of our civilization, I was naturally pleased to find that a modern scholar had reconstructed the magic ritual which supplies the connecting link between the two forms of succession in leadership. In his profound treatise *Kingship*,[1] A. M. Hocart points out that the insti-

[1] Oxford University Press, 1927.

tution of kingship can only be understood in connection with the underlying ritual of creation. In this ceremony, which seems to have succeeded the primitive custom of regicide, there was added to the sacrifice of the old king the marriage of the new king to his own sister. Hocart explains this ceremony of what might be called a primitive form of "coronation" as a symbolic enactment of the creation, which necessarily presupposes a destruction of the old. This pattern of creation is repeatedly enacted in all the traditions of the great flood and other impending disasters threatening mankind before the appearance of a new era with its new saviour.

The essential features of the creation ritual are outlined by Hocart in the following manner: around the sacred tree (the May-pole) as a symbol of ever self-renewing nature, the remains of last year's sacrificial victim were brought out with great ceremony. Laden with the sins of the group, they were thrown into the water to be destroyed. Down this same river came a youth and maiden playing the rôle of the royal-brother and royal-sister for the new year. Then came the sacrifice of the youth who had played the royal rôle the preceding year: his body was chopped to bits, parts being used for the symbolical creation of the world.[1] His blood, caught in a bowl, was mixed with clay and a human pair was shaped out of two of his ribs. This pair was then "called into life" and placed in the center of the world (as the first human pair). Then the royal siblings of the new year, formed from the skull and eyes of the past year's king, and presumably representing the sun and the moon, descended from the sacred pole as if coming down from heaven to earth. They then ate those parts of the victim which were supposed to contain his life force, and the man, after having put on the skin of the victim, had ritual inter-

[1] For the details of similar traditions among highly civilized peoples, see *Art and Artist*, chapters V and VII.

course with his sister. The whole ceremony seemed to have culminated in a general orgy in which the incest tabu was lifted; thereby not only the group as a whole but each individual member of it was supposed to share in the benefits of the rite.

Our curiosity about the presumable benefits of the ritual has to be suspended until we know more about the meaning of this creation ceremony, and especially until we understand the rôle incest played in it. For various reasons to be mentioned presently, we cannot be satisfied with the current anthropological explanation of this seasonal rite as an act of "imitative magic." By that is meant a human attempt, through the example of sexual intercourse, to stimulate to fertility the re-awakening forces of nature. Apart from the fact that such explanation does not account for the incest motif, or the sacrifice, the idea of imitative magic itself must first be explained. How does man conceive of the idea of giving, or rather, having to give nature an example of fertility and productivity? Without under-estimating the importance of a regular food supply, especially for primitive man, we cannot accept the realistic explanation that those magical ceremonies originated only in the wish for a successful harvest. On the contrary, from the material presented, it seems to follow that the strong leader, the divine king, was thought to be endowed with magical power over life and death; a power which at a certain stage of primitive civilization was applied to the control of vegetation as well. As a matter of fact, we have shown in the cult of the Heavenly Twins that primitive agriculture itself was one of the first attempts to control nature by superhuman forces. Such a presumputous idea can only be understood as an assertion of man's creative impulse aimed primarily at eternal self-perpetuation. Furthermore, the creation rite, although performed as a seasonal ceremony, obviously reaches far beyond "imitative magic" to the very creation of man—indeed, of a man-made universe. The benefit each individual member of the group draws from participating in this annual re-creation of the world and the first man is evidently an enhancement of his own self as creator and as a self-created personality.

This benefit of the individual was, however, not restricted to his participation in the ceremony itself, but carried with it a dynamic impetus which finally led to the emergence of the social self. In order to understand this process, we now have to clarify the rôle which the ritual marriage of the royal-brother to the sister—incest, in other words—plays in that dramatization of the creative impulse. Above all, it clearly confirms an earlier view of mine,[1] namely, that incest is a symbol of man's self-creative urge, which draws its strength from the belief in immortality. But only a broader conception, taking into account the magical rôle of the king as incestuous partner and sacrificial victim in this ritual, can lead to a fuller understanding of the incest-motif in its cultural and social implications. The puzzling inconsistency between the incest-ritual sanctioned and imitated by the community, and the act of incest forbidden the individual, disappears when we realize that the divine king represents a socialized hero endowed with all the characteristics of the original heroic type. Ritual incest is one of those privileges exercised by the chosen individual in a ceremony of the creation-cult at the point of transition from the belief in collective immortality to the perpetuation of the individual in his own children.

This biological fact of natural procreation was first denied, as we have shown, in favor of the magical cult of the soul whereby the individual lived on by virtue of his own immortal double. Thus the first idea of an earthly successor did not spring from any individual need to continue his

[1] Presented in a volume written in 1905 and publishel in 1912 in German: *Das Inzest-Motiv in Dichtung und Sage,* F. Deuticke, Leipzig; 2nd ed., 1926.

personal existence or life-work but emerged from social necessity. For only in the case of a preeminent personality who had proved his magical power as leader did there exist an interest on the part of the *community* in preserving his unusual qualities and transferring them to a successor. Originally the transferrence took place by way of magic (by the eating of the vital organs of the predecessor or the drinking of his blood). Later, this magical ceremony was replaced by a symbolical act in which the new king or chief was given successorship by the ruling one in the ceremony of anointment. The latter custom rests on the soul-belief that the leader originally was a self-made man and that the strength of his magical power could only be transmitted by magical means, that is, through identification, and not sexually through procreation.

The ritual marriage to the sister, as enacted in the creation rite, thus represents the first step towards a reconciliation or unification of these two principles, namely, magical and sexual perpetuation. The sister, more than any other person (even more than the mother), represents a feminine double; the son springing from this marriage, therefore, seems predestined biologically to inherit the magical qualities. In the creation-rite the two kinds of perpetuating magical power are synchronized: the new king is chosen and ordained as the successor of the sacrificed victim, as in the primitive custom of regicide; at the same time, the incestuous marriage indicates the future development into the actual custom of royal marriage between brother and sister. This custom, which we find actually practiced in the ancient dynasties of such highly civilized countries as Egypt and Peru, has prevailed in the tradition of intra-marriage between royal families throughout the history of Europe right into the present.[1]

[1] It has been said that practically all European dynasties spring from Elizabeth of Bohemia, the daughter of James I of Great Britain and Anne of Denmark.

Incestuous sister-marriage is primarily not a sexual union for the procreation of children but a magical ceremony still guaranteeing the perpetuation of one's own self in the successor. Yet the introduction of the sister in her rôle as sexual partner who replaces the original double or twin was precipitated by needs and demands of the community and only gradually and reluctantly accepted by the individual. A strange motif preserved in the creation rite seems to reflect that very transition from the double to the woman, and the resistance to it. We are referring to the episode, reminiscent of the Biblical creation of Eve, where from the victim's ribs was shaped a human pair, supposedly the first man and woman. This "first woman" as a creation of and from man, representing the most complete reversal of the most obvious biological fact, not only betrays man's tendency to eliminate his mortal origin but also shows that he could only accept sexual procreation and with it mortality by *creating* first his own woman, the "first" woman whom he dared to accept—as part of himself, hence, transmitter of his immortal power.

Such resistance to giving up magical self-perpetuation also explains why the original form of the king's sacrifice was carried along into the new ritual. Strange as it may seem to us, the sacrifice, because it belongs to the immortality rites denied the common mortal, was considered a privilege and not a punishment. The hero cannot die a natural death, either because he himself lives again after some kind of re-birth or resurrection, or because he is magically incorporated in his successor. By the same token, he is not supposed to beget children in the ordinary fashion, because, according to the myth of the birth of the hero, he himself came into the world in a magical way. With the gradual acceptance of procreation through the sister-marriage, the sacrificed and the newly created king eventually became fused into one. That is to say, royal succession could still be considered a perpetuation of the immortal self in terms of its biological re-birth.

Unexpectedly, we come here upon the biological aspect of incest, one of the most disputed topics in anthropological literature. Originally, as we see now, it was not at all a problem in eugenics or genetics except in the common interest of preserving extraordinary qualities of outstanding personalities. This "breeding of genius," as we might call it today, became necessary as soon as the "natural selection" of the successor type was interfered with by the demands of the legitimate biological successor. The need to combine the two principles, that is, to breed high qualities—instead of just transmitting them—seems to have been of such importance to the community that the people ignored possible injurious biological effects of continuous incestuous relations. In fact they were rather inclined to view certain signs of degeneration—such as epilepsy, which was called the sacred illness—as characteristics of an extraordinary personality. As time went on, the ritual and symbolism became more important than the person, especially when strong personalities were lacking. Finally a situation developed which can best be described in terms of the witty observer who once characterized the group of Bohemian artists on Montparnasse as showing all the symptoms but none of the achievements of genius.

At any rate, what strikes us as important is the realization that even all the real achievements which we sum up as "culture" have been accomplished by deviates, that is, by personalities who were either above normal or in any case outside the realm of the average. The average type shares the spiritual values of civilization only through a kind of vicarious participation, whereas the really creative type—be it hero, artist or scientist—falls a victim to his own creation for which he has to sacrifice himself in one way or another. In the eternal drama of self-sacrifice and re-birth, from the solemn custom of regicide to the gay spirit of the carnival, each individual could participate in this ritual of self-creation. A new kind of immortality through the medium of magic participation was epitomized in the social self as it emerges from what might be called a gradual democratization of immortality.

INSTITUTION OF MARRIAGE

The development of the social self as an outgrowth of the commoners' participation in the ritual of divine kingship led to the establishment of another institution equally as important for the individual's destiny as was the institution of kingship for that of the community. This, which formed the foundation of our Western civilization, is the institution of marriage. As A. M. Hocart has convincingly shown (in his book already referred to), it was from the ritual incest-marriage between royal-brother and royal-sister that the institution of marriage sprang. Marriage was at first more of a sacred rite than a sexual, social or economic institution. Originally, as a ritual ceremony which we found to be merely a sexualized form of self-perpetuation, it signified the sacred union of these two. Its purpose at first was the continuation of the salient qualities of leadership in the newly anointed king and later their transmission to the royal-child of this union. The prerogative of the heroic superman to perpetuate himself not only magically through participation but also biologically in his successor was gradually claimed by the ordinary individual, who by imitating the immortal hero in partaking of the sacred ceremony of ritual marriage became himself a hero immortalized in his children. Thus, through the institution of marriage, which descended so to speak from the king to the people,[1] every husband became a kind of king in his

[1] Such "participation" is preserved with characteristic reference to twin-symbolism in certain European customs. For example, at the marriage of

own right and his house became his castle. There he was master and ruler invested with the symbols of the magic power of a king "en miniature." Hence, the magnified figure of the tyrannical father of the patriarchal family, a late socialized product of an originally magical function.

It is easier, hence, more generally satisfying, to explain the king as an elevated father (of the country)—something which Freud attempted to do by projecting family organization back into primitive times when no family yet existed and "fatherhood" was unknown. Biological fatherhood, as we have already shown, had no place in the supernatural world-view with its belief in personal immortality. Strange as it may sound, fatherhood emerged as a very late conception and a social one at that; not a term designating the man's sexual function in procreation. Not only was there no father in primitive group-life but the development of the social conception of fatherhood bears out the basic importance of spiritual values as against social needs and even biological facts. Biological fatherhood only became important—in fact was first accepted—when social fatherhood proved of advantage in supporting the individual's eternal need for personal immortality.

In this sense, the emergence of the social self is epitomized in the conception of fatherhood finally arrived at. In order to show how this conception evolved from magic ritual, we must go back to the ceremony of the brother-sister union which became the prototype for the ordinary marriage and thus instituted the father-rôle. Strange customs, remnants of which are to be found scattered in frag-

---

Crown Princess Juliana of the Netherlands (now in exile) another "Juliana" received royal consent to marry on the same day, despite the ban on other weddings, because she and the Crown Princess had been born the same hour of the same day twenty-seven years before. The whole village turned out for the traditional ceremony of the peasant girl and her boatman-husband. A more collective example is to be found in the marriage of the since-dethroned King Zog of Albania whose ceremony was accompanied by the simultaneous weddings of 150 commoners.

mentary traditions all over the world, bear out the emergence of the later father concept from this ritual incest-marriage. In Jewish tradition, for example, as it is preserved in the Old Testament, the wife through marriage became the sister of her husband and is commonly referred to as such. Likewise, the ancient custom of the Levirate prescribed by the Mosaic code demands that a childless widow be married to the late husband's brother. Here we see how the early institution of marriage has to be made "incestuous" according to its ritual prototype and actually carries this significance, inasmuch as husband and wife become, so to speak, clan-relations. This may explain the notion some children have that their parents are related, that is to say, are blood relatives—a mistaken idea which is very understandable, since in the child a new blood relation is established.

Such isolated customs of ancient tradition as those mentioned above point to a totally different social organization than the one known throughout the Western world. To the unique work of the Swiss scholar, Bachofen, we owe our knowledge of one once widespread in which the father-rôle was not yet acknowledged and the mother, supported by her brother as the masculine head of the family, ruled the family-clan. This custom still in practice among some primitive islanders is known as the "avunculate" (uncle-hood), and the social organization of which it was an essential feature has been designated by Bachofen as the matriarchal system.[1] From all this it follows that the family, as we now know it, emerged at a very late date in the history of mankind. For centuries the social life of the primitives consisted of certain group activities divided chiefly according to sex and generation. The life of men and women was strictly separated and so, too, was the life of the younger generation from that of the matured and elders. Before maturity the children of any given clan were

[1] Bachofen, Johann Jakob. *Das Mutterrecht,* Basel, 1897.

under the care of the women, a group of "mothers" who formed the nucleus of the domestic life, just as the group of older men managed the community affairs. Those children belonging to the same clan were considered "brothers" and "sisters," not in the sense of being blood relations but descendants from one and the same totem (spirit of the dead). Hence, the ancient rule of exogamy which prevented those brothers and sisters, members of the same clan, from having sexual intercourse springs from magical sources and is not based on biological observation or social needs. The fact that this strict incest-tabu concerning brothers and sisters was only lifted in the creation-ritual, in which this very union was made a symbol of magical self-perpetuation, throws a light on the origin of the much-disputed rule of exogamy. It seems to have meant a social barrier compelling the common man to renounce his desire for self-perpetuation in favor of sexual procreation necessary for the survival of the clan. How the original marriage ritual between brother and sister developed into the legal marriage ceremony of Roman law whereby the woman was given to the man in "filiae loco" epitomizes once more the emergence of our Western concept of fatherhood from the development of the social self.

Unaware of such irrational determinants in our most common concepts, many anthropologists and sociologists, indeed, even our modern psychologists, seem to take their obvious meaning for granted. They tacitly assume that the family-unit existed from the very beginning for the benefit of its members, and, since they could not find such a pleasing "tableau" in the history of the past, they naïvely projected their own conception into it. Freud, when he had to supplement his psychology of the individual by the social aspects of personality development, even went so far as to re-interpret primitive anthropological material in the light of our present-day family-organization. In his sensational interpretation of the Greek Oedipus-saga we find the social significance of a collective myth explained in terms of the highly individualized psychology of modern neurotics. In pointing out the *social* significance which this tradition had for the Greeks themselves, I found[1] that this story epitomizes the transition from a more archaic form of social life to the later family-organization. Greek tradition reflects the struggle between individualism and socialization in the rebellion of the self-sufficient hero not only against the power of the Gods but also against the new laws of man encroaching upon his freedom of action. The Oedipus tradition, in particular, gives us an idea of the tremendous resistances on the part of the individual who at that stage felt that he lost his freedom through the family as we may now feel deprived of our liberty by the state.

As is well known, the story tells of King Oedipus who was exposed as a child because of the warning given his father by an oracle that his son was destined to kill his own father and marry his widowed mother. Freud thought to have found the explanation for these "horrible crimes," which the hero unknowingly commits, in the unconscious wish of every son to kill his father in order to have intercourse with his mother. If, however, we consult the scholarly analysis of the Oedipus material by Carl Robert[2] we realize that there is a much more primitive basis to the Oedipus tradition of the Greek drama corresponding to the creation-rite. The Oedipus of the primitive seasonal myth was originally a phallic vegetation spirit, an offspring of the earth-mother whose son was also her husband. "The child of the mother earth," says Robert, "needed no father in the beginning; and if it should acquire one then this according to primitive cult could only be an identical one, the old Year-god whom the son must kill in order to become

[1] *Modern Education,* Alfred A. Knopf, N. Y., 1932.

[2] Robert, Carl. *Oedipus.* 2 vols. Berlin, 1915.

the Year-king himself." Here we realize that the Greek Oedipus tradition simply represents a re-interpretation of the creation-rite in which the father is substituted for the brother (and the mother for the sister). In other words, what we have here in terms of Greek civilization amounts to a further sexualized version of the creation ceremony, transposed into the framework of the father-centred family. The two kings, the old and the new self, originally conceived of as twin brothers, appear here as father and son. The killing, although conceived of in terms of the struggle between generations, has the same ritual meaning. The incest likewise has the ritual meaning of self-perpetuation transposed from the magical to the sexual plane. Whereas Freud saw in it an instinctual (unconscious) desire of the son to have sexual intercourse with his mother, the tradition actually reflects the transition—accomplished in Greek civilization—from heroic self-perpetuation to man's reluctant acceptance of his biological rôle as father and his perpetuation through the generations. The resistance which both Oedipus' father and the hero himself show to accepting their respective rôles in the human drama of family relations really makes it a *drama of fatherhood* clad in the typical vestige of "the myth of the birth of the hero," who is not born a son nor does he become a father. The killing of the twin-brother, this typical motif symbolizing the hero's immortal self, appears projected back into Oedipus' childhood—where another newly-born is killed in his stead—as if to indicate that this heroic double belongs to a remote past which the highly sophisticated Greek playwrights seem eager to recapture—in vain. At this time when our present family organization was just in the making, man from the threshold of the heroic age was enviously looking back into the past stage of heroic self-perpetuation epitomized in the creation-rite. The heroic self rebelling against his biological successor was given the name "Oedipus" and invested with the old incest-ritual, because the latter formerly had been the symbol of heroic self-perpetuation which had given way to the acceptance of biological procreation.

In this sense, the Greek Oedipus-saga, in which Freud saw only the rebellion of the son, proves in the light of social developments a heroic defence on the man's part against his rôle of father. The father of Oedipus, Laios, clearly represents the type of man rejecting sexual procreation. According to the tradition he abstained from intercourse with his wife because he was told his son would be a mighty hero and overthrow his reign. When the child, conceived by accident, was born, the father, not wanting any son to succeed him, ordered his death. In the incest of Oedipus with his mother, the tradition symbolizes this universal desire to be one's own successor. Hence, Oedipus himself becomes a representative of the father who does not care to have children (the two sons whom he begets with his own mother kill each other according to ritual tradition in fratricide). This compromise to beget himself, as it were, as his mother's son and be reborn by her must fail tragically. This—not that he slew the father and took his place with the mother—is the veritable sin of Oedipus. For as little as the father wants to continue his existence in his son, just as little is the son inclined to play the part of successor to his father. In this sense, Oedipus rebels alike against the rôle of son and of father, not as son against father. This double conflict in the individual himself, who wants to be neither father nor son, but simply SELF, is portrayed in the Greek tragedy, which epitomizes the struggle of the immortal heroic self against the racial self of sexual procreation manifested in marriage and children. The inner resistance of man to his ephemeral racial rôle, be it that of father or son, is represented in the Oedipus drama as an external strife between father and son.

However, the two do not recognize each other when they meet and fight, since in King Laios Oedipus does not kill his biological father but revolts against the father-principle as such. In this sense, the father-son relation is from the beginning a generative, not a personal one, that is to say, a clash between two world-views at the transitional stage of development from the heroic to the social self, personified in the father- and son-type.

With the dawn of the patriarchal ideology, the child is no longer the bearer of collective immortality in the meaning of the old soul belief, but as the individual successor to his father he becomes a personification of the latter's immortality. Thus the conception of the son-type was first derived from the social ideology of fatherhood and only much later appears in biological terms of the mother-relationship. Against this denial of his own individuality, the son has rebelled from the time when man accepted fatherhood as a symbol of the social self. From then on, we see in the history of mankind the grandiose duel of those two principles personified in the father- and son-type, manifesting itself in social, political and religious strifes. The Greeks perished in that struggle of the pre-family-self, the hero, against the emergence of the social self epitomized in the family-types of father and son. Roman civilization, on the other hand, was built up on a further socialization of this new father principle. Just as the ritual marriage-ceremony between brother and sister was gradually adopted by the common man in order that he might benefit vicariously from such magical participation, so Roman civilization enabled the average citizen to participate in the advantages of socialized fatherhood. Every freeborn citizen had by the very fact of his political status the right to be a father, that is, to have legitimate children over whom he legally ruled. This right to social fatherhood, which proved identical with being a Roman citizen, was denied the class of slaves whose children were not sons or daughters of their fathers or mothers but merely slaves of their masters. Besides and above this general Oriental distinction between rulers and slaves, Roman civilization for the first time developed a definite class-consciousness and with it political class struggle between ruling groups. The right of every citizen to social fatherhood meant no right for the son except the one to become a father in his turn, that is, a social type prescribed by this first totalitarian state. Since the legal power of the father over his sons was equivalent to his power over his slaves (the word "family" is derived from "famulus"—servant, slave) we can justly say that the sons dominated by legalized fatherhood actually were the first "have-nots." Not that the slaves had more, but they had no hope and hence no real desire to demand or take what the "haves" possessed. It was different with the sons, who, despite their lack of legal rights, were brought up with the idea of promotion—provided they behaved—from the "have-not" into the "have" group. Hence, they could easily form the nucleus of a rebellious class striving to overthrow the ruling class of fathers. At the same time, there existed an equally strong rivalry between the members of the ruling class as to who was the strongest and thus entitled to rule the rulers.

At the height of the patriarchal rule in ancient Rome, the father had become invested with a power derived from the magic self of the hero in whose image civic fatherhood was created as a social type. Paradoxically enough, it seems that Freud's "primitive dominance of the father" who ruled tyrannically over the "herd of brothers" only existed politically in the highly organized Roman state at the peak of its power. In this light, psychoanalysis, centred around the father-psychology, appears as a last stand of the crumbling patriarchal ideology which collapsed together with imperialism in the World War. For a while, the outlived father-principle found refuge in an individualistic psychology which explained the father-son relation on the basis of personal, more specifically sexual rivalry between two individuals within the same family. On the basis of its patriarchal ideology, psychoanalysis had to explain the Oedipus-saga in terms of the Decalogue and thus appears as the last bulwark against the decadence of the bourgeois family-structure as it grew out from socialized fatherhood in Roman law. This collapse of the ideology on which the social structure of Western civilization was built occurred simultaneously in the political, economic and psychological sphere. The breakdown of the institution of kingship in the World War, followed by class struggle and disintegration of the family, led to the present chaos with its moral bewilderment and economic insecurity.

Although it may be tempting to draw a prophetic parallel between the instability of our own civilization and the collapse of the Roman Empire,[1] the difference between the two situations is nevertheless sufficiently striking to obviate any such easy historization of our problem. The struggle in the Roman Empire signifies the beginning of a social movement through the end-phase of which we seem now to be laboring. The proverbial diseases of children and the natural decay of old age are sufficiently distinct as to cause and symptoms not to be treated in the same way, although both may be fatal. The common assumption that history repeats itself seems to spring more from our emotional need for likeness than from factual observation. Far from repeating itself, history does not even seem to move in evolutionary cycles but rather manifests itself in and through crises. What does repeat itself, though, is a traditional pattern handed down in ritual cult and mythological tradition; a pattern which, clashing at different times with different realities, produces new and unique events.

[1] Haskell, H. J. *The New Deal in Old Rome,* N. Y., 1939.

The task in which Roman civilization ultimately failed was to apply an ideology of magic origin which had worked socially in creating a new type of citizen, to the final test of establishing economic equality. Contrary-wise, the problem of today's economic crisis is to find a new ideology after Western civilization has failed to maintain this universal type of citizen promoted by Christianity. When the church lost this cultural function, psychology had to divert the failure of establishing economic equality into an attempt for political equality stated in terms of the democratic type of man. Whereas in Roman times it was the first democratic government which had failed in its ultimate application, it now is the democratic type who resists his democratic government's carrying his ideology of equality too far into realistic achievement. In this sense, it is true that fascism and communism are the result of unfulfilled promises of democracy.[1] If a too liberal government carries the democratic ideology beyond the endurance of the democratic type, then there appears the paradox of the individual feeling forced—"governed"—by a government which he himself created as an expression of his type.

Here we are reminded that government—of any kind—originated in kingship, which, under the name of monarchy, has survived as the most popular form of regime. Indeed, it has been argued that any one-man rule as opposed to government by a group or class is monarchic in principle, whether it sails under the flag of fascism, communism or so-called democracy.[2] Such a political conception gains momentum from the emotional fact that the people themselves are inclined to conceive of their government in terms of a "governor," whether or not he be autocratic. When, for example, the President of the United States has been mock-

[1] See, Ascoli, Max and Feiler, Arthur. *Fascism for Whom?* W. W. Norton & Co., N. Y., 1938.

[2] Belloc, Hilaire. *Monarchy,* Cassell & Co., London, 1938.

ingly made responsible even for bad weather, we see in such a "joke" more than an echo of the "primitive's" belief in the rainmaker.

POWER AND THE STATE

This magical power over natural forces in which primitive man did believe is still the underlying ideology of our modern conception of power, be it political, economic or psychological. Here again we find the same paradox which has perverted man's original concepts of supernatural values into psychological hybrids or semi-true realities. Power is at bottom a magical concept, pertaining ultimately to man's control over life and death. The primitive conception of power clearly expresses this fundamental truth by assuming a supernatural force working for good and evil in human life. The earliest known conception of it, in the pre-animistic stage of emanism was "*mana*," as the Melanesians called that transcendental force which all primitives know under some name or other (Orenda of the Iroquois, Wakonda of the Sioux, the Tjurunga of the Australian aborigines, Brahma of the Hindus, etc.). The missionary Bishop Codrington, one of the best authorities on the Samoan Islands, explains this fundamental idea of all primitive life, strange to civilized man, in the following manner: "Mana, this concept met with in the entire Pacific region, is an invisible power which is believed by the natives to cause all such effects as transcend their conception of the regular course of nature. It is the active force in all they do and believe to be done in magic, white or black. By means of this, men are able to control or direct the forces of nature, but by means of different practices are also able to exercize to their own benefit that supernatural, invisible power."[1]. . . "It is a power of influence not physical and in a way supernatural, but it shows itself in physical force

[1] Codrington, Robert Henry. *The Melanesians,* Oxford, 1891, p. 118, note.

or any kind of power or excellence which a man possesses . . . all Melanesian religion consists in getting this mana for oneself or getting it used for one's benefit . . . it is not fixed in anything and can be conveyed in almost everything. Ghosts, souls separated from the body, supernatural beings possess it and can share it. Though itself impersonal this power appears always connected with some person who directs it, and one expects from the one endowed with it the ability to bring about the extraordinary."[1] Men who have it, and whom we would call today strong personalities (comparable to the primitives' shamans, priests, chiefs, etc.) may use it in order to gain power for themselves over others. Every conspicuous success of any one individual passes as evidence of the possession of mana.

Such a profound conception did not, however, spring from the simple observation of individuals who obviously possess some "magic" power beyond themselves which the ordinary man does not share. This simple observation would not have required a "pantheistic" theory for its explanation. It was, on the contrary, the experience of inexplicable forces operating in nature with which the strong personality became identified. The primitive hero—whether medicine-man or chief—was in that sense a real superman, being endowed with the same forces which govern the universe and thus having the power to combat and control them. By "real superman" I mean a personality endowed with this *power plus the will* to use it constructively, not an individual with will-to-power, a hyphenated psychological bastard between those two legitimate forces, the power to will in the natural human being.

In this, our psychological misconception of will-to-power, is epitomized the main failure of civilized man, namely, to translate into realistic terms the supernatural conception of power. Hence, material power which has been attained and

[1] *Opus cit.*

exerted in political, economic or psychological terms (propaganda) cannot be maintained except through a powerful personality, not driven by the artificial will-to-power but by his will to use this super-individual power beneficially. Thus, all the great leaders and conquerors in history were chiefly concerned with the problem of their successor to whom they could entrust the maintenance of their material power; and all of them saw or foresaw this external structure collapse for lack of an equally powerful successor. This failure in succession was a determining factor in the breakdown of the Roman Empire, whose material glory vanished while Christianity recaptured man's supernatural power which, however, was not of this earth. The church, to be sure, when, in the sixth century,[1] it became strong enough actually to take over the function of the Roman state, embarked on the worldly power-policy which eventually led to its demoralization, and thus precipitated the splitting up of medieval Europe into smaller national units.

From this angle, the history of medieval times represents a constant battle between the two competing powers, church and state, that is, the ultimate authority of Emperor or Pope, Caesar or God. Just as the divine power of the king became translated into political terms of imperialism, so the supernatural power spiritualized in the Christian faith degenerated into the worldly power of the Papacy. In the simultaneous struggle of these two for supremacy lies the germ of that quarrel over investitures which convulsed the Middle Ages and which finally compelled dissatisfied personalities to turn away from both Papacy and Empire.

[1] "It took Rome almost as long to fall as to rise. Her decline began in the third century, but it was three hundred years before Roman civilization became medieval. Only in the sixth century did consuls and senators vanish and the pope replace the urban prefect as the real ruler of the city of Rome. Only in the sixth century did monasteries replace schools of rhetoric as the chief training grounds for scholars and administrators." This century saw the final collapse of Roman civilization, and Professor Duckett rightly calls it, "The Gateway to the Middle Ages."—New York, 1938.

With the Reformation, the Church, having failed to control its inherent contradictions, ceased to be a cosmos. Before that time, however, up to the seventeenth century, some kind of unity existed in European political structure, after which it diverged into separate national ideologies culminating in German Protestantism, in the British Reformation and in the French Revolution, all more or less coinciding with the opening up of the New World, America, acclaimed as the long-awaited Utopia fulfilled on this earth.

In particular, the French Revolution, in its historical dramatization, epitomizes the complete confusion of man and superman, manifested in the vicarious aggrandizement of the State and its ruler: the State became more and more personalized while the ruler simultaneously became more collectivized. Thus Louis XIV, "le Roi Soleil," in whose reign monarchy reached its apogee, has been justly credited with the famous declaration, "I am the State." For the State actually symbolizes a de-personalized ruler or sovereign. This is borne out by the organization of all great Oriental empires in Antiquity built around and shaped after a divine ruler whose life was strictly regulated according to celestial pattern. The same principle is still operating in the imperialistic organization of the people of the "Rising Sun," the last expanding Orientals who revived their national aspirations around the cult of their divine Mikado. Certain English writers who have made a study of Shintoism (e.g. Sansom, Gubbins and Hearn) are generally agreed that the doctrine of the Imperial line's divine descent was inculcated by the nation's rulers at the time of the Restoration, and emphasized in the Imperial Edict on Education in 1890 for the purpose of diverting to the Sovereign the old feudal loyalties and giving to the nation, in the Throne, a new rallying centre. The state creed of a Divine Emperor, gradually identified with the Shintō Cult, has undoubtedly fulfilled its purpose by centralizing and educating a national spirit in which patriotism is combined with the racial tradition of loyalty. At the same time, the descendants of the *samurai*, the military caste, have enlarged the scope of the God-Emperor creed, making it include the claim (originally formulated by Hirata) of a divine descent for the whole race, which is therefore manifestly superior to all others, and justified in its divine mission of world domination.

At this point the fundamental difference between this Oriental and our Occidental totalitarianism becomes clear, in that the one is based on religion, whereas the other, by replacing and absorbing religion, becomes itself a new social religion. Hence, F. A. Voigt, in his recent book *Unto Caesar*,[1] could justly say that "both Marxian Socialism and National Socialism, which resemble one another closely, are modern secular religions. They are messianic, they reject the Christian doctrine of sin, and they use either the class struggle (in the case of Marxian Socialism) or the principle of race (in the case of National Socialism) as the criterion of good or evil. Both are despotic in their methods and their mentality. Both have enthroned the modern Caesar, collective man, the implacable enemy of the individual soul. Both would render unto this Caesar the things which are God's, in order to establish the kingdom of heaven (a socialist heaven) on this earth."

Man's conception of the State cannot be understood without the real meaning of power with which the State in its various forms has always been associated. The political history of the State begins at the height of Greek civilization, because it first conceived of the State in human terms and earthly principles. Not that powerful States were unknown before; but the great Oriental empires were organized as a reflection of heavenly laws and governed by a godlike ruler who, however, was strictly bound by celestial regulations. Only in the fifth century development of Athens

[1] Putnam, N. Y., 1938.

did the Greeks approximate their ideal state, an essentially democratic one. Plato, in his vision of the Utopian State (in *The Republic* and *Laws*), which upheld the old heavenly pattern, opposed it. It was his pupil Aristotle who first described the man-made State with its human shortcomings but regard for humanitarian principles. From his definition of man as a rational animal, it has been concluded by later political theorists that the State is man's own voluntary creation. Hobbes, especially, the supreme exponent of what we now call totalitarianism, asserts that man is a social animal, i.e. he deliberately created the power of the State by the surrender of his individual powers; by no other means could anarchy be ended and justice ensured. Power, according to him, is the guarantee of law, and without a supreme power to which all the members of the community are subject law cannot be maintained.

There we meet another of these paradoxes springing from the confusion of supernatural concepts and realistic politics. For this supreme power which is sovereignty—named by Hobbes "Leviathan"—has been confounded with supremacy as such—against all. The contradiction is that society demands unlimited submission on the one hand and unlimited authority on the other. It is not surprising that Hobbes, in order to avoid this embarrassing dilemma, furnishes a sound theoretical basis for democracy by demonstrating that power ultimately derives from the people. This doctrine of "popular sovereignty," which was native to medieval thought, became obscured by the rapid drift of the Renaissance towards absolutism. Out of the conflict grew Althusius' modernization of the medieval theory of the "social contract," whereby he differentiated between one which constitutes society and another which determines the relation of the people to its rulers.[1] Thus originated a tradi-

[1] Von Gierke, Otto. *The Development of Political Theory,* trans. by Bernard Freyd, London, 1939.

tion which, in opposition to that promoted by Hobbes, emphasizes man's natural rights and ultimately finds its epitomization in Rousseau's totalitarian mysticism of the General Will.

Although both these schools of political thought on whose heritage we still thrive—or rather, labor—are based on the inseparable unity of the two concepts, power and State, not one of their famous representatives explains why power was transferred from the individual to the State in the first place, and furthermore how the State redistributes power to its emasculated subjects. True, the State is man's own creation, but not primitive man's creation, nor was the tremendous power of the vast Oriental empires created by man in the sense of those political theorists. Only when the individual in the sense of our previous exposition had gained power, i.e. regained in a different form his super-individual power of primitive man, could he create the State by entrusting to it this newly acquired power. Figuratively speaking, the State thus became a kind of governmental power-"bank" into which the citizens pooled their individual power-surplus as a safeguard against its misuse by any one of them. That is to say, only when Western man became a "king" himself in his own family, through socialized fatherhood, was it possible and necessary to create that essentially "democratic" State to protect his prerogatives by checkmating the others. This development starting in Greece reached its climax in Rome with its socialized fatherhood-citizenship. That explains why any kind of democracy arises from the family and finds its foundation in it, whereas the city-states like old Sparta or pre-Bismarck Germany rest on a tribal ideology.

Civilized man's rationalization of the primitive power concept which finally appears epitomized in our idea of the State is due in the last analysis to his fear of this "naked" power (as Bertrand Russell now calls it). This naked power, which we need to cloak in various kinds of justifications,[1] represents the actual life force itself of which we have become afraid not so much because we cannot control it as because we are trying to control it too much. True, when it is allowed to operate freely it can work good and evil alike; but when we try to control it it seems to work only evil.

Man's eternal need to control this super-individual power is borne from the fear of "chaos" which lurks beyond the self we know. Hence, the superman was singled out as the divine king who became endowed with this dangerous weapon, dangerous to the bearer himself as well as to the subjects exposed to it. Since it is at bottom a power over life and death, the divine king, as we saw in primitive tradition, had to prove himself fit for his task by killing his predecessor. This was a cultic performance for which, according to the human law, he had to pay with his own life. (*Le roi est mort, vive le roi!*) In this sense, the divine king or leader was not only the trustee of the clan's magical power but by the same token the representative and original executor of this power in terms of the rationalized law. This double danger of the divine power may explain why in mythical and subsequent historical tradition the leader in times of crisis appears as a foreigner who is allowed to assume might. First of all, being alien, he takes this dangerous burden off the community shoulders, and secondly, being a stranger, he makes this strange irrational power more ac-

[1] In a highly illuminating study on "The Technique of Sovereignty," *Swords and Symbols,* N. Y., 1939, James Marshall has recently analyzed the symbols of ruling, that is, the ideological and physical means which have been in use throughout the ages to gain power and to justify its exertion. It is worthwhile in our context to quote the author's conception of the State as an "agency of sovereign power. The State is never static and the word 'State' itself has the meaning of temporary condition. The State is like a scale that is never stationary and never in balance; and the political process is similar to the attempt of a man to balance such a moving scale." p. 98.

ceptable. At the same time having—as did Jesus, Jeanne d'Arc and other historical figures—assumed this power illegitimately, the outsider, like the divine king after his term expires, is prematurely removed from the scene of action. On the other hand, there exists in every form of government a legitimate distribution of power according to a traditional hierarchy whereby the democratic impersonations of the king—from the Prime Minister down to the ordinary father-citizen—function as power symbols of the democratic spirit, expressed in the saying that everybody carries a marshal's baton in his knapsack.

The transition from traditional monarchy to republican democracy is epitomized in the history of the Roman Empire and was accomplished through the development of the social self in terms of civic fatherhood. From this social self sprang the two social institutions fundamental to Western civilization: our form of government from democratized kingship, our family from socialized fatherhood. The whole development of the Roman Empire with its external growth and internal weakness betrays itself as a struggle for and against democratization as it emerged from the socialized father-principle. This basically magical conception failed when its social ideology, that is, legal fatherhood, was ultimately faced with a realistic solution of the problem of equality in economic terms. But even before the "have-nots" had a chance to share what the "haves" possessed, this whole social structure disintegrated from within through the mere fact of its enormous scope and overgrowth.

For the whole Empire was built on this same father-pattern, with Rome as the head (capitol) of the Empire (family). Such development was possible on the basis of a much older conception according to which not only the ruler of the people was "divine," but also what he ruled over. In other words, to the divine king who actually had to live the life of a God on earth corresponded his Heavenly

City supposedly patterned and actually built on the celestial prototype. This conception we find in ancient Babylonia, in China and in early Peruvian culture,[1] and can detect its ideology in Plato's ideal government capable of creating the perfect State whose pattern was laid up in heaven. Rome itself, originally the "City of the Heavenly Twins," developed through the unity of government into an earthly centre of perfectionism and as such could represent the whole State, the Roman Empire. In its ideological conception as an entity within which the individual lived not so much for his own rights as for its perfection, the City of Rome (which played a similar ideological rôle in the Fascists' "March on Rome") foreshadows St. Augustine's theme of the "City of God" (preserved in the Pope's Vatican City). This contradiction between ideological and realistic conceptions of the State—as represented by Plato and Aristotle respectively—was reconciled in the ancient world first by the Hellenistic monarchies and later by Rome. But it needed Augustine's idea of the Heavenly City finally to bridge that gap. The political institutions of the Middle Ages owe their stability to this philosophic concept which the doctrine of divine right made applicable to human affairs.

Simultaneously with the growth of Rome's power there developed an increasing desire among the members of the ruling class to become the head, the "capitol," in a word, the father of the ruling fathers. Such rivalry among the fathers made it more difficult for the son to step into his prescribed rôle of successor even when he wanted to. Furthermore, the ideal of the Roman citizen was to become a father as good as or better than his father or forefathers, and not to be a good or better son. Hence, the successors of

[1] In the Eastern Roman Empire, known as the Byzantine State, we find the mystical conception of the Emperor as divine Priest-King with his elaborate court organized as the earthly counterpart of the Heavenly Jerusalem. See Diner, Helen. *The 1000 Years of the Byzantine Empire,* N. Y., 1938.

men in power were rarely their own sons, and Roman history abounds in examples of an adopted child becoming the factual successor of a successful man. The struggle between the democratic principle of socialized fatherhood and the temptation to exert singlehanded the power implied in its legalization eventually degenerated into a fight of mediocrity against leadership. As Fletcher Pratt in his *Hail, Caesar* aptly remarks: "Like all closed aristocracy the Roman capitol was afflicted with a declining birthrate. The supply of trained leaders began to run out just at the moment when the Republic, by virtue of its imperial position, was most in need of administrators with minds large enough to embrace the problems of millions and long enough to envisage the problems of decades."[1]

On the other hand, the fear of the group in power, combined with sharp rivalry among themselves, made them anxious to pursue the policy of finding a successor for anybody who happened to be too successful. That is how Caesar came to fall, after having practically brought all Europe under Roman dominance and being actually in a condition to fulfil his earlier promise of distributing the property of wealthy landowners among the poor. The leader of the conspiratory was Brutus, presumably his illegitimate son, at any rate his adopted protégé, but, through a posthumous adoption, young Octavian became Caesar's material and spiritual heir, bearing his name, "Caesar" Octavianus. Of this "presiding member of the Capitol friends of Caesar," who from the bloody triumvir became Augustus, the beneficent Father of his country, Buchan says characteristically: "the father of the world made an indifferent father of a family."[2] Not until after Augustus, who, despite his title "the divine" made a virtue of being human and mortal, did the real "Caesars" come to power: Tiberius

[1] Random House, N. Y., 1936.

[2] Buchan, John. *Augustus,* Houghton, Boston, 1937.

and Nero, who were not superhuman like Caesar and human like Augustus, but inhuman. With them Rome again succumbed to the tyranny of the "divine ruler," the despot of the old Orient. They failed ultimately because the problem of world dominance could not be solved simultaneously with (Caesar's idea of) world-freedom in a realistic way. As Mommsen puts it: "The history of Caesar and Roman Imperialism is in truth a more bitter censure of modern autocracy than could be written by the hand of man. According to the same law of nature in virtue of which the smallest organism infinitely surpasses the most artistic machine, every constitution, however defective, which gives play to the free self-determination of a majority of citizens infinitely surpasses the most brilliant and humane absolutism; for the former is capable of development and therefore living, the latter is what it is and therefore dead."[1] The solution had to be found, not politically on this earth but spiritually—regardless of time and place—in the Christian religion: not the son of David, who became himself a tyrant, was to rule the world, but the Messiah.

Both from his personality and the political background against which he struggled, Julius Caesar appears as a real forerunner of Christianity. Contemporary tradition equipped him with all the earmarks of the heroic type. He himself believed firmly in his "Fortune," "the mysterious emanation that led his opponents to pile blunder on blunder when they faced him in the field."[2] A story reported from his youth, which clearly shows that he held himself under the special protection of a guardian angel, is in its unshakeable self-confidence reminiscent of Christ's walking on the waters. Once when he was crossing a strait in a small boat a sudden storm raged over the sea and the boat-

[1] Mommsen, Theodor. *History of Rome,* Scribner, N. Y. Bk. V. Chap. XI. English translation by W. P. Dickson, 1866.

[2] Pratt, F. *Opus cit.*

man resigned himself to being drowned. "Fool," said Caius Julius, "take your oar; you carry Caesar and his Fortune; there is no danger." This firm belief in his invincibility prompted him to join the Senate on that fatal day of his assassination of which he had been warned not only by anxious friends but in true heroic fashion by many omens. His violent death set the world aflame as Christ's execution by Roman soldiers did not long afterwards. While Caesar's military conquest of Europe did not last, he had opened up the continent for its spiritual conquest by the Christian Gospel which promised to the poor a kingdom of their own—a dream of Caesar's which could not be fulfilled realistically. Where Caesar had failed politically and economically, Christianity succeeded spiritually. The dispossessed founded a religion which solved for them their problems through a timeless and spaceless ideology establishing them as a powerful class with an entirely new psychology.

Although the disintegrating Roman Empire was finished off by the Barbarian invasion from the North it survived spiritually in and through Christianity. The Christian doctrine accomplished this miracle by incorporating the quintessence of the declining Orient into the sublime form of Hellenistic philosophy and fusing these with elements of the Jewish religion to make a new ideology. The stateless religion of the Jew was made available to mankind in Christianity, which offered the privileges of the faithful to all "have-nots" regardless of their creed and social status. While the stateless Jews had to solve their problem of survival racially, that is, by guarding their religion as a special privilege of their tribe, Christianity solved that problem not realistically but through an international, that is, universal ideology. It thereby created first and foremost a new psychological type, the ideological background of which we will discuss in the following chapter. Here it suffices to differentiate this new type—whom we might call the "inspirational" type—from the various types which contributed to its shaping. Those types, corresponding to the cultural elements of Hellenistic, Jewish and Roman origin, we might designate as the individualistic Greek, the democratic Roman and the collective Jew. Among them the Greeks were the true psychological individualists, their individualism being based on their personal selves. The Romans were individualistic in a different way, their individualism not springing from a personality-self but shaped true to a pattern, the father-citizen type. Lastly, the Jews, highly individualistic by nature, were of necessity collective in their psychology, because each individual had to represent the state as well. In both the Jewish and the Roman psychology the father-principle stood at the centre: in Jewish ideology it was biological fatherhood stressed for the survival of the race, in Roman ideology it was social fatherhood in the service of the state for world dominance.

Christianity, in replacing both biological and social fatherhood by spiritual fatherhood, introduced into religious and social ideology the principle of love, previously a mere topic of philosophic speculation. By giving the ancient Oriental mother-cult a new human meaning, Christianity for the first time translated the psychology of the son into a mother-concept, whereas formerly it was derived from the father-relation, that is, was a social concept. In other words, Christianity lifted the father-son problem from its biological base as manifested in Jewish tradition and from its socialized crystallization in Roman law into a timeless and stateless spiritual philosophy of two ever-opposed principles. Once more we see the individual fighting to save the immortal self, which has become his real self, from being submerged, this time in the socialized self which man first created just to escape his individual fate of mortality. In this sense, Christianity can be conceived of as a revolutionary movement of the son-type against his having been forced into a social type carrying the immortality of the father. Hence, its hero-worship of the spiritualized son who saved his true self by being born like the original hero, that is, without the aid of a father.

4

The Creation of Personality

IN THE emergence and development of Christianity is epitomized not only the rise and decline of our whole Western civilization but the creation and decay of our modern type of personality. Christianity as it emerged from the disintegration of the Old World of antiquity became a spiritual mass-movement of international scope inaugurating an entirely new philosophy of living and thereby precipitating a new psychological type of man. This we designated the "inspirational" type because—for the first time in history—it was built up on a "therapeutic" ideology which, by going beyond the mere preaching of an ideal for social conduct, inspired the common man—the average—to live up to a plane spiritually much higher than he could possibly aspire to in reality.

Not that inspirational books on wisdom and the art of living had not appeared before the Christian era. To mention only the better known, there was an old tradition handed down from Solomon's "Proverbs" and carried on by Aesop, Marcus Aurelius and Epictetus. But the epigrammatic advice of these men on how to achieve a pleasant, and at the same time, good life became a mere source of convenient quotations which pragmatic writers used to lend authority to their practical guidance of unsuccessful individuals. The teachings of Jesus and especially Paul's interpretation of them, which we shall discuss presently, are different from all previous "inspirational" attempts, in that they aim at a change of personality in the individual resulting spontaneously in a different attitude towards and conduct of life.

In this sense, Christianity can be looked upon as a reversal from morality back to religion, on which all morality and with it the law representing it ultimately rests. For every secular code of conduct draws its life from ideas of religious origin.[1] Hence, the importance which the Law and the violent controversies regarding its interpretation assume in the Christian doctrine of Jesus and Paul. Jesus' violation of the law, both Jewish and Roman, and Paul's theological interpretation of it, makes it clear that the conception of law originally was and emotionally still is a religious one. The aboriginal law, the tabu, convincingly shows that the fundamental law of mankind was not only self-imposed but self-operating. The individual, that is to say, automatically refrained from certain activities which directly or indirectly seemed to threaten his own self. Since the majority felt that way, the aboriginal law appears unimposed, a requirement still of vital importance to our own conception of modern law, which is supposed to function impersonally. We obey the moral law because, with its self-preserving function, it is merely an expression of our moral self. True, this genuine moral law—as it first appears in primitive tabus—is only prohibitive, as are still the Ten Commandments according to which we live because they epitomize man's moral self. On the other hand, social law, as it appears full-fledged in the Roman "ius gentium," is no longer prohibitive but aims—at least in spirit—to provide in the name of justice equal rights for all, even the under-privileged. But when this equalizing tendency reached the point in Caesar's time where it dared to touch on traditional privileges of certain groups, then the conflict between moral and social law developed into the first real class-struggle in history. For the moral law from the begin-

[1] De Burgh, W. G. *From Morality to Religion,* London, 1938.

ning was common, that is, popular law, whereas social law was dictated by the group in power. But it was only the most powerful who dared transgress the tabu and only if he was successful was he acclaimed a hero. That is why, up to the present, the transgressor of fundamental human law is not only feared and checked, but also admired if not worshipped. Thus the powerful personality, having been successful in transgressing the tabu of the average, is likely—and often permitted—to impose his own law upon the community. Hence, the divine king as the representative of supernatural power became by the same token the representative—and executor for that matter—of the law. On the other hand, he himself as a human dramatization of nature's creative power was supposed to rule with justice and to enforce the law impersonally, that is, without bestowing favors to his own advantage or increase of power. In this sense, the divine king being endowed with magical power automatically had power over life and death, thus representing God's law on earth.

Therein lies the unavoidable danger of kingship or of the rule of any strong leader; he may, from a mere representative of God, that is, the impersonal law on earth, himself become the dictatorial law-maker. Moses, the law-maker of the Jews, received the commandments for his people from Jehovah, and thus, since they corresponded to the impersonal tabu and not to the man-made law of the leader, they could be accepted as moral law. The gradual introduction of man-made laws for the privileged into the framework of the impersonal moral law led to Jesus' and his world-apostles' historic fight against the ritualistic law of the Jews which restricted instead of furthering life. As against this ritualistic law and the man-made law of the Roman Empire, Paul preached the spiritual law of self-determination, thereby re-establishing the moral value of primitive tabu on an ethical basis. In this sense, Christianity may be looked upon as the declaration of independence on the part of Jewish proselytes who grew weary of the restrictions of the Law of Moses.[1] It became the greatest moral and political revolution in the history of the human race. It not only preached the equality of human souls—the true basis for all other equalities, political, social and economic—but it separated Church from State by the well-known statements, "Render unto Caesar," and "My Kingdom is not of this World." Christianity in this way remade the ancient world and when it was overrun by the Barbarians they also fell under the spell of the new gospel. In this unique sense, Western civilization appears as a product of the egalitarian principles of Christendom. The transition, all-important in the development of modern man's conception of ethics and justice, was epitomized in Jesus' revolt against the existing law; a revolt for which he was executed as a criminal and subsequently worshipped as a demi-God. As Thurman Arnold, in discussing the *Symbols of Government*, epigrammatically puts it, "In theology a separate personality known as the Redeemer appeared to represent benevolence and this enabled God to escape from the logic of punishment of sin."[2]

The Jewish law transgressed by Jesus and militantly opposed by Paul was most strictly observed by the Pharisees, a comparatively small sect of the Palestine population consisting of tradesmen and artisans in Jerusalem whose way of life was different from the patrician Sadducees and the rural Galileans from whom Jesus sprang. Paul himself was a Pharisee (born in Tarsus) and proud to be the son of a Pharisee. The Pharisees, whom we would now call a middle-class group, drew their inspiration from the Prophets and

[1] Blended at last in "Acts" are two originally hostile brands: the ultra-libertarian, represented by Paul, and the moderate, represented by Peter (and John). At first the moderates were favored; only after Marcion (140 A.D.) had published his Epistles did Paul become celebrated.

[2] Yale University Press, 1935.

according to their tradition women were the equal of men, the submerged the equal of the patricians, and slaves the equal of their masters. All alike were children of God created in his image. In their condemnation of the worldly temptations of luxury, licentiousness and autocracy, they resemble the Puritans of the sixteenth century in England and early America.[1] In the time of Paul, however, who was born in the golden age of Augustus and lived through the reigns of Tiberius, Caligula and Claudius to be martyred in Rome during the persecution of the Christians that closed Nero's reign, the Pharisees had become a narrow-minded sect laboriously constructing an edifice of ethical monotheism.

It is well known that Paul, born a Jew, was able to invoke his Roman citizenship and appeal to the judgment of Caesar when, in the year 60 A.D., the public authorities in Jerusalem had apprehended and were about to scourge him. Thus Paul, as the descendant of free Roman citizens, was given the privilege of Roman law. Roman citizenship was not confined to the inhabitants of that city, for the early civil wars had extended this prized status to the inhabitants of Italy, and later under the emperors it became a right available to individuals throughout the Empire. In this sense, the Roman equality of the citizen before the law, making the political status superior to blood relationship in civic affairs, was a forerunner of the Christian doctrine of religious status: the equality of the human soul in the eyes of God. This equality was expressed above all in the institution of Christian marriage in which there was no barrier between the free and the slave, Roman or Barbarian. The "Pauline privilege" concerning the divorce and re-marriage of converts created the profoundest process

[1] Finkelstein, Louis. *History of the Pharisees,* 2 vols. Jewish Publication Society, Philadelphia, 1938.

of racial and social amalgamation recorded in history—a hybridization under religious sanction which formed modern civilization.[1]

This hybridization, facilitating the emergence of the new type of man, finds its social and spiritual counterpart in the vast syncretism of Christianity in which survived the Jewish faith, the spirit of Hellenism and Roman world power. The old Oriental doctrine of re-birth welded with the Jewish belief in a messianic future counteracted the realistic rationalism represented in the Roman state. By incorporating into the new religion of the Western world a great deal of the irrationalism of the Orient, Christianity escaped the collapse of a Roman civilization which had become all too rational. Like the Jews, the early Christians put faith above everything—state and country; but with the important difference that instead of a realistic deliverance through the Messiah an inner experience and change in the individual self was the salvation. In this sense is it to be understood when Albert Schweitzer, one of our profoundest scholars in the field of Christianity, aptly reminds us, in a re-issue of a book published first in 1923,[2] that the Christian religion cannot be disposed of as a mere development of Hellenistic ideas of redemption but is an original religion of its own to which only the great religious systems of the Far East are comparable in spirituality. At the same time, it has to be considered that the early exponents of the Christian faith adopted current modes of thought as the medium of their message, using, however, only what served to express a unique faith originating in the life and teachings of Jesus. Paul's letters, especially, as Canon Knox takes pains to

[1] Joyce, George Hayward, S.J. *Christian Marriage: An Historical and Doctrinal Study,* London, 1930.—Especially the chapters on the varying relations and claims of the secular and the ecclesiastical powers in regard to matrimonial matters, and the stages by which the Roman canon law upon these and cognate subjects were formulated in 1917.

[2] *Christianity and the Religions of the World,* N. Y., 1938.

point out,[1] are an attempt to express in terms of the theology of his day an ultimate fact in the Apostle's own experience. This is epitomized in the Pauline doctrine of mystical union with Christ and was for the Apostle the one matter both of primary importance and immediate certainty. Yet the Pauline literature can only be understood if interpreted in the light of the conventional language of Hellenistic theology in which Paul expounded his message to the Greek-speaking world.

This "life in Christ," the most fundamental conception of Paul's theology, is born out by his own conversion. For the faith necessary for participation in the new spirit of life was based on the belief of the individual that "Christ was actually living in him, the spirit which was the risen glorified Lord." In other words, it was not merely psychological identification, but real identity. Yet while apocalyptic notions are found in the teachings of Jesus, it was actually Paul who presented Jesus as the "Man from Heaven" (Heavenly Anthropos) and thus proclaimed the "Kingdom of God" for all who were emotionally and spiritually ready for it. But this "Kingdom" remained a mystery until Peter's eventual confession of himself as the Messiah with which the Kingdom was set up on earth. Those who entered into it constituted a "Remnant," an idea which carried on the prophetic ideal of a Remnant of Israel through which the self shall be saved from the world. As T. W. Manson points out in *The Teaching of Jesus*[2] "this ideal of a Remnant completely fulfilled by Jesus brought the dream-figure into existence as the Church."

Long before Jesus' time, the central problem of religious movement and frequent revolt in Palestine had been the messianic hope, that is, the Jewish doctrine of a saviour conceived of as effecting a final liberation of this suppressed

[1] Knox, Wilfred L. *St. Paul and the Church of the Gentiles,* N. Y., 1930.
[2] Cambridge University Press, 1934.

people. This typical Jewish Utopia of a saviour who would end all the sufferings of the chosen people became confused with the conception of the divine king during the comparatively short time when these nomadic tribes began to settle down in conquered territory. They then "rejected Jehovah" as their leader, and, in order "to become like other people," wanted a king. Against the warnings of their high-priest, Samuel anointed as their first king, Saul, "who was higher than any other of the people."[1] When he disobeyed Jehovah's orders, David, the shepherd, was anointed his successor. The books of Samuel are full of the struggles between the king, "whom the spirit of Jehovah had left," and the anointed boy David who played the harp for his melancholic lord. As often as Saul tries to kill his living successor, David spares the life of his master, until the latter takes his own life.

With their historically belated institution of kingship, the Jews for the first time embarked on a more realistic form of political messianism, an idea much older than Hebrew prophecy. The conception of an ideal king who would not misuse his power—natural or bestowed on him—not only dominated Babylonian and Egyptian history but has actually been the basis of primitive group-life, the prosperity of which was guaranteed by the king and safeguarded by all the tabus imposed on him. In the history of the Jewish people, we clearly see the original theocracy, that is, their God—invisible and movable—serving as their leader in the desert. Hence, their earthly leader, Moses, was not, as is a king, God's substitute on earth, but merely his temporary representative. It is not surprising, then, that

[1] It is worth noticing that all coronation ceremonies in Christian countries up to the coronation of King George VI of England preserve Jewish elements based on the original ritual Samuel used in anointing Saul, King of Israel. Hence, a coronation is still essentially a religious rite; and a sacred oil, when touched to the king's head, breast and hands, supposedly endows him with a "Spiritual Jurisdiction and an inalienable sanctity."

the desert God Jahwe bears the features of Moses, the strong leader, who, however, cannot reach the promised land because he belongs only to the desert and like his people is not sedentary.

Thus, with their unsuccessful institution of kingship, the Jews betrayed their own genuine God who struggled violently against their attempt to domesticate him; hence, Jehovah's fight against the building of a permanent temple, the final destruction of which in the early Christian era ended the history of the Jews as a people. Only at one time in their past was there a chance for the establishment of a dynasty and with it a State. This was in the time of David who through his thirty-three years of reign over all Israel became the symbol of the ideal king. Consequently, he was to establish the succession of his family, indeed, of his house forever. His famous discourse with Nathan about the building of a temple foreshadows the whole messianic struggle of later centuries. The building of a permanent house, the temple, for the wandering God of the desert goes hand in hand with the establishment of the house of David as reigning kings of Israel. "Jehovah will make thee a house, when thy days are fulfilled, and then shalt thou sleep with thy fathers. I will set up thy seed after thee, that shall proceed out of thy bowels, and I will establish his kingdom. He shall build a house for thy name, and I will establish the throne of his kingdom forever. I will be his father, and he shall be my son."[1]

This sounds quite Christian and, for that matter, is, inasmuch as in Jesus' time the burning question still was whether the Messiah can only be a son of David or a God-sent hero from heaven, as David himself seemed to have been. Thus the Jewish people were faced from the beginning with the vital problem of succession which the primitives had solved in the ritual killing of the divine king by

[1] II Sam. 7-14.

his magical successor. From David's time on, the messianic hope of the Jewish people aspires in two different directions, representing the popular as against the scholarly solution of the saviour's predestination. It became a vital issue every time one of these many self-styled prophets claimed to be the Messiah, and, as borne out by the famous reference in the Gospel, was a crucial problem in Jesus' time. Only once does Jesus raise this theological question with the Pharisees: "how can the Messiah be the son of David?"[1] Only at this point is the question of his birth brought up; later eschatologies merely mentioning the "appearance" of the Messiah. The position of the rabbi of Nazareth appears, according to Schweitzer,[2] an original and simple solution of the problem presented by the rivalry of the two eschatologies.

With this famous question to the Pharisees as to how he can possibly be King David's son *and* the Messiah, Jesus carried the traditional struggle of the prevailing succession-ideologies ad absurdum. But he himself could only prepare for, not find a solution for it, because he, a simple Essenen preacher, was committed to teaching the eschatology of John the Baptist. Jesus, having been brought up on the Jewish eschatology of the Messiah who brings about the resurrection of the nation, was driven through his persecution by Jews and Romans alike into the Messiah ideology combining the earthly with the celestial kingdom. His "parables"—like Hamlet's—I understand not only as a means to hide but also to reveal and find himself. Only through a miracle, then, could he become the Godsent Messiah; not through a miracle which could be explained as magic but through the miracle of his own resurrection, which Paul not merely testified to but actually experienced and lived through in his conversion. Since an individual's

[1] Mark XII. 35-37.
[2] *Op. cit.*

life cannot be continued, Paul actually signifies a new beginning based on the *now* resurrected Christ. He is not like Jesus, a fulfillment of the past tradition as represented by the old Prophets, but a fulfillment of the future in the present.

Thus we find as the focal point of Jewish-Christian controversy the magical versus the dynastic origin of the saviour, in other words, the problem of succession which may here be defined as the idea of the *eternal* survival of the fittest. We have seen how the primitives solved this community problem not only by magical transmission of the supernatural power of the leader but also by subduing the strong individual to the rules of their ritualistic tradition. The mighty empires of the ancient Orient overcame this difficulty with their dictatorial rulers through the patriarchal ideology, according to which the offspring of a great king was able to rise above his own ancestors. We have seen how this ideology in ancient Rome was made the basis of political citizenship, in that the son had to become a better father than was his father and all forefathers.

The Jews, this restless and stateless people, preserve in their history the struggle of a wandering tribe trying to settle down through the establishment of divine kingship, but unable politically to solve the problem of succession. To this, their lack of political leadership, we owe Christianity, which emerges from the inherent dualisms in the messianic ideology. The Jews had to put the arrival of their Messiah in an indefinite future, the eschatology of the final day of judgment. At the same time, he was supposed to be the anointed one (the Greek "Christos"), that is, the saviour-king of the end-period whose manifestation in the flesh simultaneously fulfils and crushes the unreal hopes of the Jews. Hence, the delay in the arrival of the Messiah, the so-called "Parousia," became the real dynamic force in the dramatic development of early Christianity.

Because it is just from this clash of the future hope of the Messiah with the need for an immediate salvation in the present life that Christianity emerged. By giving to the Jewish conception of the resurrection in the flesh on the final day of judgment the Hellenistic interpretation of the revelation of the spirit, Paul saved the early Christian sect for humanity.

Since we are interested here in the new type of man and his spiritual ideology introduced by Christianity, we have to focus our attention on Paul as the actual propagator of the Christian movement and the real creator of the universal type of man patterned by this moral revolution. In this—our emphasis on Paul's "educational" importance—we feel the more justified since we conceive of the drama of Jesus' life as a new enactment of the creation-myth lifted from its purely ritualistic significance into the realistic realm of social movement. In the drama of Christ we find all the elements of the ritual of the divine king in a quite new and far-reaching revaluation: the brief period of disputed kingship with the final killing of the divine king, and the liberation of his "double," the acquitted criminal—cast onto a world-wide historical background out of which emerges not merely a new conception of immortality but beyond it a new type of living man.

Yet it was not Jesus and his simple rabbinical teachings which created the new type that was to build the new Western world. Strangely enough, this universal type characteristic for modern man sprang from the highly abstract and sophisticated doctrines of Paul, who, through his personal experience, brought Christianity to life, indeed, to eternal life—as far as its 2000 years of past history is concerned. In the light of our conception of Jesus' life-story as an enactment of the short life and death by killing of the divine king, the much disputed question as to whether Jesus really lived, that is to say, whether he lived the life ascribed to him in the Gospels, becomes of secondary importance. In his dramatization of the creation of a new world-age we recognize the operation of a fundamental principle, indispensable to the comprehension of the creation of personality types, regardless of time and place. It is the living tradition that the heroic type, who precipitates revolutionary change, has to live a life according to the creation-ritual in order to justify his mission. That is to say, the hero actually patterns his life after the mythical tradition, as Jesus' life was foretold by the Prophets and appears to be fulfilled in the Gospel. This is the timeless living-force incorporated in the Gospel, which does not speak of "progress" but of dying and rising again, thereby revealing the pattern of history not in terms of evolution but in a succession of crises.

During the times of the acute struggle for the maintenance of a permanent, everlasting personality type, climaxed in the socialized self of the Roman citizen, Jesus enacted the creation-rite in terms of the dynamic religious ideology of his time, namely, messianic kingship. Through Paul's philosophic interpretation, this new creation of man and his world furnished the ideology for the personality of the average type who in turn patterns his life after the heroic or moral leader. This entirely new revaluation of the divine king's life and death became necessary in a world of social upheaval and spiritual confusion, and was made possible by virtue of the extraordinary experience of one man, Paul. While the primitive creation-rite was enacted for the maintenance of the existing order of things through their magical revival, Paul, in the rapidly changing order of things as he experienced and witnessed them, found a lasting philosophic solution for the problem of creative renewal in and for the individual himself.

After Jesus, as the prophetic son of David, had failed in his political rôle of leading the Jewish people, the other conception of the Messiah as the final liberator in a hoped-for future was ascribed to him. To this second rôle belongs the resurrection. In it Jesus appears not only as the beginner of a new Jewish era, but also as the one who ended the late Jewish ideology of a future saviour. Jesus' philosophy represents a synthesis between the Prophets and Daniel's conception of the Messiah. The old idea of the kingdom of the Messiah is interpreted as the eternal Kingdom; hence, the resurrection takes place at the beginning, not at the end of the time of the Messiah.

Paul's eschatology is even more complicated in that he achieves a synthesis of Jesus' ideology and the apocalyptic visions (in Baruch and Esra). Paul accepts from those scripts the separation between the kingdom of the Messiah and the kingdom of eternal blessing. Thus, rejecting Jesus' identification of the two principles, the temporal and the eternal, he had to change the time of the resurrection in order to restore the dwindling faith of the community in Jesus' mission. Their faith had broken down when the political Messiah, predicted by the Prophets, was crucified; on the other hand, the interpretation of Jesus' life and teachings in terms of the resurrected Messiah of the eschatology was not sufficiently realistic. Hence, Paul could only restore their faith by again separating the two ideologies of the kingdom. Since the physical liberation of his people was impossible and the spiritual liberation in a messianic future not workable, Paul found a solution in their spiritual liberation in the present. Through a change of attitude, he restored their faith in themselves and life.

In a word, everything hinges on the interpretation, or rather, re-interpretation of the parousia, that is, the *time* of the arrival of the Messiah. With Jesus' death, signifying the collapse of the new movement, politically as well as religiously, Paul was confronted with a new situation which called for a new solution. He found it by changing the Gospel of Jesus so as to separate the kingdom of the Messiah from the eternal kingdom of God. Since Jesus announced a general resurrection in the eternal kingdom of God, Paul himself had to become the first to be resurrected in order to prove that the kingdom of God had arrived. The whole doctrine of Paul is an endeavor to reconcile Jesus' death and resurrection with the Jewish eschatology of the future Messiah. Jesus, the rabbi, presented a realistic solution, Paul, the mystic, a spiritual solution—as the only possible one; the first corresponds to the thought of the Jewish prophets, the second to the Christian Apocalyptic. Without Paul, who gave to Christianity the livable ideology of the life in Christ through re-interpretation of the parousia, no world-religion would have developed from it.

Thus the Christians began to live the messianic Kingdom in reality, starting even a new world-age with the birth of Christ, while the Jews continued to wait for the messianic kingdom in an indefinite future. It was this eschatology, that is, the futuristic beyond-theology, which Paul converted from its ideological conception in the Jewish faith into a dynamic life-force. From an enemy of Jesus, Paul through his conversion at Damascus became his most ardent disciple, indeed, his living incarnation after the death of the Master. He is the one who makes Jesus the Messiah by bringing him back from the dead—in himself—and thus reverses the whole eschatological sequence in terms of time. He says, the *NOW* is here! Jesus' life and death was the forerunner of the Day of Judgment which is coming in the future. Maybe tomorrow; you'd better be ready; join Christ, that is, identify yourself with him and you will be —as he is—risen from the dead, alive, no longer waiting for an indefinite future to live the life on earth. Through this re-valuation of the time element Paul succeeded in putting the pull towards an indefinite future behind man where it could operate as a push in the present: an impetus which has been dynamically effective in enabling man not only to survive the collapse of Antiquity, but by the same token to create a new, our Western civilization.[1]

In making his resurrection available as a personal experience to everybody in the present, Paul, in his unusual experience, spiritualized the magic participation of the commoner, the average man. Thus the exceptional type, the deviate who through his own personal conversion was "twice-born" and thereby acquired a new self, became the prototype for the average man, in fact, for mankind. Paul taught that anyone who can believe in Christ, that is, the resurrected Jesus, will himself be resurrected, that is, have a new life, a new self such as he himself had acquired. Discarding the Oriental conception of re-birth as well as the Jewish conception of resurrection in the flesh—which did not actually mean deliverance of the individual but implied a cosmologic ideology based on eschatological belief—Paul carried those traditional concepts beyond any kind of immortality ideology. His was a new kind of living immortality achieved in the creation of personality.

Thus we see in Christianity as propagated by Paul an entirely new interpretation of the age-old problem of succession, which in essence is a time-problem and was solved as such by the world-Apostle. From the spiritual conception of immortality in the primitive, who dispensed with biological succession by virtue of his double, and the magical preservation of extraordinary qualities enacted in the ritual of kingship, we meet in Christianity a spiritualized conception of succession for every individual—not only for the privileged individual or group, but a real democratic ideology which the Roman Empire had failed to put into practice.

[1] Compare in *Seelenglaube und Psychologie*, F. Deuticke, 1930, the discussion of a similar re-valuation of time in modern physics: Einstein's relativity, Heisenberg's conception of the future influencing the past and Bergman's conception of the NOW.

This complete re-valuation of the problem of succession carries with it the original germ of a development which culminated in the emergence of what we call personality. While Jesus, a Jewish sectarian who tried to liberate his fellow-believers from the "law," only succeeded in freeing himself from the patriarchal ideology of his people, Paul, through his spiritual interpretation of the resurrection, established what might be called not so paradoxically the individual's own succession in his own present self. What Jesus achieved with his rebellion was an ideological succession in spiritualized fatherhood, while Paul, his real successor, with his dynamic therapy created Selfhood. True, Jesus' preaching went beyond the existing law, both Jewish and Roman, in that he first denied the father and then announced—and this is how I understand his message—that everyone can be "king," not only "father" as the Roman law had decreed. It was not his own realistic kingship he proclaimed and aspired to but the universal kingship for men, that is, the equal right to immortality for everyone, even the dispossessed and the slaves. In this sense, I understand his free-willed death according to his saying: "No man taketh My Life, I lay it down of Myself." This is no sacrifice or atonement for a rebellion against God-father, but an expression of the liberated individual who feels master of his own life and death and free to choose a father if he wants to. As a matter of fact, we are reminded by Dr. Manson[1] that Jesus seldom spoke of God as Father except to his disciples and only to them after Peter had made his confession at Caesarea-Philippi.

Paul, on the basis of Jesus' crucifixion and resurrection, fully restored the idea of spiritual succession which primitive man symbolized magically and which at the climax of Greek culture was manifested in the master-disciple relationship of the great philosophers, artists and scientists.

[1] *Opus cit.*

Paul, however, carried this Hellenistic conception beyond human relationship, in that he animated the individual to become, so to speak, his own successor by developing a new personality of his own. Thus the life in the Double was shifted from the hereafter into the present, whereby the individual was fulfilling his Double-life during his own lifetime. By participating in Christ's resurrection, man thus was actually "twice-born" in life instead of re-born after death. In this philosophy of self-succession I see the basic element of our psychological personality concept. The Greeks had intellectualized this problem of succession in their master-disciple relationship; the Romans legalized it in civic fatherhood; and Christianity spiritualized it, thus bringing the original magical conception of immortality back to an individual plane. While Jesus was still caught in the community problem as to who might be the authentic successor, Paul established the individual's own right to succession and self-succession in his "life in Christ."

Although the Christian institution of marriage, or rather, inter-marriage, as distinguished from the strictly racial codes of the Jews and the political discrimination of Roman law, solved the problem of succession for the Christian type of man, the idea of succession as we found it religiously maintained remains most important for our search into the beyond of individual psychology, because in it the individual problem meets with the community problem. Originally signifying the individual's concern for his survival in his double, succession became a community problem with the need and desire to preserve one outstanding individual's unusual qualities in another person, his successor, who thereby would be enabled to "succeed" as well as his forerunner. Such magical succession, lifted from the Greek master-discipleship into a mystical plane of spiritual identity, is at the basis of the self-styled World-Apostle's relation to his master Jesus. Historically speaking, the problem of

Christianity's origin lies in the question: what is the relation of Jesus to Christ? That is to say: how did the Jewish preacher Jesus become Christ, the founder of a new creed? The answer is: through Paul, who calls upon himself—by virtue of his vision—as the one chosen by Christ with whom he identifies himself. This identification, though, signifies real identity and thus becomes creative succession, in that Paul lives Jesus' life as he himself might have lived it. Such spiritual twinship, embracing both the magical Double of primitive belief and the intellectual discipleship of Greek civilization, also goes beyond the legalized succession epitomized in Roman law. The fatherless Jesus teaches that every son who loves his freely chosen father and is loved by him is a Messiah in his own right. Thus Jesus prepared Paul's final step by his "self-calling" through his baptism which lifted him out of the commonest clan of the Essene as a chosen individual.

Thus, in the history of mankind, we encounter three solutions for the vital problem of succession which developed from the individual desire for immortality into the community problem of preserving the qualities of the fittest. These three solutions—the magical, intellectual and biological—correspond to three types of civilization, namely, the primitive with its magical succession in the Double, the Greek with its intellectual succession in the disciple, and the Roman with its legalized biological succession in the son. In combining all those conceptions, Christianity reaches beyond them in conceiving of the father—who is biologically denied—as representing the son's own future, whereby a "choice-father" replaces those former relationships. Thus the ancient concepts of re-birth and resurrection were welded into the personality type of self-succession. The prototype of our own "psychological" concept of personality was thereby created. In this sense, all psychology is at bottom mass-psychology and as such beyond the individual.

But it is "beyond" also in another, deeper sense, inasmuch as the individual personality-type always seems to be derived from an outstanding personality deviating from the average in one way or another. In this sense, too, the prototype who furnishes the model for the average is always beyond the psychology of the common man, who, however, behaves according to this type.

All mass-psychology, on the other hand, is shaped after the outstanding individual as an "inspirational" self. Thus the personality-type of a certain time and age is patterned *between* the outstanding type of the leader and the average man who through magical or spiritual participation is striving towards this ideal. Hence we have to distinguish between mass-psychology as it is created from this ideal and mass-psychology as it is applied—if necessary forcibly—to the average man. In Christianity we find both those processes epitomized in the creation and propagation of the Christian type of man. This essentially timeless type, naturally taking on the prevalent ideology of his age, merely consists in the capacity to create a personality according to prevailing standards.

Thus in the shaping and re-shaping of personality types within our Western world there are three principles simultaneously operating: on the basis of the common inspirational type, which is susceptible to all sorts of influences, new personality-types are created during social and spiritual crises of religious, political or economic origin. Such crises manifesting themselves throughout the ages in the struggle between temporal and eternal values demand and facilitate the emergence of a strong leader. Finding before him a task similar to that which was the lot of previous men of action, he shapes his goals and correspondingly his personality according to the heroic tradition of leadership. Thus he precipitates the creation of a new order and with it a new type of man who shapes himself after the prototype of the leader whose skill it is to follow this general development in his own personality.

Parallel with such periodical change of personality types precipitated by mass-movements there exists a permanent undercurrent of deeper personality development independent of those sweeping social influences. I mean man's desire and need to maintain his individual personality as the inspirational successor of his own true self. While the first more hectic change is precipitated by an increasing awareness of group and class differences and achieved through affirming differentiation—often hateful and hostile in its manifestations—the second process of developing one's own true self is stimulated and accomplished through love. This love-principle, as Paul expressed it in his so-called "hymn to love," (I Cor. 13), is different from any previous conception of love. It is a true characteristic of Christianity's inspirational psychology, stated in Paul's mystical credo, that we move through faith and not through insight.

Thus the conception of personality and with it the different personality-types of various civilizations are in the last analysis derived from the deviate, who in turn shapes his outstanding personality according to heroic tradition, although in terms of his time and culture. This tradition itself sprang, as we have shown, from the need to organize the individual's daily life in terms of a man-made ritual which, however, has become increasingly socialized and institutionalized. Whereas in primitive and ancient times, the hero, as distinguished from the people, created single-handed the elements of culture, later, with the democratization of the institutions of kingship and marriage, the average man became an active participant in the development of civilization. Thus the fitting of the individual's life into the heroic pattern of the outstanding personality starts through the ritualistic ceremony in which the individual is temporarily lifted beyond his socialized self. With Christianity, however, this lifting experience was made permanent, that is, into a psychological type of personality. The whole process of creating personality by patterning it according to tradition became conscious, as borne out by the statement of the Gospel that the word of the Prophets became flesh in Christ. As Christ's life was continued in Paul, so Christ's word became flesh in Paul and through the Apostle in mankind.

Yet, while the hero and the religious leader appear self-sufficient, indeed, self-created, the average man, who lives, so to speak, beyond his psychological means on heroic tradition, needs to have this "lifted" self supported by various props. Originally this was achieved by real participation of the group members in the magical ritual of renewal enacted by an outstanding personality (hero, divine king, priest). Such experience was more deeply rooted than our psychological "identification," which is but a faint individualistic echo of a uniting communal experience that is quite different from modern man's vicarious mode of living. But no matter on what emotional level such participation takes place, it always needs another person, not only for its initiation but likewise for its maintenance and continuous operation. Although it strives to make the individual utterly independent, that is, self-sufficient in his own right, it necessarily fails in that achievement through the personality's constant need for support and justification. The more individualistic our type of personality grew, the more it needed for its sustenance another person of a complimentary or supplementary type, without thereby fully replacing the collective security of the group. The primitive type, on the other hand, being as much a real member of his group as he feels himself to be an individual, stands much more strongly by and on himself; he does not even become involved in sexual relationship, for sex to him is merely a function of his mortal self.

Love, as we came to conceive of it through Paul's theology, on the other hand, was unknown to the primitive and non-existent in the world of Antiquity. Among the most primitive tribes (in Madagascar) the fear of incurring the ancestors' displeasure was the main stimulus to socially acceptable behaviour. In the Old Testament, there still reigns the moral code of reward and punishment. Jehovah commands righteousness under the threat of punishment. The Prophets first spoke of love, the love for God which makes you good. The Christian God was supposed to love you whether you were good or not, an idealistic doctrine which, as is well known, was soon abandoned by the Church fathers in favor of the old Jewish discipline. Yet this desire to be good was instilled in the true Christian type who eventually carried it beyond its religious and moralistic meaning into the realm of personality development. By creating his personality in an effort for heroic immortalization, the individual at the same time had to resort to his true personal self. Thus, in saving his immortal self through accepting the Christian conception of love, the individual rescued his own real self from living on and in the "borrowed" self of the leader.

Time and again the individual self had to save itself from the coercion of conforming mass-psychology which guaranteed the collective immortality of the tribe or nation. Be it in terms of magical self-perpetuation in the double, or in social terms of legalized fatherhood, or by the creation of a personality shaped after the pattern of a superhuman hero, it always amounted to an overlapping of the natural self living in this temporal world of affairs and the personality-self living in and for another world and a more or less indefinite future. The spiritual self-succession in the personality build-up follows the heroic pattern in the striving for independence by denial of the parents to whom the individual owes his natural self—thereby precipitating in one way or another a spiritual crisis comparable to the experience of the twice-born type. In other words, the average man of the Christian era patterns himself after the personality of the twice-born, whether or not he is capable of such an experience. In this way he is able to participate in the psychology of the twice-born type without really having it. What he has, though, is a sufficiently effective symbol for the really liberating experience of the "super-man," namely, baptism, the religious meaning of which—liberation from original sin—at the same time symbolizes the second birth of the average individual. Thus, through the spiritual conception of the Church, the child becomes a participant of Christ's resurrection in his own life-time. Hence the Christian type of personality starts his life, so to speak, on a secondary plane of experience, leaving behind him not only his own biological past but all past history before Christ, that is, psychologically speaking, the magical self, the heroic self and the socialized self—all of which we found synchronized in the spiritual self of the Christian type.

This prototype of all later inspirational movements and personality patterns consists in a flexibility which has survived to our day in the "adjustable" type of modern psychology. Just as this archetype has been derived from the individual experience of a deviate, so our present psychology was derived from a deviate type, the neurotic. This statement, however, does not imply that our psychology of the neurotic type is retroactively applicable to all the deviates in the past who made history. Jesus, with his seeming self-sacrificial attitude, was "masochistic" just as little as Paul—in spite of his epileptic fits—was simply a neurotic. Both appear as highly creative personalities who, by destroying outworn values, liberated new life forces. For in every individual there exists a genuine desire to conform, improve, develop, in a word, to be good. From this innate desire to change and to be loved for his achievement spring good and bad traits in the individual's character. According to his temperament, man either tries to immortalize himself in his work, as does the creative type, or more wilfully attempts to preserve his own physical self by cutting himself off from the natural life-processes, as does the neurotic. But the price they all, even the average individual in our modern world, have to pay for this personal independence from the group is another kind of *individual* dependence which we call relationship. Paradoxically, the individualistic personality tends more towards the development of relationship and not, as it may seem, towards aloneness. Such highly individualistic relationship, however, in its emotional make-up and even more in its spiritual evaluation, resembles the magical double- or twin-relationship of primitive man. In this respect, the meaning of marriage changed from a magical ceremony promising self-perpetuation and from legal agreement guaranteeing biological perpetuation in the children of the family, into a symbol of highly individualistic relationship which is bound to fail because one partner cannot play the rôle of alter-ego for the other.

Here we come upon the age-old problem of good and evil, originally designating eligibility for immortality, in its emotional significance of being liked or disliked by the other person. On this plane of individualistic relationship, personality is shaped and formed according to the vital need to please the other person whom we make our "God," and not incur his or her displeasure. All the twistings of the natural and the social self, with its artificial striving for perfection and the unavoidable "relapses" into badness, are the result of these attempts to humanize the spiritual need for goodness. The struggles and conflicts resulting from such futile attempts can never be solved through the magic of will, be it by willing oneself different or by trying to change the other person will-fully into what we want him to be. All the guilt with which modern man is filled springs not so much from the necessary failure of such use, or rather, misuse of the other person, but in a deeper sense from willing against the self and the natural fulfilment of it within the realm of a given civilization or community.

The neurotic and the criminal type only represent outstanding examples of such failure in individual relationship, as our modern basis of personality development. The fear of personal power and its dangers, which prompted primitive man to check and limit it collectively through regulated renewal of the existing order, breaks ever so often through all the inhibitions and tabus which man created to protect himself from his irrationality. In personality development we can detect the same dynamic cycles within the individual's life which we have found operating in the "dialectical" movements of history. We find anarchy, hierarchy, bourgeoisie corresponding to the impulsive, neurotic, creative type of personality determining the individual's reaction to his environment, which, however, is no longer a natural one but epitomized in the man-made social order prevailing at the time.

In times of social crises this need for goodness-aspiring immortalization is shifted from the individual to the social order as a whole, as was the case with the Christian movement and as still holds true for our present secular movements to reform society in order to establish the kingdom of heaven on earth. While during the Christian era historical reality, then in the making, clashed with the all-powerful mythical tradition, now, on the contrary, the traditional ideology of the inspirational type of man is clashing with economic and political realities which he is unable to cope with. The French Revolution and its aftermath, the emergence of American democracy, were the first social movements carrying the Christian doctrine of the individual's equality into the realm of political realism. Communism, which in its fundamental ideology resembles so much early Christianity, seems to signify another step in that direction, whereas Fascism represents the opposite principle of difference, symbolized in its doctrine of racial superiority. Such nationalistic movements are, however, not new in the struggle of European nations to free themselves from the yoke of Rome. For the future historian, the Nazi's propagation of their Teutonic pageantry might be considered the logical conclusion of Luther's protestant fight for an independent German religion.

Once more we realize here that not only is the average individual's psychology shaped and patterned according to the outstanding personality, but also history on a large scale is made according to mythical tradition, which is bound to clash in one way or another with the existing realities of life. In this sense, history is actually made from mythical stuff—which afterwards is segregated as "unhistorical." The hero, for all we know, may not be historical himself, but historically speaking he is more real than history because he made it, shaped it, according to mythical tradition. In fact it is just that ability which makes him a hero. Thus we see that the patterns of historical development are just as much "borrowed" as are the patterns of personality types. We know, for example, that the impulse for the French Revolution of 1789 came from the England of 1788, just as the American Revolution was borrowed, though vastly improved upon, from the French. This world-revolution was actually lived through in France, whereas England checked it economically and Germany applied it ideologically. On the virgin soil of America it could be worked out politically, in a new kind of democracy, which however had its birth in the West where the Continental immigrants became real Americans.

Yet revolutions are not only contagious, as borne out by

other simultaneous social movements,[1] but also seem to have served as convenient excuses and justifications as they spread from foreign countries. Not unlike the syphilis which was called in England the "French disease," and in France "the Spanish plague," while the Spaniards claimed it was brought back from America by Columbus and his men, social evils and upheavals are likely to be labeled as of foreign importation. Be that as it may, the universal fate of historical personalities who changed the world we find epitomized in Christianity. The new personality-type seems always to be promoted not by the one who actually creates it in real living but by one who applies this living experience of the other. Although the one who actually lives it furnishes the prototype for the creation of the new personality-type, it always needs the theorist, be he theological, political, philosophical or psychological, to furnish the ideology by which the average is measured and towards the fulfilment of which he strives. Thus not Jesus but Paul, not Robespierre but Rousseau and in Germany, Kant, provided the ideological framework for a new personality-type which had emerged spontaneously. The same holds good in our time for the neurotic type and his interpreter, Freud, who thought to explain neurotic symptoms as an exaggeration of normal behaviour, whereas in reality the psychology of civilized man is at present "neurotic," which means, distorted by the battle of irrational forces against their suppressor, reason.

In view of those paradoxical facts one wonders whether this clash of personalities, ideologies and traditions as manifested in different civilizations might not be the very spark of life for the creation of true culture and with it new personality-types. At any rate, the diffusion of cultures, which

[1] Merriman, Rogers B. *Six Contemporaneous Revolutions,* N. Y., 1939. The following six revolutions took place concurrently in seventeenth century absolutistic Europe: the Catalonian, the Portuguese, the Neapolitan, the English Puritan, the French Fronde and the de Witt republican pensionary movement in the Netherlands.

we shall discuss fully in the last chapter, seems to reflect on a large scale the average individual's absorption of the outstanding personality's psychology. Usually it is not only introduced by a stranger but typically borrowed from a foreign civilization, thus carrying out culturally the mythical tradition of the hero who comes from no-man's land as a saviour transmitting civilization. For such absorption of "borrowed" personality seems to enable the individual to save his own true self, just as the borrowed elements of foreign civilizations seem to provide the very fertilizer for the development of a true genuine culture.

5

Two Kinds of Love

IN OUR endeavor to show how ideological and collective motivations of a bigger order determine the individual's behaviour and personality-formation beyond psychology, we finally reach a point which seems to set a limit to such an undertaking. For what could be more personal than love, more individual, indeed, individualistic? And yet, just love —not only its various conceptions but the actual way we love and want to be loved—has been prescribed for us by speculative philosophies and mighty ideologies like those which determined our religious creeds and moral standards. Such a statement, however strange, appears plausible and even acceptable once we have realized that philosophies and ideologies—just as much as religions—are not merely explanations or even interpretations of existing phenomena, but rather, create new phenomena and with them new types of personalities precipitating new events.

Be that as it may, love is not, as is tacitly assumed, as old as mankind. No conception of it exists among primitives and hardly any among the most highly civilized peoples in Antiquity. Save for the Old Testament in which love for God and one's parents and neighbors is rather a command of righteousness, and Plato's philosophy, there exists no real conception of love in the pre-Christian era. The very first love-ideology, in Plato, appears merely as a sentimental reflection on the part of the great moralist upon his decadent age. According to Nygren,[1] Plato's conception

[1] Nygren, Anders. *Agape and Eros* (translated by Watson, Philip S.), second part of *The History of the Christian Idea of Love.* London, 1938. (First published in Swedish, 1930.) See also the more philosophic treatment of the subject by Gruenhut, L. *Eros und Agape,* Leipzig, 1931.

of Eros is symptomatic of a general decline in the force of the original vital Eros; a view still echoing in the deprecatory implication with which we are accustomed to refer to the idea of "platonic" love.

Conceptually, though, Plato's philosophy of the Eros implies three different meanings: the desirous love, which we would call, "libido"; the egocentric love, which we designate as narcissistic self-love, and only third and last, the divine sublimated love (for example, love for wisdom: philosophia), which is commonly considered "platonic" love proper—perhaps rightly so, since it is most characteristic for Plato, who admits only one direction for the development of the Eros, (from below) upward. Only through Eros, is his message to the decaying Greek civilization, can man rise from the world of the senses into the world of ideas; implying our conception that ideas in themselves are powerless unless they are carried by the life-force of Eros into dynamically powerful ideologies.

This, however, did not happen with the ideology of love until the Christian era, when Paul, inspired by the teaching and experience of Jesus, professed "the law of love" as an active life-force. This new Christian love, Agape, was not conceived of as the opposite of Eros but as of an altogether different kind—no sublimated Eros or "platonic" love, but an entirely new attitude towards life which, translated into actual experience, created a new type of man. It has been argued as to whether Antiquity collapsed through the emergence of this new love-concept or whether—as is more likely—the expansion of Eros, spiritually with the Greeks and physically with the Romans, led to the collapse of Antiquity and the birth of the age of love. In any case, what happened was that the urge for powerful expansion and domination characteristic of the world of Antiquity was replaced and finally complemented by a desire for yielding and surrender manifested in the need to be loved. This yearning for surrender was not a defeatist attitude, a negative giving-up; it was a voluntary yielding in and to love, a release of outgoing emotion in the opposite direction from that of the egocentric will-ful Eros.

In his profound work, Nygren shows that in the early days of Christianity fellowship with God was conceived of in three different ways—by Judaism, by Hellenism and by Christianity, respectively, that is to say, by man's fulfilling of the Law (nomos), by man's desire for heavenly values (the platonic Eros) and by God's own love freely bestowed on the sinner (Agape). He also shows—and that is his main thesis—that the Agape-motif had to uphold its own against the powerful compulsion of the law and the libido. After the Apostolic Fathers had failed to rescue "the Agape-motif from the clutches of nomos" the Eros-motif "overwhelmed Christianity as a flood" in Gnosticism until a compromise was reached in which the influence of the Eros "becomes greater with the passage of time."

In this struggle of the Agape principle for survival, the power-ideologies were not only victorious on the whole but a great deal of confusion was created by a more or less purposeful misinterpretation or misrepresentation of the Agape. Even in modern times, Nietzsche ridiculed the Christian ideology of love as decadent, weak, slavish, and Freud misrepresented it as "feminine," masochistic, in a word, neurotic, because he—as well as Nietzsche—was only interested in restoring the will-ful Eros of Antiquity as a means of individual therapy. While the Jew was commanded by his God to love lest he be punished—which really means respect out of fear—the Christian conception of love is based on the idea of being good through being loved. But this meant being loved by God not by man, as it was realistically interpreted, i.e. misinterpreted from the beginning right up to our day. When we speak of God here, we do not have to interpret that religious conception psychologically, because from a certain time on in history God just means "God" to the individual, with all the implications any term we use loosely may carry. Yet, in our language, we might say that this Christian love is a purely internal experience justifying the Self; for being loved by God, manifesting itself as love for God, can only be experienced on the basis of self-acceptance.

The difference between the love-philosophies in Antiquity and the Christian era can be stated as the difference between coercive possessiveness versus yielding. Correspondingly, the Jewish God was a God of punishment and revenge, whereas the Christian God was one of love and forgiveness. In a word, the religion of hatred changed into the religion of love, which in turn changed the individual's attitude from will-ful wanting into a desire of being wanted, that is, loved. In this sense, the personality of man changed from the will-ful into the loving type; psychologically speaking, the will to want turned into the will to be wanted (loved).

This change of attitude is epitomized in the changing conception of good and evil, this most fundamental problem in human life. The Jewish creed rested on righteousness: if you follow the commands of your God, that is, respect his laws, you are good. The Christian faith rested on being loved by God, which made you good. On the other hand, the origin of evil, the problem of problems, cannot be solved objectively (that is, in God), but only in the human being. The first psychological solution of this problem is to be found in the Jewish doctrine of *"jeçer,"* the original psychology of man, stating that our own attitude condemns something in us as "bad." This "jeçer" corresponds to Freud's conception of "libido" to such a degree that N. P. Williams, in his notable Bampton lectures,[1] felt compelled

[1] 1924. Published in London, 1927, under the title: *The Ideas of the Fall and of Original Sin,* p. 68 ff.

to compare the two concepts. The author elaborates the parallel by stating this Jewish doctrine of original sin in terms of the Hebrew conception of "jeçer": this evil spirit is localized in the heart, that is, in the innermost self, its nature is ambivalent and its origin is individual not hereditary, meaning, it is implanted by God in every single man.

This first psychology of the sinful desire appears, however, as the end-process of century-long Jewish speculation and as the unavoidable result of the history of the Jewish people. Contrary to the great religious systems of the Far East, the Jewish doctrine of the fall (and original sin) conceives of evil as temporary and avoidable and not as an inherent dualism in the nature of man. This *unique* conception of the Jews seems to be the result of their unique experience in exile, the sufferings of which they naturally had to conceive of as temporary and avoidable. To give a meaning as well as a justification to their tragic fate in history, they had to assume that it was through their own fault (sin), in not having obeyed the law of God, that they had to endure all those evils; and at the same time they had to believe that God had provided for them a special mission in history by putting them through all those sufferings.

Such an explanation of their unique psychology is corroborated by the findings of scholarly research which indicate that before the Babylonian experience there was no conception of original sin and that the Story of the Fall of Man (Gen. III) can only be understood as a reflection upon their life in exile. The Paradise-episode does not betray any idea of original sin: the change came in with the experience of exile, which was conceived of as a punishment for the people's sins. The first recorded incident of sin (later elaborated in Henoch) is the sexual intercourse of the Angels (sons of God) with mortal woman (Gen. VI). Whether this story epitomizes, as I am inclined to believe, the sinning of the Jews in exile with strange women

—transgressing one of the severest tabus of the Jews—in any case, the idea of original sin grew stronger in the post-exile period (see Psalms). But since this does not account for the sin after the Flood it was replaced by the doctrine of the Fall of Man; that is to say, the idea of original sin, obviously a post-exilic product, was pushed back into the beginning of things.[1]

This theory clearly shows that the Jews maintained an attitude of self-reproach and self-accusation, the result of their tragic experience in exile, even after their liberation, and through the diaspora it became part of the universal psychology of mankind. We are not surprised to find mankind taking over this unique psychology of an exceptional tribe as their own, although the corresponding historical experience was lacking for the rest of the world. Such assimilation of one kind of psychology by a totally different type has occurred frequently in history. Here it suffices to point out that through this vicarious adoption of his unique psychology by the rest of the world the Jew was made the scapegoat in a much deeper sense than we are accustomed to believe. In this respect, Christianity appears as a spiritual revolution on the part of the rest of the world by which it sought to free itself from the self-imposed morality of a totally different type. At the beginning of the Christian era there were current two theories of sin: the popular conception of a moral fall and original evil in apocalytic writings of the lower classes (amhorez) living in the hope of a messianic deliverance from the yoke of tyranny; and the learned rabbinical theories of an evil impulse in the individual. Christianity united the two, that is, without fully

[1] While the Fall-story reflects the more popular conception of apocalyptic theology, later rabbinical teachings of the psychological cause for sin are based on the conception of "yeçer ha-ra" (evil imagination) derived from an interpretation of the Biblical text in Genesis (VI, 5). This doctrine of original sin was first indicated by Sirach (beginning of the second century before Christ) and later elaborated in the Talmudic scripts (the Hebrew literature in between is lacking).

succeeding, tried to liberate mankind from the inescapable curse of sin. The apocalyptic ideology, on the other hand, was relinquished by the Jews after the fall of Jerusalem (70 A.D.) and the suppression of Bar Kochba's revolt (135 A.D.), because with those events the hope for a brighter future of their people definitely vanished.

Meanwhile, from the Christian movement, there had emerged this new hope through an ideology of love not based on the evil will but on the desire to be good so as to be wanted (loved). This was the new Gospel: man loved by God is good, not bad, if only he lends himself to be loved by God instead of taking the whole responsibility for the evil in the world on himself. The Jews did that, because with them the people as a whole felt guilty of having sinned. Theirs was a collective sin and a corresponding collective guilt, which found expression in the messianic redemption of the whole people who would be resurrected as a nation among other nations on the day of final judgment. This group-psychology of an exceptional experience of a people was made the basis of a general psychology for every individual of mankind. Christianity tried to break through this vicious circle of mass-psychologism by going back to the original meaning of the Fall-tradition, which plainly implies that man was good by nature and having fallen off this path can be restored to righteousness. Hence, the original Fall-tradition became part of the Christian doctrine, whereas the psychological explanation postulating as the "cause" of sin the evil will of the individual remained the Jewish tradition, which, however, became just as universally accepted in man's psychology.

Those doctrines represent the two dualistic principles in human nature: the will which in and by itself is conceived of as evil,[1] and the moral principle of good and bad, the solution of which depends essentially on the individual's attitude

[1] See *Truth and Reality*, Alfred A. Knopf, N. Y., 1936.

towards love.[1] This problem of duality in ethics is as old as mankind and remains unsolved despite theological and philosophical controversy carried on throughout the ages, up to Luther's unresolved will-puzzle and Kant's categorical imperative. For it arises in every man's daily conduct from the fact that morality as duty-doing and as pursuit of the good cannot be reconciled on the monistic basis which rationality requires from our behaviour. Christianity, as far as we know, represents the only successful attempt to form a reconciling principle in the reciprocated love of God to man. Though not a final solution of the problem of evil and freedom of will, this axiom of Christianity that "God is love" established at least ideally a new livable basis for human action.[2]

It is no final solution, because the love of God for man, the "Agape," not only presupposes man's willingness to be loved but also implies his reciprocal love for God, that is, faith. What stands in the way of this achievement is the fact that in the individual's subjective experience, the strong impulse, the will, is always felt to be bad or evil, not only because it may be harmful to others but chiefly because it endangers the own self. Thus the conception of sin and guilt in the individual is bound up with his consciousness and self-consciousness. But again with the Jew, it was not so much the non-acceptance of the self-doomed death, as it was the non-acceptance of their fate, that is, life. Hence, the Jewish psychology is pessimistic, hostile to life, whereas Christianity promised to every individual the chance for a better, indeed, a good life.

[1] Characteristically enough, the two words for good and evil in the Hebrew language have no moral connotation whatsoever; they simply have the practical meaning of useful and harmful (tōbh and rā).

[2] See de Burgh, W. G. *From Morality to Religion.* London, 1938. Augustine's conception of Love which dominated not only medieval theology (of Bernard, Acquinas, Dun Scotus and Luther) but still exerted its influence in modern times has recently been expounded by John Burnaby: *Amor Dei,* London, 1938.

Herein is anchored the true democratic ideology of Christianity, promising every man equality before God, that is, in his own self, whereas our political democracy, praiseworthy as it may be, always remains an unattainable ideal of the heavenly kingdom on earth. Interestingly enough, early Christianity proves to be more realistic in that respect than later periods of social planning. By proclaiming that man is not fundamentally bad, Christian doctrine simultaneously claimed that things were bad and had to be changed. While the Jew was constantly blaming himself for not meeting the ideal requirements of his God, the early Christians with Paul as their leader were keenly aware of the need for a change of order.

This change of order, which finally precipitated the collapse of the ancient world, was, however, brought about first by the change of the type of man through the new idea of love. This new ideology, purely conceived of as being loved by God with the meaning of accepting one's own self as fundamentally good, was bound to be misunderstood, misinterpreted and misused in the course of time until we find it in our day thwarted and twisted in the neurotic type who is either fighting it willfully or giving in to it too "masochistically." But, in one way or another, this genuine need of the human being to be loved became the strongest motive for the molding and building of personality-types. Yet, while the curse of the evil was overcome by being loved, meaning, being good, the trouble with this humanized love-ideology was that not being loved made the individual bad. In a word, the moral integrity of the personality became so utterly dependent upon the other person's love that the individual either had to deny it willfully or submit to the insecurity of a personal God.

This humanization of the spiritual love-principle reached its climax in an era known as the Romantic period, which left its imprint on modern relationship in an ideology called

Romanticism. This eighteenth century philosophy of love was prepared for in the Renaissance, which, as a cultural movement, evolved a new conception of love entirely original and quite different from that of the Middle Ages. While the ancients considered love a pleasure whereby human beauty was accepted as a mere aspect of nature's beauty, for the Middle Ages it had been sin, and feminine beauty was looked upon as a temptation by man who no longer saw woman as a means of pleasure but as a cause of perdition. During the Renaissance, however, feminine beauty as its all-powerful stimulus became, together with a new conception of love, the object of philosophic speculation and the admitted source of poetic inspiration. In the synthesis, not entirely heathen and not fully Christian, which Renaissance culture represents, love was considered sensuous as well as spiritual, and woman was looked upon as fully equal to man, that is, endowed with gifts of mind as well as body.[1] Contrary to the thought of the Middle Ages, love was no longer considered subordinate to virtue, or beauty denounced as a source of peril. In a word, the conception of original sin changed to the conception of original love. Love, that is to say, was appreciated not because it was a *means* of becoming good, but because it *was* good, which means not only pleasurable but beautiful, that is, part of nature.

In the Romantic period which flourished in Germany, this free philosophy of love could not be accepted. There it was not the beautiful woman who was appreciated and thus loved; it was woman as a group or class who became idealized. The leading intellects of that period, shaken in their fundamental selves by the repercussions of the French Revolution, saw in fully developed womanhood the perfect, that is, emotional expression of the true self. In a period of col-

[1] Tonelli, Luigi. *L'Amore Nella Poesia e Nel Pensiero Del Rinascimento,* Florence.

lectivistic ideologies glorifying folk-traditions, folk-lore and folk-art, woman became, so to speak, collectivized as the carrier of racial continuity. The challenge to love no longer appears epitomized in sheer beauty but in an abstract notion called the "beautiful soul." Although this idea was taken over from Plato's "Banquet," the actual love-life of the poets in the Romantic period was anything but "platonic." In fact, Wieland, to whom is credited the romantic conception of the "beautiful soul," indulges in erotic phantasies bordering on the pornographic; whereas his English predecessors, the philosopher Shaftsbury and the novelist Richardson, had given the "beautiful soul" a moral connotation.[1]

In this idealization of woman we recognize a reaction against her moralization brought about in the Middle Ages by the Church, which, in the obsession of witchcraft, had identified her with the evil symbol of mortality—sex. Through this about-face of romanticism man suddenly lifted woman into the rôle of representing the immortal soul-principle hitherto usurped by him. This rôle of the soul-bearer, in primitive conception, had been ascribed to her religiously in the soul-belief of totemism and socially in the institution of matriarchy. There, the man could still preserve his personal immortality in his belief of self-perpetuation, whereas in the romantic conception of the woman-soul he actually renounced his better self to her. She became the beautiful *soul of the man*, his eternal, immutable, immortal side as against the mutability and transitoriness of his individual self. This we saw struggling during that same period with the bad, condemned ego epitomized in the persecuting double.

Thus, in romantic love, the Christian love-ideology, as applying alike to both sexes, became divided up between

[1] Schiller, in his famous poem, "Anmut und Wuerde" (1793), defined the beautiful soul as the perfect balance between moral feeling and physical emotion.

the two sexes and thereby created a confusion under which we still labor in our sexual psychology. While during the Middle Ages man had made woman the symbol of evil, now by virtue of representing the beautiful soul she was supposed to make him good by allowing him to love her. This reversal of the moral evaluation had two far-reaching results. Through the collective ideology of the beautiful soul applied to her, the woman became, so to speak, "collective," that is, promiscuous, as borne out by the not so "romantic" but highly sensual relationships among the leaders of the romantic movement, who may be said to have introduced the modern divorce vogue into our sex life. Secondly, this promiscuity, together with the freedom of emotional expression permitted her, gave women a decidedly masculine appearance, which basically was determined by her having been made the bearer of man's soul-ideology.

As the woman was allowed so much freedom and encouraged to play the rôle of soul-saver for the man, he soon felt too dependent upon her; she threatened to dominate his whole life and even the hereafter. Thus in his eyes she became bad again. This change of attitude found expression in literary fashions and types, such as "The Fatal Woman," or "La Belle Dame sans Merci," which can be traced right to our own times in the writings of Oscar Wilde, André Gide and Gabriele D'Annunzio.[1] In those man-made literary fashions which were instrumental in creating corresponding types in life, the woman not only appears unwomanly but hard and cruel in a masculine manner. Here we first meet the types of sadistic-masculine woman and masochistic-feminine man, who, although in their time they were accepted, indeed, highly estimated types, in our day have been diagnosed as "neurotic." Their strange behavior started the first psychological speculations about the basic difference

[1] See Praz, Mario. *The Romantic Agony* (transl. from the Italian), London, 1933.

of the two sexes.[1] Just as this difference, in view of nature's bisexuality, does not imply any clear-cut distinction, so is there no sharp line to be drawn between sensual pleasure and pain as we find those sensations coupled in romantic sado-masochism. While this sexual terminology has actually been derived from two outspoken perverts, the psychological relation between pleasure and pain expresses a deep-rooted bond based on the duality of the life-principle itself. As sex naturally implies death in the surrender of the individual to the collective life-principle, we meet in romantic love a moralization of this very life-principle whereby man became submissive and created the picture of the fatal, cruel, in a word, sadistic woman. Side by side with this type, we encounter as a reaction to it, the satanic and diabolical man in the literature of the same period. This type is epitomized in the notorious Marquis de Sade and his "sadistic" writings, which influenced all modern writers up to the rank of such authors as Flaubert, Baudelaire and Swinburne.

For the "beyond" of psychology it is particularly important to realize the order in which those types surviving in our sexual psychology appear in romantic literature: first, the masochistic man in bondage to the merciless woman, and only afterwards the sadistic man in an attempt to liberate himself from this self-imposed submission. The sadistic type, the creation of a decadent male, has produced another artifice of our psychological wax-cabinet—the masochistic woman. This invention followed when the man had again to divest the woman of the masculine characteristics he had bestowed on her. By making her "masochistic," that is, completely submissive to him, he had to picture and thus make her womanly in an extreme fashion. True, this submissiveness is her basic self, but submitting to nature, not to the man. Such natural "sacrifice," in fully accepting

[1] On this subject, one of the most famous scientists of that period, Wilhelm von Humboldt, wrote an essay, "Ueber den Geschlechtsunterschied," 1795.

her biological rôle, is different from the woman's artificially "sacrificing herself" for the man, which she can do only in true "masochistic" fashion. This sacrificial tendency, which might be conceived of as an exaggerated form of Agape, is deeply rooted in woman's nature and not just a masochistic perversion in the sense of our psychology. As long as it satisfies the individual's desire for happiness, we have no right to stigmatize it as "neurotic" or "perverse" just because we are not capable of understanding its vital significance. The Christian martyr can be as little explained by being labeled "masochistic" as, for example, can the Japanese soldier for whom sacrifice and self-sacrifice represents one of the highest virtues. The Freudian concept of "self-punishment," derived from his masochistic interpretation of sacrificial tendencies, has been erroneously explained as the neurotic's perversion to gain pleasure from pain. The pleasure derived from suffering has to be ascribed to the triumph of the individual will over pain, which thus ceases to be inflicted and becomes self-willed.

The masochistic submissiveness of modern woman reveals itself in the light of those moralistic ideologies as less neurotic than the narrowing psychoanalytic viewpoint makes it appear. Basically, such submissive attitude is an essential part of woman's biological nature; its exaggeration and subsequent exploitation, however, is man-made and betrays the influence of man's ideologies on woman "psychology." Not a few women act masochistically, i.e. as if they derived pleasure from pain, for two admitted reasons: first, from a desire to give the man they love pleasure, if he is insecure enough to need their masochism to boost his ego; secondly, in order to be changed, that is, to be made submissive to their own nature, which has been distorted by masculine ideologies. Those classical cases of masochism which have been described not only in fiction but even in textbooks, belong to the same kind of romantic literature which produced the original type. In reality, those women were "masochistic" only once in their lives, i.e., in relation to one person; at other times they can be quite will-ful and resistive. Their "masochism" represents a period in their lives when they permit themselves to submit to one particular person so completely that only their volition to do so makes it possible. In this sense, their "masochism" becomes a will-ful, instead of a natural, acceptance of their feminine submissiveness. It is here, in this area of non-acceptance of the self, where the neuroticism of this type lies, and not in masochism, which merely represents an attempt to counteract its original selfish nature. The only justification I can see in labeling the masochistic woman "neurotic," is in the unreality of the type itself.

All our neurotic terminology and ideology, in fact, originated from the unreality of personality behaviour and patterns, the reality of which has been lost. For example, the outstanding women of the Romantic epoch, which produced the type, were not considered neurotic but just strong personalities, at least, stronger than woman had formerly been allowed to be; sufficiently strong, at any rate, to scare the man into his sadistic psychology. This sado-masochistic ideology of the male, which still confuses psychoanalysts, sprang from an attempt on the part of the romantic type to extricate himself from his own conflict between dominance and surrender. The solution he found by dividing the two kinds of love—represented in Eros and Agape—between the two sexes led to our sexual psychology created from man's need to justify himself and uphold his age-old prejudices.

The first prejudice, namely, that the sexual act is necessarily pleasurable, is obviously contradicted by nature herself. We have only to look at the animal kingdom to be convinced that as a rule it is a painful struggle, to be avoided, if possible; one which the human being had to idealize in order to accept it at all. Closely related to this widespread illusion is another assumption taken too much for granted, that every human being wants to live as long as possible, or for that matter wants to live at all. To risk death, or even to seek it, is not necessarily an unbiological gesture. There are people who want to die, without justifiably being diagnosed as "suicidal." Especially when death comes suddenly and painlessly, it need not represent an escape but can be real deliverance, particularly when one's life has been fulfilled or is to be fulfilled by dying. Last, but not least, is the prejudice which includes all others, namely, that everyone's happiness is the same. For this assumption causes us to designate as "neurotic" any other whose ideas of happiness do not coincide with ours. Herein lies the greatest sin of psychology: that it sets up absolute standards derived from a rational interpretation of one prevailing type by which to judge not only our fellow men but also to interpret personalities and behaviour of the past.

In the realm of our own discussion we have only to take one of the greatest saints, Catherine of Siena, in order to illustrate the difference between psychological reality and unreality. In spite of her amazing asceticism, we could not call her "masochistic," nor, despite her single-handed fight against the mighty Pope, could she be classified as a megalomaniac. In his recent study of Catherine, Joh. Jorgensen[1] points out that her vast assumption of authority is the very reverse of egotism, springing as it does from complete self-surrender. The core of Catherine's teaching is the need for absolute renunciation of self: it is St. Francis' doctrine of poverty under a transcendental aspect. Here again is shown how man's and woman's nature and behaviour differ—even where saintliness is concerned. Being a woman, Catherine was able to completely identify her will with the will of the

[1] Saint Catherine of Siena, N. Y., Longmans, 1938.

Church, which, representing the Bride of Christ, made Catherine the same through the mystical marriage. Thus she could become the conscience of Christendom, not because she was so presumptuous as to aspire to it but because she had emptied herself so completely of self-will that she felt the divine conscience working through her.

Experiences like this, and others in the past, could manifest themselves as powerful realities just because they were spiritually real. Not that these personalities were "neurotic," but that they had, besides their neurosis, something else which enabled them to be creative in spite of it; in truth, they experienced really in themselves what we may only allow to remain a shadow or sham experience, that is, a neurotic one. In other words, it is not what the individual experiences, but how he does it, which makes our true conception of neurosis independent of any content, i.e., a matter of attitude. In this sense, the woman is not neurotic because she *is* "masochistic," but is neurotic, one might almost say, because she is not *really* submissive and wants to make believe that she is.

The same holds good for the masculine counterpart, sadism, which we characterized as a self-assertive reaction against the presumable dominance of the woman. From a human study of the Marquis de Sade,[1] the father of sadism, it clearly follows that it is not an original perversion exaggerated to pathological proportions by a neurotic personality. It is no sexual problem at all, in fact, but a problem of the man's ego, thwarted by his hatred of women and mankind in general. He was as full of hate for the whole world as Catherine was full of love for God, but with both of them it was a real experience. The "psychology" of de Sade can only be understood from his fundamental hatred, which means it is at bottom a moral problem of good and evil, not merely a sexual aberration. As a matter of fact, the prob-

[1] Flake, Otto. *Marquis de Sade,* Berlin.

lem of love itself cannot be fully comprehended without the phenomenon of hatred. The simple observation that love so frequently changes into hatred when the individual feels disappointed or hurt indicates a deep-seated relation between the two emotions. Of course, love does not simply "change" into hatred, but both are manifestations of two opposite life-forces: the tendencies toward unification and separation respectively, that is, toward likeness and difference. This explains why hatred appears not infrequently as the result of a heightened love-emotion which carries the individual too far away from his own self to an over-identification with the other.

It is important to realize that love, even in its most extreme form of masochistic surrender, is not negative will just as it is not "sublimated" sex, but the positive affirmation of the will wanting to surrender to something bigger than the Self. Such self-surrender of the will affords for its understanding a totally different psychology from that of the grabbing and possessive Eros, from which the individual will originally springs. In that respect, Eros is willing selfishly and greedily, whereas Agape is willing universally, that is, as a part of nature. Both, however, are operating positively in the service of self-preservation, and only their volume, as it were, is different. There exists, though, in human nature also negative willing, which is neither Eros nor Agape but manifests itself actually as the negative, the opposite of love, namely, as hatred. The manifestations of this human emotion are just as important, though much less spoken of, as the popularized love-emotion. A historical perspective of this problem leaves the impression that the love-ideology had been created to stem the increasing tide of hatred between individuals, groups and nations. The Christian doctrine of "love thy neighbor as thyself" means above all not to will antagonistically against him; as Gautama, the Buddha, expressed it: "Never does hatred cease by hating; by no hating does it cease: this is the ancient law." Such aspiration can only be fulfilled, in the deeper sense, on the basis of self-love, which means, self-acceptance. For only inasmuch as the individual accepts himself can he accept others as they are and in that sense "love" them. The non-acceptance of the other, manifesting itself through assertion of difference in hatred, springs from the non-acceptance of the self, conceived of as being bad and therefore rejected. Thus self-hatred is the basis for hating others or the world at large. For self-hatred, being really unbearable, is easily justified by making the others and the world bad so they can become the object of hatred instead of the own self. Thus, pessimism may be called the philosophy of hatred, or, as Nietzsche termed it more subtly, of *"ressentiment."* A pessimistic philosopher like Schopenhauer expresses himself not merely in general terms about the misery of life; the pessimist is quite definitely a misogynist and usually an anti-feminist and anti-Semite, regardless of whether he be Jewish or not.

For the Jewish religion, being essentially pessimistic, is a philosophy of hate—and also anti-feministic—because it springs, as Theodore Lessing has convincingly shown,[1] from a deep-rooted self-hatred in the Jew. This strange characteristic of the Jew, which we traced to self-blame for sinning against Jehovah, is borne out most obviously in the curious phenomenon of the anti-Semitic Jew, a frequent type, of whom Lessing gives a number of outstanding examples. Herein is epitomized the fundamental difference between the Jewish and Christian philosophy of life. The one is based on self-hatred, leading to persecution not through their faith but through their own self-depreciation; the other is based on self-love, in the meaning of an acceptance of the self as fundamentally good, which leads to an opti-

[1] *Der Juedische Selbthass,* Berlin.

mistic philosophy of life grounded in the experience of grace and resulting in a forgiving attitude towards others.

Just as love and hatred are not static concepts in the individual but dynamic factors operating as the basic life-forces of alternate unification and separation, so in the life of nations the two forces manifest themselves racially and culturally as alternations between identification and differentiation (des-identification). In this historical process of assimilation and dissimilation, the Jew has become the symbol of the two antagonistic tendencies which he carried out in the diaspora. His far-reaching assimilation, coupled with a stubborn assertion of his racial and religious difference, almost exhausted the race, but at the same time provided the energy which kept it alive. Surviving the two kinds of love historically represented by Eros of Antiquity and Agape of Christianity, the Jew lived on his religion of difference and hatred, which has been revived at present in Nazi tribal fanaticism representing as much a religion of racial separatism as Communism is the religion of the early Christian brotherhood in terms of economic equality.

There are at present in our democracies hopes for a revival of the Christian philosophy of life to counteract the anti-Christian ideologies of modern secular religion. Whether we can evoke a new Christian type of man or have to find another positive antidote will depend at large upon our ability for any kind of really deep experience, religious or otherwise. So far these voices calling for re-establishment of a new Christian order seem to sound a hopeless note in that respect. The few intellectual promoters of such religious revival—presumably freed from theological fetters—cannot silence the cries of the masses for political and economic freedom, which the Christian ideology, especially in its Protestant democratic application, failed to deliver to them. On the other hand, those masses are still deeply engulfed in religious traditions of their forefathers, and the mere fact that a handful of intellectuals have introduced a few new terms into popular language does not alter the deep religious feeling most people, including those intellectuals themselves, still cherish in spite of their denial.

To label sin by the misleading term of "guilt"—which is the result of it—does not in the least change the individual's inner experience concerning it. The neurotic type suffers from a consciousness of sin just as much as did his religious ancestor, without believing in the conception of sin. This is precisely what makes him "neurotic"; he feels a sinner without the religious belief in sin for which he therefore needs a new rational explanation. The need and desire for a humanistic Christianity is one thing and the ability to lead a Christian life—to be "un vrai chrétien"—is quite another. The totalitarian movements, with their anti-democratic ideologies, have already fulfilled a great cultural mission in having awakened the saturated and self-satisfied democracies to a revision and revaluation of their fundamental principles. For democracy, which grew out of the original Christian philosophy of life, was never a true expression of that spirit and finds itself suddenly faced with the lack of any basic philosophy. Our democracy, which sprang from the Reformation, became a Protestant "liberal" one, that is, represents the practical application of a spiritual ideology to the modern world. Thus, in effect, Protestantism represents the secular religion of democracy.

This state of affairs has been recently discussed in a most impressive manner by Jacques Maritain, in his treatise on *True Humanism* (Humanism Integral).[1] He points out that no revival of a new Christendom is possible without a real fulfilment of democracy, which so far has been only symbol and image. "It is only in a new Christendom, in the future, that the ethical and affective value of the word democracy, which corresponds to what may be called a popular

[1] N. Y., Scribner, 1938.

civic consciousness, will be really achieved." As against this hope of an ardent Catholic, whose thinking follows St. Thomas Aquinas, we hear the voice of G. A. Borgese, who sees the Western world as now divided into three different religions: Catholicism, Fascism and Communism, and who doubts that the Church can save democracy or may even want to do so. For the Church and liberalism are incompatible, and the Hierarchy of the Catholic Church, with the doctrine of the infallibility of the Pope (re-stated in 1870), is more akin to the Hierarchy of Dictatorship than to Protestant liberalism. Furthermore, as in every hierarchy, there exists in the Catholic Church an abyss between the individual Catholic and the Priesthood, a split equally true of the Fascist or Communist rulers and the man in the street who becomes their helpless tool. As T. S. Eliot summed it up, after the Church of England conference at Lambeth in 1930: "The world is trying the experiment of attempting to form a civilized but non-Christian mentality. The experiment will fail; but we must be very patient in awaiting its collapse."

The present dilemma takes on a different significance as soon as we realize that this need for a truly religious ideology does not spring merely from the necessity to counteract the impact of secular religions upon democratic ideology. Such need is inherent in human nature and its fulfilment is basic to any kind of social life. Once more this bears out not only the predominance of ideologies over realities—a conception which I expounded in 1930[1]—but more so the need for a religious philosophy broader and deeper than any political or economic ideologies which happen to be operating. This reaching out for something bigger than any kind of government, state or even nation, originates in the individual's need for expansion beyond the realm of his self, his environment, indeed, early life itself. In this sense, the

[1] *Modern Education. Art and Artist. Seelenglauben und Psychologie.*

individual is not just striving for survival but is reaching for some kind of "beyond," be it in terms of another person, a group, a cause, a faith to which he can submit, because he thereby expands his Self. Such expansion differs distinctly from a mere enhancement of the ego springing from Eros, which remains will-ful even in the individual's seeming subjection. In contradistinction to the power-ideology of Eros feeding on "borrowed" strength, the love-ideology of Agape creates this other, bigger world in the individual himself. The former type may also produce new and important things, but they always turn out to be bigger than his Self, leaving him ever dissatisfied and greedily grasping for more. Contrariwise, the creativity springing from the love-expansion of Agape always remains bigger than the individual achievement. In a word, the truly creative type is bigger than his tasks or accomplishments, and never finds or even seeks fulfilment in the world of reality but only in the true spiritual world of creation. There he produces the real work of genius, almost as a by-product of his own inner greatness. Such superhuman dimension does not result from borrowed strength, as in the case of popular power-ideologies which always remain egocentric, be it in a good or bad sense. For the individual's need for expansion beyond his Self can be satisfied in creative as well as in destructive ways. That is to say, both Heaven and Hell are symbols of the beyond. The neurotic gains a sense of presumptuous superiority in creating his own hell, similar to that of the notorious criminal who believes in his fate, as does the creative personality in his mission.

The general run of the population, however, who cannot find any support for their ego one way or another, seek it in personal relationship, be it that of parent and child, pupil and teacher, friendship or sexual relationship. There it becomes evident that nothing in reality—least of all, a personal relationship—can carry the weight of this expansion-drive in the individual, particularly when his moral values are bound up with it. It seems to be difficult for the individual to realize that there exists a division between one's spiritual and purely human needs, and that the satisfaction or fulfilment for each has to be found in different spheres. As a rule, we find the two aspects hopelessly confused in modern relationships, where one person is made the god-like judge over good and bad in the other person. In the long run, such symbiotic relationship becomes demoralizing to both parties, for it is just as unbearable to be God as it is to remain an utter slave.

Here we see how the theological conception of being loved by God has been lost in human relationship, through a confusion of this moral principle with the highly individualized conception of sex in modern man, who wants to love and be loved will-fully by one particular person only. Thus the Christian love-ideology has been interpreted in our age in terms of a sexual psychology, which—not unlike Plato's philosophy of Eros—represents the last attempt of a morbid civilization to recapture the lost value of the original Agape. Just as Plato, before the rise of the Christian love-conception, tried to recapture the waning power of Eros, so in our day, with its renewal of collective ideologies, Freud tried to regain the lost Eros for the individual in sex. But man, being a theological rather than a biological being, never lives on a purely natural plane. Hence, sexual expression, hailed as the therapeutic liberation for the individual will, had to be tabued by the same psychology which eulogized it as a healing factor. The moral principle of love, which does not figure in Freudian psychology, has been confused with sex, modern man's symbol of mortality. In this sense, love was used to make sex acceptable, that is, "good," instead of making man good in the meaning of Agape. No attempt to overcome neurotic fear of death by sex can ever be successful, because sex implies death and its acceptance. Agape, on the other hand, can overcome the fear of death, for it is the most positive expression of it. In the yielding love-emotion, the individual voluntarily accepts the dissolution of the Self by freely submitting to something bigger than the ego and also bigger than the other person, the Thou. Thereby the individual conquers death, and with it sex, in a willing surrender to the bigness of nature.

The Christian faith that real goodness can only be found in selfhood has been misinterpreted psychologically in terms of the ego, which has to be made good by the Thou. Real selfhood, as aspired to by the true Christian type, paradoxically enough, needs a collective ideology for its maintenance, namely, the love of God. Our individualistic interpretation of that love in moral terms of good and evil, on the contrary, leads to the loss of the self in the other. This moral self lost in the other is the most fundamental cause of neurosis, which the French rightly call "maladie morale," and in the Freudian interpretation of which sex merely figures as a moralistic symbol. The more personalized this need to be loved became, the more it had to carry the whole religious impact of Godhood, which no human relationship can endure. For such an individual does not achieve goodness by being loved—as in the religious experience—but wants to be constantly *made* good through being loved. This confusion of personalized love and individual morality makes for failure in both spheres and precipitates that utter sense of despair which has been termed psychologically a feeling of "inferiority," a term borrowed from our democratic vocabulary of equality. In reality, this inferiority indicates the lack of true inner values in the personality, which he then has to find in others while blaming his own inadequacy on competitive grounds. Such loss of inner values which are basic to human nature becomes at times epidemic. For the moral self constitutes an essential part of the natural self, which we came to call "primitive," implying thereby that it is a product of civilization created, according to psychoanalytic theory, by social inhibitions of the instinctual self.

As early as 1905, in my first book on the artist,[1] I opposed this Freudian conception from a deeper understanding of the neurotic type as suffering from frustrated creativity. I assumed a self-inhibiting instinct operating in the individual just as vital and genuine as are all the other self-preserving and self-expressing instincts. Since then, I not only could confirm this viewpoint from my therapeutic experience with frustrated types but also found its philosophic basis in a human understanding of religious experience. In fact, some modern scientists do not hesitate to speak of a "religious instinct," as, for example, the biologist, von Monakov, who recently acknowledged it as one of the fundamental vital impulses. In other words, the individual produces those moral values genuinely from within and is not forced by his social environment to accept them against his will. Least of all can religion as such be blamed for the indoctrination of moral values, because the moral self inherent in human nature produced religion as a common codification of those fundamental inner values. Such codification and formulation ascribed to one religious leader merely gives those essentially human values a realistic form as law. This process has the effect of leveling the different degrees of conscience in different individuals to a collective standard applicable to the daily conduct of life. Thus the law represents the secular form of a human absolute, which is the moral self. In it is epitomized the earthly representative of the spiritual self; hence, to be good means really to be better or bigger than yourself, in a word, means immortality. In this sense, we may say that man re-creates continuously the fundamental moral laws by accepting them

[1] *Der Kuenstler,* Wien, 1907.

freely. When people lose this ability, i.e. their genuine moral self, they have to replace it by imposed social laws. Thus, another man-made principle begins to operate, first on the basis of, and later instead of, the moral self, namely, conscience as the result of consciousness of the moral self. This explains why the Jews, who had been living in exile under foreign law, had to have their own moral values codified before embarking on their quest for freedom.

Human nature, however, is neither as bad as Jewish doctrine made it out to be, nor as good as the Christian love-ideology wants to believe. In striving one way or another towards such an unattainable goal, which could only be approximated in collective brotherhood, the individual is caught in all the intricacies of an ideal of perfection which separates him from his real self without giving him the satisfaction of personal improvement or real achievement. This "disease of perfection," as Flaubert called it, is the moral evil par excellence of modern man. It not only prevents the individual from doing his best and thereby achieving whatever he can at any given moment; it creates the neurotic feeling of inadequacy and inferiority, in a word, moral badness. Such irrational striving for perfection likewise manifests itself in a morbid sense of responsibility assumed by an individual's hyper-conscience. This morbid conscience, from which the neurotic type suffers in our time, appears as a cancerous overgrowth of the moral self natural to man. In this sense, the morbid conscience of modern man appears to be an individualized moral self, collective by its very nature. Such personalized conscience, as we find it epitomized in the Protestant doctrine of free will, represents in the last analysis another attempt on the part of the individual towards autonomous control over his life—and death. To be the final judge over his own actions and at the same time to ensure his immortality by being as it were "extra-good," is the Protestant Puritan's idea of a perfect life. Unfortunately, this static concept of perfection not only blocks life itself, but is the very cause of "neurotic," that is, man-made imperfection in its most morbid form.

While this striving for an absolute goodness is at least comprehensible as an ideal, the strange phenomenon of conforming to a pattern of badness seems incomprehensible to our rational mind. Yet this was just the case with the Jewish conception of the evil spirit, which, in terms of sin, became the accepted ideology of the whole people. Likewise, in our age, such "perverted love" has become the centre of fruitless psychological discussion in terms of maladjustment, anti-social and neurotic behaviour. The individual who is not loved, that is, not accepted in a self which he himself is unable to accept, automaticaly turns to badness of one sort or another. Herein again is shown the double rôle of our psychology of personality. While it presumes to explain the existing type of man, it challenges at the same time the average man to conform to its ideological pattern, regardless of whether it makes him good or bad—as long as it makes him alike. But such conforming to any existing collective ideology on the individual's part is only possible through a denial of the other side of his nature, be it the good or bad one. If he is too good, that is, too loving and forgiving, the badness breaks through in occasional resentments and fits of hatred; if he feels all "bad" he is likely to over-compensate in a false goodness, the artificiality of which is just as bad as the real evil.

As far as the two sexes are concerned, this moralized love-ideology manifests itself in two different ways, taking manifold forms. The evil in the man is more of an active badness, springing from the will-ful Eros and manifesting itself as guilt (for willing); whereas in the woman the feeling of badness arising from not being wanted (loved) takes on the form of shame. In the modern individual, however, those natural reactions appear mixed, just as everything else appears as a paradoxical mixture of an effeminate male and a masculinized female. The conflict between likeness and difference originally epitomized in the difference of the sexes finally appears in modern man as the neurotic struggle between his natural self and the personality-ideology to which he tries to conform.

Thus the platonic explanation of the desirous Eros yearning to unite again with his other half from which he has been severed takes on the modern form of two halves in the individual himself striving simultaneously to unite internally and to find objectification outside the self in the beloved one. In a word, modern love is no longer Eros or Agape but has become Psyche, that is, basically, not a sexual but a psychological problem experienced in moral terms of good and bad. We have developed in ourselves both tendencies of love, the masculine Eros and the feminine Agape, the simultaneous expression of which makes human relationship into a symbiose of two parasites feeding on each other's "goodness." Such relationship revives the primitive twin-conception of an alter-ego which modern man tries to find in the other sex, thereby denying its natural value as a symbol of difference. His ego wants likeness to support his yearning for personal immortalization, while his personality needs difference in order to complement the denied part of his natural self.

6

The Creation of the Sexual Self

THE IDEA of succession, as we found it in the centre of personal and collective psychology, raises the question as to why such complicated ideologies became necessary, both for the individual and the community, when the obvious solution seems to have been provided by nature herself. The answer, as we have shown, lies in the paradox that man is primarily not concerned with biological succession, either personally or socially. Primitive man is entrenched in what seems to us an obsession with personal immortality; an obsession which, however, is counter-acted by the clan-spirit for group survival promoting a succession of outstanding personalities, through a kind of selective immortality enacted in the magical creation of leadership. Such collective immortality epitomized in a chosen leader foreshadows the idea of State and Nation, symbols of racial continuity of a special type of man. At the same time, sex, not being accepted as the individual natural means of succession in one's children, was looked upon as a mere pleasurable function of the ego. Just as little as there is a social self in primitive group-life, which carries in its traditional activities whatever collective security the individual needs, is there a sexual self differentiated from the total personality, as we find it in modern man. A deeper understanding of such revaluation of sex from a natural function of the ego to an expression of the personality leads far beyond psychology to the irrational roots of man's ideologies determining his behaviour.

It may be difficult for our modern mind to perceive in the strange beliefs of the primitives anything but a form of superstition. Yet our previous examination of the solutions modern man has tried to find for this eternal struggle between personal immortality and racial survival has revealed how much wishful thinking still creeps in wherever man's fear of the final destruction of his ego is involved. We also have shown that primitive man solved this eternal conflict of his existence by means of a supernatural ideology which guaranteed the individual's self-perpetuation not through sexual procreation but collectively through the group-spirit. Hence, in primitive societies we find the sexual rôle of the male strictly divorced from the procreative function of the woman, whose impregnation is supposed to take place through the reviving of the spirits of the dead symbolized in the totem of the clan. It is fascinating to pursue the highly complicated, often sophisticated ways and means by which this irrational ideology is arrived at and maintained. It was possible, however, only on the basis of primitive organization with its strict system of separation between different groups within one and the same clan. Not only were children of different age and sex confined to separate groups but—and in this, primitive society is to be clearly distinguished from all conceptions of society in modern times—the place held by woman was given special significance.

Women were not considered—as even in our most liberal democracies—a mere variation, usually inferior, of the male, but were acknowledged as a genuine species; hence, permitted expression in their own folkways. Woman, admittedly, had a quite different psychology of her own, the mystery of which man dared not penetrate—though he had to protect himself from its unknown dangers. Woman's traditional habits and customs were handed down as a sacred secret from generation to generation within the female group, whose activities were strictly separated from the social life of the male group, except when they met at naturally determined times for sexual intercourse. In a word, woman's essential difference from man was fully accepted in primitive society; indeed, was stressed to the point of her sexual function being completely divorced from that of the male.

I am referring here to the puzzling fact, well-known to anthropologists, that primitive man separated in his mind the connection between the biological facts of sexual intercourse (conception) and pregnancy (childbirth). This strange outlook was not the result of ignorance regarding cause and effect, but, as I have already said, was due to the vital urge in man's ego to maintain his belief in self-perpetuation. The long and winding path which man has travelled from this first supernatural philosophy of life-immortal to its scientific interpretation in terms of bio-psychology, I have traced in a book following the developments of psychology as it grew from its primitive base, the belief in the soul.[1]

When the belief in an immortal soul in its naivest form of the shadow or double was first shattered, man, in order to save his soul—in the literal sense of the word—took refuge in what might be called the earliest socio-religious system, totemism. This aboriginal soul-religion, resting on the belief in personal immortality, ascribed the conception of children to the entrance of a spirit (of the dead) into the mother's womb. These spirits were thought of as residing in animals or plants, which, by entering the woman, impregnated her. This naive notion of the continued existence of the ego in a somewhat different form excluded the acceptance of sexual procreation through children. Indeed, this biological fact was flatly denied and only accepted at a much later stage in the idea of the re-birth of the father in the son. Thus what actually constituted the totemistic

[1] *Seelenglaube und Psychologie,* F. Deuticke, Leipzig, 1930. In process of translation.

belief in the soul was a compromise between the untenable notion of a body-immortal and sexual procreation in one's own children, a biological fact still denied. Hence, the actual father played no rôle, yet at the same time the idea of personal survival through one's own soul was already renounced in favor of a collective soul-belief which permitted the spirit of the dead to force its way into the woman in order to be reborn.

The transition between those two world-views, the supernatural and the natural, is to be found in this earliest system of soul-religion, called totemism from the Australian "totem," which signifies an animal, plant or object adopted as a symbol by certain tribes who consider themselves descendants of one and the same "totem." This totem-animal is made responsible for the necessary supply of food, if it happens that the clan feeds on that particular animal. The tabu against killing it except on festive occasions corresponds somewhat to our conception of a "closed season," although the reason for the tabu was not so much the protection of the particular species as the assuring of a steady food supply to the community. In this sense, the totem represents the first collective, i.e., tribal planning, since it is held responsible for the stability of the population as well as for its necessary nourishment. At the same time, the totemistic system by uniting in one hand care for the two vital needs of human existence, hunger and sex, represents, so to speak, the first "social contract." It implies a mutual agreement between the primitive community and the outside world, that is, the particular environment, to respect each other's right to live: man refrains from exterminating the animal in order to be permanently supplied by it; he does not kill so as not to be killed himself.

These main characteristics of totemism, it seems, are to be found correlated only in Australia; a fact which is the more remarkable since the Australian natives are among the most primitive peoples known. Unlike the North-west coast tribes of North America, they have preserved for us the most elaborate form of totemism, embracing all its features: the belief in descent from the totem, a totem food tabu, magical ceremonies to increase totemic animals, belief in reincarnation, clans with totemic names and last, but not least, clan exogamy.

The confusion among scholars over this widely discussed problem in anthropological literature results from the inclination of most authors to single out some one of its features which fits into his pet theory, instead of viewing the problem as a whole. Professor Goldenweiser, in his survey of this field,[1] after having rejected the search for "first origins" as "unscientific," suggests a rather too "scientific" definition of totemism when he merely sees in it "the tendency of definite social units to become associated with objects and symbols of emotional value." Such caution towards any theoretical commitment is no more helpful to students of the subject than the conviction of other scholars that their narrow explanation is the only possible one. This latter holds good especially for Freud's purely speculative hypothesis[2] that the "origin" of totemism is to be found in the Oedipus-complex. The two main features of totemistic religion, the worship of the totem (animal) with the corresponding tabu against killing it (except on special occasions) and the exogamic rule against marriage of a clan-member cannot be explained by the civilized child's urge to kill his father in order to sleep with his mother; because those conceptions of our Western family structure had no place in primitive man's experience. On the contrary, the totem bringing the offspring to life through rebirth of the dead and then feeding them with its flesh plainly represents

[1] Goldenweiser, Alexander A. *History, Psychology and Culture,* N. Y., Knopf, 1933.

[2] *Totem and Tabu,* N. Y., Moffat Yard, 1918.

a symbol of motherhood, i.e. of woman's two vital functions—bringing the child to life and nourishing it. The whole totemistic system, with its intricate religious and social conceptions, it follows, emerges from man's need to deny his biological origin from the mortal mother. By lifting his origin to a supernatural plane of spiritual, that is, non-sexual conception, and by replacing the nourishment from the mother through the feeding animal, he erects not merely a social structure supporting his need but is forced to create a supernatural world-view out of which grew religious and social concepts. This universal meaning of totemism was first stated by the German philosopher, Ernst Cassierer, thus: "Actually the differentiation of the various clans according to their totem is not confined to the narrow social circle that it primarily concerns, but extends more and more widely till it embraces finally every sphere of existence, natural and spiritual. Not only the members of the clan, but the whole universe, with all that it contains, is articulated, by the totemistic form of thought, in groups which either belong together or are separated from each other according to definite kin-relationships. All things, animate or inanimate, are eventually swept into this structure in some way or other."[1]

Basically, however, totemism, as we saw it, consisting of a system balancing supply and demand in the realm of population and food, strives for a solution of the most vital problem of the tribe. The underlying idea of this primitive regulation, akin to our economic planning, is a belief that the totem, symbolizing tribal ancestry, will not create more people than he can feed. Hence, the restrictions concerning sexual intercourse have the same effect as the tabu on the killing (hunting) of the animal who provides the food at "open" seasons. In other words, primitive man, by denying his part in the procreation of children, puts the whole re-

[1] *Die Begriffsform in mythischen Denken,* Leipzig, 1922.

sponsibility for the welfare of the community, indeed, for its survival, on the totem. The shifting of man's responsibility is a true earmark of any religious conception and makes totemism mankind's first religion, which, as Durkheim first suggested, is essentially a social one. This aboriginal religion springs, as, in the last analysis, all religion does, from the most powerful fear in man—not so much his fear of natural death as of final destruction. Yet the actual creative force expressing man's belief in personal immortality as against racial survival appears as a manifestation of his will for eternal survival. In this struggle, hunger, with the daily need for its immediate satisfaction, represents the individual and temporal survival, while sex expresses racial, that is, collective immortality. Man, by resisting impersonal survival in favor of his belief in personal immortality, reversed the basic principles of human nature by making food, in terms of surplus-production, an economic symbol of immortality, while at the same time conceiving of sex as a mere temporary activity of the self. Originally, however, man lived from hand to mouth, not only because of the scarcity of food, since he felt no urge to increase the amount of that, but because his need for eternal survival was taken care of by the religious beliefs guiding his social behaviour. Even the most primitive tribes, as for example the Pygmies in Central Africa, do not kill unless they need food, and then only the amount necessary for the immediate purpose. At the same time, this killing and distributing of the kill is made a ritual ceremony in which certain pieces of the prey have to be consumed by given individuals in a definite order lest the tribe suffer. The best-known illustration of such ceremonial killing and eating has been reported from the Eskimos and described in full detail by Rasmussen.[1] That which has so aptly been

[1] Rasmussen, Knud Johan Victor. Intellectual Culture of the Copper Eskimos, Copenhagen, 1932. Intellectual Culture of the Hudson Bay Eskimos, 1930.

said of the Bedouin, that he is a parasite of the camel, is equally true of the Eskimo and the whale, which provides the most important supplies for his living. Although the Eskimo feeds on fish and seal on the coast, and lives off the reindeer inland, yet the catch of a whale is made the most important ceremony of the tribe. This is so, not only because of the variety of stuff this largest sea-monster provides but also because of the awe it inspires.[2]

The supernatural significance which primitive man ascribes to this ceremonial killing and eating—still preserved in our "table manners"—can be inferred from a touchingly naive myth of the Luisenos, a tribe of Californian Indians which lacks even the usual products of primitive art. During community debate on the problem of whether men may die and live again, this tribe is said to have conceived the idea that stags would be good to eat. "They talked about it with the stag, but he replied: No, he was a shaman and very powerful." The story then describes how the stag was saved from being killed by the fact that he himself possessed all the magic by which men threatened to kill him, and was therefore, even in this respect, identical with men. It was not until he was shown a flint arrow that he gave in; here was a magic he did not possess. In another remarkable story of the Yoghuts we are told that, after the transformation of two boys into stags, there was a hunt, the killing, disembowelling, dividing and consuming being described in such terms that Lublinski, who collected these myths, had the impression that "what was here represented was the first attempt at killing a stag for eating purposes."[1] In this tradition is clearly preserved the biological identity of man and beast basic to the primitive's belief

[1] Even today, among Northern hunting tribes, the prey when killed receives almost divine honors before it is cut up ceremoniously and eaten according to traditional custom.

[2] Lublinski, Ida. *Eine weitere mytische Urschicht vor dem Mythus, Zeitschrift fuer Voelkerpsychologie,* 1930.

in the immortality and migration of the soul.[1] That is to say, by eating the totem-animal man not only absorbs its strength but also the particular animal-qualities which guarantee survival in his environment. This made the totem-animal not only the provider of food but the symbol of life both for the individual and the community—which is precisely the meaning of totem.

On the other hand, the tabu against killing the totem indiscriminately springs not only from an economic fear of exhausting this vital supply by premature extinction of the particular species but from a religious, that is, "soulish" motive—the belief that man and the animal feeding him are identical, one flesh, so to speak, just as are mother and child. Hence, arises such "tender-hearted" concern with regard to the animal's killing as is borne out by a primitive hunt-motif discovered by Frobenius among various rock-engravings in Africa. In this picture,[2] a hunter aiming at his prey is connected with a praying woman by a curved line running from his navel to the womb of the woman, who thereby symbolizes his mother. She not only prays for his luck in the hunt, but also sanctions his killing of the animal on whom he feeds as he fed on her. Here, as in similar traditions, it practically becomes a question of asking the animal's permission to kill it for the necessity of man's own survival. Hence, the protective ceremonies before the hunt, the hunter's disguise in the mask of the animal he is after—which is not so much a ruse of the marksman as a declaration of the essential identity—and the ritual distribution of certain pieces supposed to contain special qualities. The fasting with which Indians and other primitives usually

[1] The doctrine of the wandering of the soul seems to me to be derived from the observation of the process of decay, a kind of wandering of the flesh, borne out by the true perception that out of the dead body there emerges something living. I have recorded the evidence for this belief in the tradition of the "soul-worm" among the tribes of Madagascar. *Art and Artist,* Alfred A. Knopf, N. Y., 1932, pp. 129 ff.

[2] Reproduced in *op. cit.,* p. 261.

precede the hunt seems to be a rite of justification for killing the animal for food; because from a practical point of view this fasting could only weaken the hunter's strength and thus minimize his chances.

Other activities in primitive group-life, similarly, were determined by this totemistic belief in the soul. As each clan held its own totem-animal (or plant) responsible for the preservation of the community, sexual intercourse with women of the same clan was unnecessary for the purpose of procreation. Their restrictions of intercourse, therefore, did not aim at preventing "incest" with relatives (since all descendants from the same totem felt "related"), but represented their belief that woman was impregnated by the same totem, i.e., without their aid. This theory, which saves man's belief in immortality, presupposes knowledge of the male's function in propagation. At the same time, man had to deny this knowledge in the interest of his belief in the soul, even at the price of a purely matrilinear organization whereby the children belonged to the group of mothers. In this sense is it to be understood that all the children of a clan on the mother's side were considered "brothers" and "sisters," since they all came from the same totem that had spiritually impregnated the mothers and consequently made superfluous sexual impregnation by the men of the clan.

With these remarks we have ventured into an explanation of one of the most puzzling problems in anthropological study. This custom of *exogamy*, one of the earliest collective regulations of the sex-life, makes it prohibitive for the man to have sexual relations with the females of his own clan—"as if" he were too closely "related" to them. Yet this strict tabu goes back to a time before any family unit in our sense existed; indeed, before the rôle of the father in procreation was recognized. As to the origin and significance of this exogamic regulation in primitive society, there is today no general agreement among scholars. From the most recent works in this field we learn that, after sifting all previous theories, there remains only a modicum of facts, which however contradicts the Freudian view according to which exogamy aimed at averting incest. Neither the concept of, nor the social conditions for, incest yet existed in primitive culture. The only fruitful approach to this, as well as all other folkloristic traditions, seems to lie in an acceptance of their supernatural origin first expounded by Durkheim. Applied to the problem of exogamy, this conception has been formulated by his follower, Levy-Bruhl,[1] as part of a more general tabu, which is "supernatural"; his "theory of transgressions" explains prohibition of incest as a means of holding at bay an evil influence. Lord Raglan, in his recent survey of the whole subject,[2] goes a step further, holding the magical origin of exogamy to be the only satisfactory explanation of the known facts and suggesting that the solution to the riddle must be sought in the belief in immortality.

Some years ago, I myself in my book *Seelenglaube und Psychologie* (1930), had arrived at this conclusion, showing there that even in the earliest times soulish motifs not only distorted biological facts but also exercised a decisive influence upon the formation of social institutions. By "soulish" motifs I meant, however, not psychological ones, or even those claimed by the so-called "depth-psychology," but the magical and supernatural ideologies which rest on the belief in the soul and which we find instrumental in the formation of religion. In order to understand this process we must first clarify the very nature of the purely biological sex impulses. The sexual impulse as a source of personal pleasure has a distinct individual character; as a means for

[1] *Le surnaturel et la nature dans la mentalité primitive,* Alcan, Paris, 1931.

[2] *Jocaste's Crime,* London, 1933.

procreation of the species, on the other hand, it betrays definitely an anti-individualistic tendency. Starting from this two-fold aspect of the sexual urge, I emphasized that the dualism is not brought about by external restrictions, which on the contrary represent the result of this innate division. The primitive, especially, whose whole attitude towards life rests on the naive presupposition of personal survival, shows a strong resistance to sexual activity for the purpose of procreation, since this is in opposition to his firm belief in individual immortality. Hence we have, as I have said before, primitive man's denial of any connection between the sexual act and pregnancy, and his subsequent explanation of the birth of children in some supernatural fashion such as is preserved in myth, customs and beliefs of all peoples throughout the ages.

The individual's inner resistance to the biological sex urge, insofar as it does not serve the aim of purely personal pleasure, must be taken as one of the most fundamental facts of human life and as the starting-point of any investigation of social behavior. There exists a fundamental dualism in the masculine sex-impulse, highly estimated as a pleasurable function of the ego while simultaneously rejected as a coercion to propagate—hence, feared as a symbol of man's mortality. This inner resistance of the primitive self and even more so of the civilized personality to the racial coercion of sexual propagation makes intelligible all the sexual tabus, different from our notion of inhibition, as a positive and vital expression of the individual guarding his personal immortality. With all his astonishing regulations of the sexual life, primitive man was actually creating a sexual self, that is to say, he set man-made sexuality as against natural sex.

It was this newly created sexual self of the male who invented all the varied and complicated tabus of woman for his own self-protection: first of all, the most inclusive *tabu of impregnating the women* of his own clan as expressed in totemistic religion and the social prohibition of exogamy. This fear of impregnation, deeply rooted in man's desire for self-perpetuation, can be detected in various customs carried over into Western civilization. It was the sacred duty of the high priest in ancient civilizations to perform the rite of defloration on newly wed maidens, and in medieval times we find the same right granted to the landlord in the "ius primae noctis." To what extent modern man's resistance to having children, which he is inclined to justify economically, still feeds on this irrational motivation is borne out by the analysis of neurotic inhibitions of that kind in the causation of which sufficient practical motives are lacking.

Accordingly, we find from primitive times on, not only a complete sundering of the individual's sexual impulse from its generative function, but also a corresponding division of women into two groups. One, which may be called "mothers," because they still serve the function of reproduction, originally were thought of as being impregnated by the same totem, hence, tabued. The other group, serving the function of pleasure-giving, lives on in a type called from the Greek, "Hetaera," signifying a woman who foregoes marriage for the sake of giving pleasure—and not merely of a sexual nature—to many men (the Japanese Geisha, the French "cocotte," etc.).

It has been clearly established that human organization begins with extensive sexual regulations between groups (as we find in exogamy) and not with special incest prohibitions between individuals, be it parents and children or siblings.[1] To be sure, the exogamic prohibition at the premarital stage, introduced by man himself for his own pro-

[1] The late incest-tabu proper prohibiting sexual intercourse among "blood" relatives simply represents the former exogamic rule applied to the family organization.

tection, seemed to have turned against him when he first accepted individual marriage and with it biological perpetuation in his children. For monogamous marriage signifies an attempt on the individual's part to take care of his own immortalization, independent of the community to which all mothers (woman) belong collectively. Hence, the community declares, if you want a woman of your own and all to yourself, you must find her elsewhere and leave our women to the clan which needs them for its own maintenance. Thus developed what seems to have been the first form of individual marriage, the "matrilocal" form, so called because the man emigrated from his native hearth in search of a wife and established himself in her house or that of her mother.

This custom of the husband dwelling in the home of his wife as long as he is married to her has been practised among most of the peoples of North and South America, among all the African tribes, and among the Malays of Indonesia and Mikronesia, as well as the more aboriginal races of Asia and Polynesia. According to Robert Briffault, who has dealt with this topic in a thorough-going study,[1] the matrilocal marriage is a result of the natural predominance of the mother in the rearing of the offspring. This "local" situation of the sexual problem is, however, different from our marriage in other respects also, in that it is not necessarily permanent or monogamous. The husband can have other wives in different places with whom he lives in turn ("a girl in every port"), and can also live in each of these places with several women, usually sisters.

This leads to the consideration of another still earlier form of pre-marital organization, namely, the group-marriage preceding and leading up to our individual marriage. Indeed, there are traces of an ancient custom to be found from the time when the numbers of men were not yet re-

[1] *The Mothers,* 3 vols. Macmillan, 1931 (London, 1927).

duced by war, in which all the brothers of one group lived in sexual communion with the sisters of another group. This marriage custom seems to be in opposition to the exogamic avoidance of sexual intercourse between brothers and sisters, yet it may even find its explanation therein. For when the "brothers" of a group were forbidden marriage with their own clan "sisters" it could easily happen that they sought a substitute in a group of sisters belonging to a strange clan. This brother-sister relation, however, had nothing to do with our conception of "incestuous relation" because it was conceived of by the primitives not in the sense of blood-relationship but in terms of group-relationship—a conception by which all children of one and the same generation considered themselves collectively as "brothers" and "sisters." The sexual restrictions imposed upon them were exogamic ones, irrespective of whether it was a question of a real sibling or merely of a member of the same totem-clan.

Such a "group-marriage," first designated by L. H. Morgan[1] as the most archaic of all known systems of relationship (found among the Malays), represents, according to an up-to-date definition, "a contract between clans and division of clans which is impersonal, into which every member of the group (social band) enters by virtue of his membership as soon as he becomes of age, without its being necessary to ask either his consent or anybody else's." What such primitive unions, in which groups of brothers have their wives in common and groups of sisters their husbands, might have been like can be inferred from the so-called "Punalua marriage." This relationship, practised by certain natives, Morgan amplified into the conception of a group-marriage, since he took brothers and sisters in a classificatory sense; on the other hand, he again restricted this meaning when he reported that in the Punalua group blood-

[1] Morgan, Lewis Henry (1818-1881). Ancient Society, N. Y., Holt.

brothers and sisters were frequently united. Lorrin Andrews, the first reliable specialist on Hawaii, also reported (1860), "that two or more brothers and two or more sisters were accustomed to possess their mates in common," meaning here, furthermore, blood-brothers and -sisters. Later, Hiram Bingham found in Hawaii that the marital union between brothers and sisters was "deemed very respectable in the highest circles."

In view of these unclear and in any case fragmentary traditions, it seems to me not justified when some modern sexologists, encouraged by psychoanalytic theories, draw the conclusion "that the earliest form of sexual relationship was incestuous," especially when they must confess, to be sure in parenthesis, that these "sibling marriages" do not necessarily concern blood relation. Such confusion fostered by psychoanalytical misconceptions is due to a neglect of group psychology in favor of individual psychology. If we have learned anything from the study of primitive life, it is the lesson that the early regulation of sexual activities was originally not individual but social; that is, for the purpose of maintaining the group as against man's individualistic tendency for self-perpetuation. To prevent the marriage of relatives was not the aim of primitive tabus, as is amply borne out by the historical traditions of sibling marriages, which on the other hand cannot be taken as proof of an original strong incest-wish in man since they were enforced as a traditional ritual on certain outstanding individuals and families (as among the Kamtschadalas, in Siam, Polynesia and lower India).

These individual sibling marriages—the cultish origin of which we have shown—have moreover nothing to do with the group-marriage spoken of by Morgan, which tells us nothing about the incest-wish of the individual or of any tabu prohibiting it. The best proof of this is supplied by the form of group marriage found among peoples of

India, especially among the "Nairs," the noble warrior caste on the coast of Malabar. "They live in great club houses, the membership of which is constituted by a number of related families. The relationship passes only through the female line, the father not coming into consideration. The members of the club possess everything in common. The administrator of the common property is the oldest man, while the oldest woman presides over the inner affairs of the house. The men are not married, but live in a free love relationship with the women of their caste and are received as lovers in other houses. The household is not run by their wives or lovers but by their respective mothers or sisters. Love and household are thus among the Nairs completely separated; the organization of the maternal family makes possible free love in such degree that Buchanan could say with justification: "no Nair knows his father. Strictly speaking, the group-marriage of the Nairs is a combination of polyandry and polygamy." In polyandry, the marriage of a woman to several men, especially prevalent in Thibet and parts of India, the men are usually brothers. Rousselet says of this: "The marriage of several men to one woman is apparently the type of the oldest social organization of the aborigines of India and the western Himalaya." According to Mueller-Lyer, polyandry is associated with the formerly existent mother-right.

From these data it follows that the institution of group marriage fortified the position of women. The gradual dominance of the mothers, not only over the children of the clan but ultimately over the men, as borne out by the "matriarchal organization," was seemingly a slow process resisted by man who still defended his supernatural origin and survival. As he was conceived from the spirit of the dead and lived on in his double he had to keep free from the mortal origin of woman, the mother. Thus, motherhood, strange as it may sound, was not accepted from the beginning as a matter of course; the conception of the mother as the bearer of life appears comparatively late, although at an earlier stage than the conception of fatherhood, emerging, as we have shown, from the socialized self. Originally, "the mother herself is no more than the host, as it were, of the child who decides to be born of her body; she is in no sense its shaper or genetrice. Motherhood and fatherhood both, in Australia, are essentially social; they are based upon and fulfil certain fundamental social needs . . . there is nothing of any biological or physiological nature nor any concepts of consanguinity associated with these relationships."[1] From this denial of motherhood on the part of the man leads a long uneven way to the modern individual's famous "mother-complex." This emotional tie—far from being natural—is the ultimate result of a development which started when man first accepted biological fatherhood in place of his own self-perpetuation. For then and only then did he have to be sure that the children were actually his own, begotten from their mother, his wife. Strange as it may sound, but intelligible from our point of view, man accepted the mother as the source of his children's life long before he admitted his own mortal origin from woman, the mother.

This is borne out by the rôle of woman in matriarchal society, especially as it appears reflected in religious concepts of the mother-goddess. One of the most striking examples has recently been brought to light in the history of *Petra, the Rock City of Edom*, drawn chiefly from Biblical sources by M. A. Murray.[2] In the early days of the matrilineal succession to the throne, when kings ruled by right of their mothers (or wives) and not as sons of a royal father, the deity of Petra was a goddess who, in the course

[1] Ashley-Montagu, M. F. *Coming into Being among Australian Aborigines*, N. Y., 1938.

[2] *Petra, the Rock City of Edom,* Blackie & Son, Glasgow, 1939.

of time, changed her sex and became masculine. This change was effected through three successive stages: first, she was provided with a divine son who tended to become her consort, then her father, and finally apparently herself. In this religious development, as documented from the history of Petra, I see reflected the early rôle of woman who first was accepted as mother of the offspring, thus acquiring a son who then became a husband of herself, the mother, and thereby took on the rôle of father to her children.[1] This rôle, making the woman again into a mother, closes the cycle from the mother of the tribal offspring to that of the father's children; a cycle which leaves no room for the man's own mother and subsequently no room for the woman who is to the man the feared symbol of his own mortality.

Thus the son's emotional attachment to his mother, the ill-famed "mother-complex" of our rationalized psychology, is explained not as the result of the biological dependence of the helpless child but is understood as a secondary reaction against the dominance of the father who is forcing the son to become his identical successor. Against this compulsion towards likeness the son, so to speak, takes refuge in the mother, thereby creating an emotional dependence which only increases his innate fear of the woman. This fear of the other sex, springing from man's desire to survive in his own image, betrays once more the individual's dislike of difference and his longing for likeness. The difference of the woman is least objectionable in the sister (or other relatives); hence, the desire for incest as a

[1] In the full-fledged patriarchal family organization, as we know it from Roman father-right, there appears an almost complete reversal of the family conceptions prevailing at the matriarchal stage of primitive group-life. In ancient Rome, at the marriage of the daughter, the paternal power was transferred to the husband: the woman was passed over in *manum viri*, and as wife she was *filiae loco*, that is, according to the law, she became the daughter of the husband, who thereby accepted the father-rôle (today she still exchanges the name of the father for that of the husband).

compromise between egotistical and sexual perpetuation in the idea of re-birth.

This solution of the problem of succession we found epitomized in the sacred marriage of the brother to the sister in which the man could still maintain the idea of being his own offspring (later, "incest.") There was no mother yet, and "the husband," as we have seen, through marriage to his sister, became the "brother." As marriage became more common—not only a privilege by which the extraordinary type preserved his unusual qualities—the man could still keep aloof from participation in the procreation of the clan by accepting his wife as "sister." A number of ancient customs serve to illustrate this stage of development. For example, among the ancient Jews, it seems that the wife became by marriage a sister, while among the Baganda, on the other hand, a sister is viewed as a wife. Among many Australian tribes, the bride is bartered for a relative (usually a sister) of the bridegroom. This custom is sometimes mitigated to the naming of an unrelated mate by some designation of relationship ("sister" or "cousin" among the Egyptians, Arabs and Bataks). As in these ancient marriage customs, the origin of which we found in magical cults, the wife becomes, so to speak, a "blood" relative of the man, so, too, does the child become a blood relative of the man, by means of this "marriage of siblings." In earlier stages of the exogamic group marriages, the children were only considered blood relatives to the mother. Even in our socialized marriage, there develops an emotional relationship which not infrequently turns the partner into an "incestuous" sex-object. This emotional confusion accounts to a great extent for marital difficulties and failures in our civilization. The well-known assimilation between married couples often extends far beyond the mutual adoption of habits and tastes to physical resemblance and emotional twinship resulting in sexual inhibition.

Why, then, in the development of the sexual self, was the sister so important as the first object of sexual tabu as well as the symbol of ideal marriage—a contradiction which is still reflected in our confused emotional relationship between man and woman? In the magical rite of "coronation" for the divine king, we found the sacred marriage-ceremony between brother and sister to symbolize the transition from magical to sexual perpetuation. The sister, by tradition as well as by feeling and appearance, was the predestined female substitute for the double, heroically symbolized as the twin-brother. A child from her was bound to preserve all the desired qualities of the man; indeed, was emotionally identical with the reborn hero himself. Thus we realize in the marriage of the sister a symbolization of the sexualized double or twin-brother, whereby self-perpetuation in the one was renounced in favor of perpetuation in a real successor resembling the self as much as possible.

This important shift in man's conception of immortality we found epitomized in the late Greek myth of Narcissus, whose self-love appears explained in another version as the result of his love for his identical twin-sister, the death of whom caused him to seek consolation in his own image. The Narcissus tradition shows us, then, the way by which man's self-love, springing from the longing for immortality, is transformed into love for the other, for the person like the self. On the level of our patriarchal family organization, the somatic, characterological or emotional likeness of members of the family can be substituted for this self-relatedness, since the father finds himself again in his (identical) son, the mother in her daughter, and the brother in his sister. Incestuous love proper appears, then, only at the stage of the individual family unit where it expresses the earlier love for one's own ego in the language of the sexual self. We clearly recognize here how the biological urge, by its very nature anti-individualistic, finally becomes individualized through love for an "identical" person resembling the self in one way or another.

This development once more confirms our view that the sexual regulations of the primitives did not aim at avoiding incest by rule of exogamy, but implied commands compelling the individual to sexual intercourse with strangers, that is, with women whose difference was not mitigated by any symbols of likeness. Because of his inner resistance to biological procreation, primitive man practically tabued sex; or, at least, had to be induced by "law" to marry and produce children—a practice similar to that of the totalitarian states in our day which still feel compelled to do so on the basis of their "tribal" ideology. Since woman as the incorporation of natural biological sex was so much tabued that there was hardly room for any relationship with her, primitive man had to be induced to overcome this instinctive fear of woman—that is, the fear of difference—through the establishment of certain conditions under which sexual intercourse was permissible. By channeling his natural biological urge to serve the needs of his ego, man from time immemorial has tried to avoid his rôle as the bearer of the procreative life-principle of which his Self is but an ephemeral manifestation. In reversing this natural state of affairs man turned sexual intercourse, which is shown by the behavior of higher animals to be a battle of nature, into a mere source of pleasure.

Be that as it may, man's innate resistance to procreation, enforced by his ideological fear of woman as a threat to his immortality, betrayed itself in innumerable tabus imposed on his sex life and that of the woman. Those aboriginal tabus, especially that of the menstruating woman, clearly show that such restrictions were self-imposed in order to protect the man from his fear of sex.[1] This

[1] Already A. A. Crawley, *The Mystic Rose,* London, 1902, explained the narrower incest-tabu as an offshoot from the general tabu against sex which became effective for the man at the time of woman's first menstruation.

genuine fear of sex in the individual I traced in the *Trauma of Birth* to the shock the child experiences in parturition, and on that basis interpreted the shrinking from the female genital (which Freud explained as a "castrated" male organ) as a shrinking from the symbol of mortality. The womb as the place of birth likewise symbolizes death, and the return to the mother (earth) implies just as much a dying as it does the possibility of re-birth. In this deeper sense, which the Greek Oedipus-saga conveys, the desire for incest with the mother—as different from the narcissistic incest with the sister—expresses the basic need for immortality in the language of the sexualized family-self. It epitomizes the individual's longing for eternal survival by being re-born, a longing which the man can only satisfy biologically in procreation through his children. Accordingly, the incest-*tabu* expresses the group ideology of generative procreation, thus upholding the natural law of mortal sex as against man's immortalized sexuality. In transgressing this incest tabu, the individual once more tries to recapture heroic stature, thus overcoming the fear of death by being reborn through his own mother. We have seen how, because incestuous origin was considered an earmark of supernatural qualities, the ritual incest with the sister was imposed as a duty upon the immortal hero. In this sense, Nietzsche, referring to those folk-beliefs (in particular among the Persians), saw in Oedipus' incest and parricide only a manifestation of the superman swerving from the course of nature. Such supernatural influences can still be detected in the Oedipus-tradition, where the marriage to the mother is linked with a curse resulting in the barrenness of the whole country. Although Oedipus lifts that curse by conquering the Sphinx, he brings upon his country a similar curse of sterility by having intercourse with his mother and thus interfering with the natural cycle of procreation. Since the hero's sexual offense not only brings about general sterility but is punished by threatening famine, Oedipus' transgression of the incest-tabu at a time when the feudal structure of the Greek city-state gave way to more "democratic" family-communities reflects on this new plane the totemistic correlation between sex and hunger.

This interplay between the two main natural forces of hunger and sex, negligible in times of prosperity, becomes a vital problem when times of crises produce a shortage in the one or abundance in the other area. Climate, weather, seasonal changes, natural disasters (such as the flood which in the Biblical story calls for a preservation of animals lest men starve), epidemics, war and other calamities may precipitate an acute awareness of this interdependence between sex and hunger. In our own day we are faced once more with a vital disproportion between population and food supply; a problem which carries sex far beyond its being merely a topic of parlor conversation or a personal problem to be discussed in a consultation room. This time man faces the issue on the biggest scale ever experienced by him, and, what is more, entirely on his own responsibility. Not only is a totem lacking to take the blame for the disproportion between population and food stuff, but also every God has been thrown overboard who might have shared this responsibility with man, who thus pays the price for his presumption in seeking to master nature. While economists seem to agree that there could be sufficient food for the world's present population, a few eugenists assert that still more babies are what the world needs for "recovery." Professor Hogben's population studies[1] show that fertility in industrial society is declining rapidly. Of still greater interest to us is his general conclusion confirming our view of primitive man's sexual regulations—namely, that the common opinion that human reproduction proceeds of its own mo-

[1] Hogben, Lancelot, in *What is ahead of us?* The Fabian Lectures, The Macmillan Company, N. Y., 1937.

mentum unless checked is a delusion. Hogben points to some obvious factors in modern life which contradict this tacit assumption. For one thing, urban congestion sets up a more or less conscious resistance to parenthood: dwelling places are small and the home as a family centre has been weakened by commercialized entertainments. "It is beyond dispute," he concludes, "that high density of population produces low fertility, and that low fertility points directly towards race suicide."

The same observation seems to hold good for entire nations, as well as for certain classes within a nation. European observers, especially, are startled by their paradoxical findings that poor countries, like poor families, produce the most children. As no one seems able to explain this curious fact we welcome Professor Pearl's frank though winding admission that "there are certain indefinable or obscure factors at work about which literally almost nothing of a precise character is now known."[1] This reluctant profession of some irrational elements still operating in human nature carries the more weight that the author expresses himself most emphatically against birth control, easy access to which he blames for the declining birth-rate, especially in America. Hence, different economic and social classes have different fertility rates, largely "because of their own volition and intent, they want to have them."[2] These facts, in my opinion, prove conclusively that the fluctuation in the birth-rate is not, as most people like to believe, exclusively determined by economic factors. As a matter of fact, sex is the very sphere in which irrational elements beyond the human will, together with all sorts of social factors determined by the particular community life, are always operating.

This, our present world-crisis, with its manifold aspects

[1] Pearl, Raymond. *The Natural History of Population,* N. Y., 1939.
[2] *Op. cit.*

of individual and social problems, economic and emotional, can in the last analysis be reduced to a disproportion between population and food supply created by man himself. For he not only assumed the complete responsibility originally ascribed to the totem but also the complete management of the food supply which is no longer left to nature, although still essentially dependent upon her. From the first sexual tabus of the primitive to our direct and indirect forms of birth-control (the latter, perversions), man created this sexual self against nature, for whom, essentially, the whole individual—man or woman—is nothing but a sex-cell. Man's need to differentiate himself as an individual, or if possible as a personality, from his purely biological function precipitated the split between him and nature from which he suffers, but which has enabled him to achieve human culture.

The restrictions and tabus which primitive man introduced into his natural sex life and later applied to the breeding of domesticated animals originated, as we have shown, in his desire for eternal survival, that is, personal immortality. This purely egotistic attitude would have had disastrous results for the species had not other equally strong factors counteracted such "suicidal" tendency. This was not only the power of the sexual urge which drove man to procreate himself against his own will; it was another factor, man-made, namely, the realization of death as finality—not merely as a transition from one life into another. Whereas primitive man resisted procreation that he might live on himself, civilized man, realizing the futility of such a wishful conception of life, accepted immortality collectively, that is, through his children in the tribe, community or nation.

This inextricable dilemma between over- and under-population only reflects the eternal conflict between personal and racial survival in the individual. As unique individuals we want not to procreate but to survive eternally; as male or female cells we not only have to procreate but we want to, in order to survive at least collectively. In a word, while low fertility results from the desire for individual survival —which seems to operate automatically in densely populated areas—surplus population indicates the predominance of the strife for racial survival. Hence are derived, on the one hand, the opposing ideologies of the totalitarian states, with the submission of the individual to the race; and on the other, the various forms of democracy with more or less freedom on the individual's part to perpetuate himself and thus preserve his possessions within the narrow realm of the family. Yet in effect there is not much difference between the two kinds of planning—that left to the parents or that undertaken by the State. For the State, no matter what its form of government, is always requesting children from its citizens; if not directly, then through certain economic and social measures. Thus, in a different way, sex is just as much determined, that is, controlled by the State, as it was through tabus in primitive community. This age-old clash, between the individual's desire for his sex freedom and the inherent racial urge of sex, expressed in all kinds of social regulations, betrays itself in the secretiveness with which the individual guards his own personal control over his sexual function. This latter is not only borne out by the individual's indulging in various "unnatural" acts—such as masturbation and other perversions—but also in our whole attitude towards sex, which is guarded as a big secret not merely from children but also from the community at large. Hence, the totalitarian production of "cannon fodder" brings with it—as for example in Germany just before the present war—a wave of crude jokes about sex, whereby the individual seeks an outlet for his curtailed personal pleasure. The deliberate mass-production of population is justified by the need for imperialistic expansion into new territory conquered for the same surplus population which perishes in acquiring it. In this sense, sex always was and still is a powerful political weapon wielded not merely as the means for producing a warrior-class or a soldier type, but for the ultimate purpose of conquering other peoples. There we find a "sadistic" element not only in the individual but inherent racially in the drive for the multiplication of one species to the detriment of another. In our time, however, this urge for racial survival appears rather as a fear of racial extinction, which is likely to arise in a conquered people like the Jews in the Diaspora or the Germans after the World War.[1] Spontaneous reactions like these throw light on the well-known fact that the conqueror, the victors, are likely to perish, while the conquered, the meek, "inherit the earth." This was true throughout history, from the conquest of the Jews by the Egyptians and the Christians by the Romans; it was true of the Middle Ages and it is true now.

Yet another truth to be remembered at this point, is equally important. Not only nations and classes in power which are regarded as superior are "less fertile than the general run of the population,[2] but also superior individuals, such as men of action, great artists and scholars, produce none or at best inferior offspring. A consideration of this important fact introduces into our discussion of population-quantity the equally important problem of quality. Those two dynamic factors in social life, represented by the correlation between leader and mass, operate in a strange manner of interplay. A full-fledged leader needs the capacity for expansion implied in more people, while this surplus popu-

[1] Haldane, J. B. S. *Heredity and Politics,* Norton, N. Y., 1938.

[2] According to statistical figures recently published by Rudolph Binder in "The Eugenical News," Germany, in the 15 years that followed the World War, lost between 10 and 12 millions, several times the number who succumbed to bullets, gas and lack of food.

lation needs a leader to direct their course of action.[1] Yet we see, right now, in the totalitarian state, with its mass production of population, one strong leader with no successor in view, when there is a greater need for a strong man than in the democracies, where a group of leading men select one supreme executive whose power is checked.

As a characteristic illustration of how modern man has tried to solve biologically the problem of leadership, which primitive man solved "magically," I would mention here an experiment attempted in the twentieth century. In the beginning of this era, when Japan became Westernized and its growing population demanded expansion and leadership, the Nipponese government arranged a prize contest, open to scholars throughout the world, for the best method by which to breed genius. It seems that no contribution was received, but the raising of the question inspired a German scientist, Wilhelm Ostwald, to write a book which he called, *Great Men.*[2] In it were given the biographies of about a dozen individuals, all showing genius in the realm of science. Most of them suffered, throughout their life from early childhood, not only handicaps of all kinds, physical, mental and environmental, but even definite disadvantages as far as their future achievements were concerned. Ostwald, in his objective presentation of those life-stories, did not draw any conclusions but let the material speak for itself. These men, obviously, achieved what they did, not only in spite of adverse circumstances but really—at least as far as physical handicaps were concerned—in spite of themselves. Granted the difference in the breeding of genius—be it in the realm of science or art—and the training of political leaders, the same principle of spontaneous development, as

[1] The German demand for "elbow-room" is explained by Bernhard Koehler, head of the National Socialist party's economic commission: "Germany has too few people to master her tasks, and too little land to feed the people she does have."

[2] Grosse Männer, Leipzig, 1909, also French edition, Paris, 1912.

borne out by the collapse of the Roman Empire from lack of sufficient leadership, holds good in either sphere. Today we see the totalitarian states, especially Germany, chiefly concerned with this problem of future leadership; a concern which accounts for the emphasis laid on youth-movements and the early training of the younger generation in the spirit of the party ideology.[1]

Thus any community, large or small, has to be concerned with three major problems: first and foremost, the food supply for the living generation; second, a livable balance of the birth- and death-rate in view of available food stuffs; and last but not least, the providing of adequate leadership to manage these problems within a given environment. It seems that the solution of all three problems, especially the last one, depends on the size of the community, notwithstanding climatic conditions and racial heritage. This explains why small tribal communities could and still can succeed on the simple totemistic organization, whereby the responsibility for the balance is shared by the whole community adhering to the tabus imposed by the totem as a fictitious leader.

With the growth of the community this fictitious leader becomes personified in the chief, the king, who, as we have seen, is made responsible for the welfare of the community in the same way as was the totem-animal which regulated the birth-rate as well as the food-supply. In the fictitious leadership of the totem is foreshadowed the ideal leader of civilized nations, namely, their God, who finally crystallizes into the absolute notion of the State. With the twilight of the Gods, man himself took on more and more of this responsibility for his own soul and the welfare of the community, until there emerged the form of leadership char-

[1] In one of his recent Reichstag speeches, Adolf Hitler emphasized the urgent need for "Fuehrer-Auslese" and warned that the future revolutionists will be recruited from the neglected "Fuehrer" type.

acteristic of all civilization from Antiquity until modern times: the king as God's representative on earth, and as the representative of the state replacing God's kingdom on earth.

With the dawn of Christianity there was revived an older form of leadership, namely, a sharing of the responsibility between the earthly ruler, represented by the King and his State, and the Heavenly Lord, epitomized in the Church. For almost 2000 years humanity has been battling with the question as to what, or rather, how much belongs "unto Caesar" and what unto God. In our day, this human problem has precipitated a new crisis which the totalitarian states are trying to solve through their secular religions, that is, by welding into one unity the two aspects of government. Their leaders profess to be no longer representatives of God on earth but of the might of the masses from whom they emerged; in reality, however, in their godlike dictatorship, they are as scornful of the people as the people are afraid of them.

This emphasis on the masses[1]—a true characteristic of our times as it was of the Christian era—implies a more realistic attitude towards life, in that it automatically minimizes the importance of the leader, or rather, puts him in his right place. True, leadership of any kind, from the legendary hero who creates culture to the artist and scientist who enrich it, is necessary for the constant stimulation towards cultural achievements. But civilization is produced, or at least maintained, not by the comparatively few leading spirits, political or otherwise, but by the masses of people. And in times of crisis, as in the present period, it is not the few intellectuals shouting most loudly that civilization has to be saved who really save it. It is the masses of the

[1] With his exhortation of the masses on whom the leader relies, he really does not mean the people themselves but rather a dynamic symbol of the creative power from which he feeds, as a child from the mother.

people who through their mere existence and procreation—which the leader-type resists—guarantee the continuance of life and with it any particular civilization. No matter how great the creative genius and his achievements, he needs an audience to appreciate his work lest it be unproductive. Indeed, as has been said of God, he would not even exist if man were not here to worship him and admire his works.

In speaking of the masses and their importance for the perpetuation of any specific civilization or the human race in general, we do not overlook their economic struggle, because it is inextricably bound up with the problem of procreation. Yet it is more than mere economic need or social ambition which spurs the individual to rise above the mass and become distinguished through wealth, power or creativity. In such success is expressed the individual need for self-realization and fulfilment in terms of his personal immortality. Hence, we have man's ideological resistance to sexual procreation, by which he aims to protect himself from this powerful racial instinct threatening to devour his personality. Thus the individual will is set against the will of nature manifested in sex. In his personality the individual will triumphs over the procreative instinct. In this sense, all the tabus and restrictions which modern man finds so inhibiting in his sexual life were originally will-ful expressions of his ego in subjugating the sexual instincts. All the sexual inhibitions from which modern man claims to suffer and which he blames—supported by psychoanalytic theories—on his environmental heritage, were originally positive expressions of an irrational ideology invented by man to save his ego from the ultimate destiny of sex: death. In this way he built up a sexual self which finally lost its positive function when the cultural climate in which it was meant to function, namely, the magical world-view with its will to immortality, was replaced by a rational philosophy of life.

Thus we find the sexual impulses of man developing in two different directions, according to whether the power of sex over the individual is accepted and submitted to or resisted by way of will-ful control. This latter attitude distinguishes civilized man from his primitive ancestors because it also leads to the achievements of human culture—not, however, without man's growing need to submit to the coercion of sex through the yielding love-emotion. The only way, evidently, in which the individual is able to accept the coercion of sex is by yielding it will-fully to one, the beloved person. It seems that only then can sex take on the significance of life for the individual; otherwise, the natural association of sex with death operates as an inhibiting factor. This connection explains, in the last analysis, the individual's innate resistance to sex; for with the acceptance of it as a dominating force of his nature he simultaneously accepts death as the natural twin-brother of sex (in Greek tradition Eros and Thanatos were always pictured as inseparable). This also is the meaning of the Biblical Paradise-story, where the discovery of sex brings death into the world. For the personality is ultimately destroyed by and through sex, regardless of whether he accepts or denies it. In the latter case, however, this destruction is self-willed and set against the ever-threatening destruction which nature in any case has in store for the ephemeral ego.

7

Feminine Psychology and Masculine Ideology

It has become a truism that man from time immemorial has imposed his masculine way of life upon woman, both individually and collectively. Traditions, likewise, seem to agree that woman not only willingly submitted to any man-made ideology which happened to prevail but was clever enough to assimilate it and use it to her own advantage. Less obvious, though of greater importance, is the complementary process, namely, that man, while imposing his mentality on woman, usurped some of her vital functions and thus unwittingly took on some of her genuine psychology, differing fundamentally from his own masculine ideology. Herein lies the most paradoxical of all psychological paradoxes: that man, who was molding woman according to his own sexual will, should have taken over into his ideological philosophy the love-principle so deeply rooted in woman's nature. The conception of Agape, as we have seen, revived the vital principle of woman-love which had been lost in Antiquity, particularly in Greek civilization, where the original mother-goddess was finally replaced by the masculine ideal of the self-created hero.

This gradual replacement of an original mother-culture by the masculine state-organization appears reflected in the development of ancient religion, especially in the Near East, that is, in Asia Minor. Of particular interest to us is the recent study, already referred to, of such development which, documented by Biblical tradition, enables us to follow the successive steps leading from the one form of social organization to the other. The material in question concerns the story of Petra, known from Biblical sources as "the Rock City of Edom," which, from the time of Moses and possibly before that, controlled, for many centuries, a great transit route. In its early days of matrilineal succession, the deity was a goddess who, by acquiring a son first for the rôle of consort and later father, finally became masculinized herself in the form of a god.

Such development, characteristic of all early religions of civilized peoples, seems to reflect the gradual emergence of our later conception of family-types from an undifferentiated mixture of biological facts and supernatural ideologies. Yet, in a sense, this symbol of an originally bisexual mother-goddess reveals to us the real story behind the mythical conception of the "first" man, as presented in later Biblical tradition. In order to be impregnated by man, woman had first to give birth to that man as her son, who, when matured, could become her mate and thus a father. The Biblical story presents, as it were, the end-phase of this development in a masculinized reversion of the fact that man is born of mortal woman. Primitive religion, on the contrary, abounds in pictures of a self-sufficient or (later) hermaphroditic goddess who originally creates life without the aid of man before creating man, who in turn creates her in his own image. Such speculations about the origin of man necessarily lead to an incestuous beginning, which, however, does not reflect biological facts but expresses an ideological need in man to blot out the mother-origin in order to deny his mortal nature. Herein is to be found the dynamic drive for man's religious, social and artistic creativity through which he not only proves his supernatural origin (religion) and capacity (art) but also tries to translate it into practical terms of social organization (state, government).[1]

[1] A German scholar, Ernst Bergman, designates these two antagonistic tendencies of human civilization in terms of the difference of the sexes as

The primaeval mother-goddess, later associated with her son-lover who eventually as father usurped her place, seems to have been the prototype of the "Heavenly Queen" characteristic of all Near-Eastern religions, in which invariably a mother-goddess appears sexually related to a son. From Babylonian and Egyptian to Persian and Greek tradition we find this same pattern symbolized in the relationship of Istar-Tammuz, Isis-Horus, Maja-Agni, Tanit-Mithra, Kybele-Attis, Astarte-Adonis and Aphrodite-Hermes. Even in Christian tradition, traces of a similar relation of Christ to Mary can be detected, as Robertson[1] has suggested on the basis of an earlier myth of a Palestinian God—probably named Joshua—who appears in the alternate relations of lover and son to a mythical Mary. It is important, however, to bear in mind that Christianity does not represent a mere parallel to those ancient conceptions but rather a revival and re-interpretation of the original mother-concept which had given way to the masculinization of Eastern civilization. For in Christianity, this incestuous relationship is interpreted as a symbol of spiritual re-birth. This conception is expounded in Jesus' answer to Nicodemus' question as to how a man can be born when aged? Is it possible for him to enter a second time into his mother's womb and be born again? Christ's well-known answer to this tricky question bears out his spiritual interpretation of the ancient tradition.

The gradual masculinization of human civilization, in my opinion probably the most enlightening clue to history, is borne out by mythical and religious tradition as well as by the development of social concepts and artistic creation. Mythologically, it is epitomized in the transition from an

"Erkenntnisgeist und Muttergeist" (Breslau, 1931), meaning the spirit of knowledge as against the spirit of motherhood. He even speaks of a sexualization of woman by man.

[1] Robertson, John Mackinnon, *Pagan Christs*. N. Y., Truth Seeker Co.

original moon-goddess characteristic for all early religion to the masculine sun-god who obliterates the moon. The transition—paralleling the above-mentioned religious concept of a mother-son relationship—is found in the widespread tradition of an originally female moon-goddess who was first supplemented by a masculine counterpart, a moon-god, in the rôle of son or brother, with a later development to husband and father. "These mythological traditions of all civilized and most primitive races have their sociological counterpart in the fact that the remains of the moon-cult also point to primitive conceptions of society, in which the woman still played a greater part than that which we find allotted to her in the patriarchal organization of high cultures with their sun-cult."[1] The best documented example of such masculinization, implying the denial of woman's importance, is to be found in Egyptian tradition with its violent suppression of the moon-cult epitomized in the ancient Isis-religion by the sun-cult of Ra forcibly introduced by the heretical king Tutankamon. According to the original moon religion in ancient Egypt, the child was named after the mother, a matrilineal rule still reflected in the legend of Moses, the fatherless child. In this, as in all other traditions of the myth of the birth of the hero, the father was not eliminated, as Freud saw it in the light of his patriarchal philosophy, but was unimportant if not altogether unknown.

As the repressed mother-cult is presented in such fragments of an earlier civilization, so we may find in other relics of ancient tradition further evidence for the once universal veneration of female creativity which was denied by man's need of an immortality of his own. How far-reaching and in what unexpected directions such a search may lead can be illustrated by a suggestion of Dr. Murray's, which she presents in connection with her discussion of this

[1] *Art and Artist,* Alfred A. Knopf, N. Y., 1932, p. 125.

change of sex in the early religion of Petra. She points out that among the gods whose images—often merely oblong stones—have been found at or near Petra were several who were also honored at Mecca in the "Days of Ignorance." This conjecture makes it likely that the "Holy Carpet" which covers the Kaaba was once the outward image of a goddess, which therefore had to be decently veiled. Such interpretation would explain the ceremonial circumambulation of the Kaaba during the ceremonies of the Haj as a relic of the ritual dances long ago, when pagan Arabs capered round it naked and priests of Baal leaped up and down before the altars of a god who required human sacrifices. Both through their racial relatedness to the Arabs and the religious influence from Babylonia the Jews seemed to belong to this same cultural development to which they also appear geographically bound. Petra, which during its long history had changed hands frequently, was always snatched from earlier settlers by one of the many Arabic desert tribes attracted by its riches. In the Bible it is known as Edom because in its early days it was occupied by the Edomites, descendants of Esau and kinsfolk of the Jews. They had captured it from the Horites, who in turn had taken it from the Kenites under whom it was first known. The Biblical sources from which most of Petra's history is drawn provide many examples showing how primitive and crude the Jews were in the day of their power.

There is one incident recorded from a later period which is completely out of place as far as religious ceremonial is concerned and which seems to have preserved in it another relic of an original mother-cult among the Jews, whose monotheism appears as the result of a long struggle against foreign gods who still betrayed the earmarks of an earlier mother-goddess. The episode referred to is King David's dance before the Torah, an unheard-of sacrilege not only in the times before the building of the first temple but even in the early days of the Golden Calf—another mother-symbol. In the light of Dr. Murray's suggestion about the original "sex" of the Kaaba it seems quite possible that the Torah which guided the nomadic Jews through the desert represented an original female symbol, a relic of the great Asiatic Mother-Goddess who had been replaced by Jehovah through the man Moses, in whom appears epitomized the transition from the mother-cult of ancient Egypt to the father-cult of monotheistic religion. The Torah proper, containing the new masculine Law of Moses, was—not unlike the Kaaba—carefully covered by the rich vestments inside of which it rested invisibly.

Christianity not only openly restituted the early importance of the mother-cult but likewise did away with its highly masculinized substitutes in Jewish religion and Roman statecraft. By spiritualizing the Oriental mother-cult, the Christian religion extended this genuinely biological conception into a universal love-ideology applicable alike to man and woman. We have shown how this spiritual love-conception of Agape gradually became contaminated with earthly, that is, sexual love-desires—a confusion of the two principles culminating in the romantic love-emotion. This semi-religious development precipitated what one might call a feminization of our Western world, resulting in our psychological type of man. The will-ful Eros and the yielding Agape were translated into psychological terms of "wanting" (will) and "being wanted" (loved), a moral re-valuation which not only brought about a change of personality types but a change in the general mores of modern times.

This change of psychology in modern man calls for a new evaluation beyond our moral classification of masculine and feminine which shall take into account the more fundamental difference concerning the functioning of the will in the personality of the two sexes. Whereas man's will in its free expression is simply "wanting," in woman's psychology we meet the paradoxical will-phenomenon of wanting to be wanted. Such reversal in the expression of the will raises the question as to whether we are to see in it another perversity of human nature or a genuine expression of woman's natural self. This latter assumption would then presuppose that there always was and still is a woman-psychology, which has not only remained unrecognized throughout the ages but has been misinterpreted religiously, socially and psychologically in terms of masculine ideologies. First and foremost, through this confusion of the feminine Agape and the masculine eroticism, the religious conceptions of good and evil have been interpreted in sexual terms of "masculine" and "feminine"; that is to say, our social standards and values concerning masculine and feminine traits have become inextricably bound up with our moral notions of good and bad. According to this moral code, which Western man set up by interpreting nature in moral terms, masculinity became identified with strength, power, if not creativity—in a word, goodness; whereas femininity designates silliness, weakness, if not wickedness—in a word, badness.

In view of our previous discussions, it becomes obvious that what we meet in those moralistic qualifications is the age-old struggle of the rational self against its irrational nature. From the point of view of man's rational psychology, "feminine" traits of emotionalism appear "irrational," whereas in reality they represent human qualities of a positive nature. Since modern psychology is not only masculine but derived from our neurotic type of man, a great deal of its terminology originated from a misinterpretation of woman in terms of man's sexual ideology. Such misinterpretation, as shown for example in the psychoanalytic conception of masochism, is not a modern invention but is deeply rooted in human language. For language, which originated as a free expression of the natural self, gradually developed into a rational means of communication voicing the predominant ideology. Thus, in contrasting masculine ideology and feminine psychology we have to guard against becoming involved in the intricacies of linguistic confusion inherent in human speech. In other words, we must first step beyond language in order to remain "beyond psychology," made up as it is from a language already sexualized. Contrary to common belief, human language did not emerge like the love-call of birds and other animals as an expression of the male's sexual urge for the female. True, language is masculine, but only in the sense that it was created by man to be used as a most powerful instrument with which to produce a world of his own by interpreting the existing world in terms of his masculine sexology.

The creation of the universe through Jehovah's word, as the Old Testament presents it, gives testimony to man's presuming to re-create the natural world in his own words. The Biblical story called "The Tower of Babel" epitomizes man's ambition to change language from a means of self-expression into a tool for universal communication. The moral of this parable seems to imply a warning against man's presumptuous attempt to "understand" everything by putting it into words. The fallacy of such an undertaking betrays itself in the vicious circle created by man who first named things in his own language, only to use the same language afterwards by which to "explain" them. Thus it seemed easy to prove—be it in religious, sociological or psychological terms—that this man-made universe was right. In reality, however, this creative ambition of man has produced ever-increasing confusion since the time of Babel, until in our day the world is actually at war about the meaning of words. Terms like communism, fascism, democracy seem to evade any clear definition, because it is not so much their semantic meaning which counts as the way they are used and the means they are used for.[1]

In trying, at least temporarily, to keep out of this ideological word-war, we go back to the undeclared war on the border of the two sexes, that is, masculine versus feminine ideology. Here, because the only terminology which psychology furnishes us with which to explain woman is a masculine one, we find ourselves confronted by the same difficulty concerning human language. While the story of the Tower of Babel impresses upon us the linguistic confusion between man and nature in terms of national differences, here we encounter a more fundamental difference in the language used in traffic between man and woman. There actually are two different languages characteristic of man and woman respectively, and the woman's "native tongue" has hitherto been unknown or at least unheard. In spite of her proverbial chattering, woman is tacit by nature; that is, she is inarticulate about her real self. Man, in his creative presumption, took upon himself the task of voicing her psychology—of course, in terms of his masculine ideology. This fundamental misunderstanding between the two sexes, speaking as it were different languages, appears in Biblical tradition at the beginning of things when Adam listens to the voice of the serpent, speechless by nature, and simply understands it his way. Mark Twain, an unsurpassed master of language, expresses this dualism in human speech when, in his "Diary of Adam," the first man constantly complains about Eve's interfering with his joyful task of naming things by suggesting different names for them.

The question as to whether or not this aboriginal dualism

[1] Soon after the German occupation of Czecho-Slovakia, Berlin sent a daily radio-hour to Prague in order to explain the political terminology of the Third Reich to its new subjects.

of verbal expression in man and woman is reflected in the two genders of various languages has become a source of heated debate among linguistic scholars. In approaching the problem from a new angle, that of man's creative urge,[1] I was disposed to assume, in conformity with the general view adopted in this book, that what we have to deal with is not a growth of language out of sex-acts or sexual activity but a comparatively late sexualization of language as a manifestation of the human creative urge which gradually usurps the parenthood of everything by bringing sexual connotations into its nomenclature. This sexualization of language is itself, then, a metaphorical way of expressing a "just-like"; that is, it gives name-forms to everything that man creates, "just as if" they were produced by him as the child is.[2] It is very tempting, of course, to adduce the existence of genders in almost all modern languages as evidence of the sexual origin of languages; but such a conclusion is so superficial that most scholars, even when attempting to prove the sexual origin of languages, scorn it as unscientific.[3] A really scientific approach proves for our living languages what Powell had already established as a result of his thorough investigation of Indian languages, when he says: "The student of linguistics must get entirely out of his head the idea that gender is merely a distinction of sex. In the North American Indian languages

[1] *Art and Artist,* Alfred A. Knopf, N. Y., 1932, Chapt. VIII. "The Formation and the Creation of Speech."

[2] A rather curious example is provided in the famous "Indian Bible," as the first translation made in the colonies was called. Some scholars claim that the translation by the Rev. John Eliot was so faulty that the Indians could not understand it. But recently Prof. S. E. Morison came to the rescue of the translator by pointing out some of the difficulties under which Eliot labored. "Throughout the Bible, wherever the word 'virgin' occurs, Eliot uses a word that means 'a chaste young man.' That was because chastity was accounted a masculine virtue. They had a word for 'virgin,' but seldom any occasion to use it. No doubt it seemed much more suitable to the Indians to have the bridegroom met by ten 'chaste young men.'"

[3] See *Art and Artist,* Alfred A. Knopf, N. Y., 1932, for discussion of this subject.

(and probably in the Bantu and the Indo-European also) gender is usually a classification method." We find the classification of "higher" and "lower" beings, that presently became one of "male" and "female," in the Semitic languages, which, even thus early, breathe the moral outlook of the East. Here, too, the primitives disclose to us the deeper sources, for (according to Powell) the main principle of their classification is to divide animate and inanimate objects.

Thus the inclusion of primitive languages within the scope of our study has shown this phenomenon of grammatical genders to be but a part of a much wider and more complex system of classification; and this makes it all the more interesting to follow the phenomena of transition. Opposed to the two-gender system of the Indo-European, we have the Indian classification that we have just been discussing, based chiefly on the distinction of "soul" and "no-soul" (living and non-living), though, to be sure, there attaches to this a certain valuation as "personal" and "impersonal," which reappears in the distinction of "masculine" and "feminine." Most interesting of all are the transitional languages, which show the beginning of sexualization side by side with the old basis of classification. According to Meinhof,[1] the developed system of the Bantu languages has more than twenty classes with special prefixes; and between them and our two-gender system we have, for instance, the Hamitic Ful, in which, above the old classification of nouns, is an overlying new system with only four headings: persons, things, big and small, whence, as the big pass into the class of persons, and the small into that of things, a twofold system is developed, corresponding to our division into masculine and feminine. This gives us a glimpse into the valuation-principle which *eventually* iden-

[1] **Meinhof, Carl, Introduction to the phonology of the Bantu languages. Berlin, 1932.**

tifies persons, living, big and important things with man, and non-living, small and unimportant things with woman.[1, 2] This provides a striking parallel to the primitive's belief regarding the immortality symbols (i.e. the shadow) of man or woman respectively, stressing the immortality claim of man's soul as against woman's mortality, and subsequently assigning values to everything by dividing the world into things animate and inanimate, i.e. good and bad. The only problem here is: why does woman always come into the class of the evil, dangerous, and less valuable? This, as I have explained, arises from man's urge to eternalize himself personally, an urge threatened by sexual propagation, of which woman is the representative; and so woman passes into what I have called the Not-I class, which includes dangerous as well as unimportant (and neutral) things.[3]

This brief summary of the origin of human speech bears out man's utter egocentricity, which can be supplemented by the fact that among the first things he named were the parts of his own body. Centuries before the Greeks formulated this basic egocentricity in the slogan of their whole civilization: "Man is the measure of all things," it operated naively in primitive man. Starting from his own body as his "first field of experiment in his efforts to solve the problem of the ego and to discover its relation to the surrounding world," man divided the visible universe, as it were, into two categories, the "I" and the "not-I." The things he accepted, liked or needed he classified as belonging to the I-class, relegating everything else to the not-I class. By virtue of his belief in personal immortality, in

[1] *Art and Artist,* Alfred A. Knopf, N. Y., 1932, pp. 245-6.

[2] In Bedauye this is still quite clear. Thus, a cow is masculine because in these lands it is the chief support of ordinary existence; the flesh is, however, feminine because relative to the whole cow it is of less importance. (Reinisch: *Die Bedauyesprache,* II; Vienna, 1893; p. 59.)

[3] Cf. Holma, Harri, in his fundamental work on the names of the parts of the body in Assyrian and Babylonian, Leipzig, 1911.

which woman as the bearer of sexual mortality did not participate, she automatically became identified with the not-I class (wo-man—no man). Hence, all not-I things, which later formed the neuter class in European languages, were first considered feminine. Thus language, like all other basic human inventions, originated from the supernatural world-view and not from practical motives or rational considerations. Such origin explains the powerful rôle of words in magical practice, whereby the knowledge of the right word, kept as a secret in priestly tradition, could call a person or thing into being as well as destroy it.

While this genuine magic of words still echoes in our political and scientific slogans, language, which was at first religious, gradually became secularized. Hence is explained why any profanation of language was forbidden, and still is, for that matter, until language itself in its every-day use became profane. This process of deteriorization, known to linguists as "change in the meaning of words,"[1] ultimately also led to the sexualization of language as a part of the whole masculine interpretation of the world.

In this brief summary of certain linguistic characteristics, the two grammatical genders, we have said, had originally a classificatory meaning of good and bad. This good and bad—as the Hebrew connotations for it imply—can be translated as useful and harmful respectively. Thus in the

[1] In that process which reflects the changing mores, words tend towards a baser standard. Examples of such "moral degradation" of words can be amply found in every modern language. Not being sufficiently familiar with the history of the English language, I am taking a few examples from a letter to the *New York Times*. Mr. Jacques W. Redway, of Mt. Vernon, N. Y., writes, on June 21, 1938: The opposite process, the covering up of a bad meaning by a nice word known as "euphemism," applied essentially to everything which has to do with the two basic "unmentionables," sex and death. Examples abound here, too, for every category; so we will just mention one which, having found expression in law, definitely characterizes the social philosophy of our times. The good old English word "bastard," which is avoided in ordinary speech has been formally banned in New York by a statute approved April 9, 1925, and for it is to be substituted in all legal documents the term, "child born out of wedlock."

beginning they were quite rational, but in their extension into a whole system of "Weltanschauung" they appear to us irrational. In fact, this very word itself only designates the absence or negation of the rational, as does the unconscious of our modern psychology the lack of consciousness. In this sense, the change in the meaning of words epitomized the gradual condemnation of irrational terms expressed in language and their replacement by the rational. Since any positive designations for the irrational elements in human nature are lacking, woman's psychology, which still preserves those irrational elements, is non-existent because un-describable. Hence, civilization means increasing rationalization whereby man's importance and power is augmented at the expense of woman's right to herself. In particular, he took over her love-ideology in the Christian Agape, and at the same time—by denying her—interpreted her psychology in terms of his masculine ideology.

Man's denial of woman's world, as so often with successful denial, first operated creatively and enabled him to build up his masculine self-sufficient world not only in the supernatural symbols of religion, art and philosophy but also, though to a lesser degree, in theories of social organization, meant to change natural society according to his supernatural views. In order to pursue that aim, man, having masculinized the world, had to change woman according to his masculine ideology, that is, to sexualize her in his own image. Although this resulted in making her a willing instrument of his erotic desires, it was not primarily aimed at that but sprang from man's basic psychology which is contrary to that of woman. This basic difference, all-important for the understanding of human nature and its destiny, can be stated briefly thus: Man born of woman never accepted this basic fact of being mortal, that is, never accepted himself. Hence, his basic psychology is denial of his mortal origin and a subsequent need to change himself in order to find his real self which he rationalizes as independent of woman. Woman, on the contrary, fundamentally accepts her basic self, that of motherhood; at the same time, having taken on the masculine ideology, she needs constant confirmation from the man that she is acceptable to him, an assurance which she can only get by living up to his ideals and demands. Furthermore, woman seems to have a resistance to revealing her own psychology: first, because it is her last weapon against the man, the last refuge of her crushed and submissive self; second, because, as has often been said, her psychology is a mystery not only to the man but to herself, a secret which, by her very nature, she is never tempted to penetrate or to give away—except in living, which can never be grasped by psychological knowledge but only by human understanding. This *real woman*, psychologically, can only be described in negative terms, because her reality is irrational (intuitive, *sybille*). On the other hand, the woman is not permitted just to be, instead of having to know what she is, because the man wants to preserve her riddle in order to penetrate it. This interference on the man's part with the woman's natural being forces her to react in two extreme ways: she fights the man with his own weapon either by becoming masculine and psychological (sophisticated) as he is, or by so completely submitting to him as to become what he wants her to be. In either case, *his* attempt to discover her feminine psychology, makes her more and more like him; hence, in the age of Psychology, we see more masculine women than ever, especially of the latter imitative type; whereas the other fighting type is more primitive, and probably always existed.

This fundamental different psychology of their basic personalities is reflected in the ancient traditions of the first woman, showing that woman had to be made over by man in order to be acceptable to him.

There exists a little-known Biblical tradition of the creation of the first woman, antedating the widely propagated story of her emergence from Adam's rib.[1] This first woman, Lilith, molded as was Adam himself from the same clay, was, according to this anti-Paradisical version, a complete failure; hence, was replaced by the man-made woman, Eve. With all Eve's docility, however, she inherited seemingly from Lilith, who was a rebellious and mischievous demon, the curse of badness, which man, because he had to tame her, make her over, put on her from the dawn of memory. In these two versions we see epitomized man's need for a woman created by himself whom he therefore could accept, and woman's willingness to take on this rôle of man's creation which is her biological lot. At the same time, in order to create the woman as a sexual being, that is, a real self, man himself had to be born first by her, thus completing and at the same time breaking through the eternal cycle of creative perpetuation.

This strange story of the first woman, Lilith, neglected in favor of her more popular competitor, Eve, also implies the existence of two types of woman: the weak, dependent, child-like woman who all her life remains, so to speak, a daughter, and the independent strong woman of pre-familial matriarchal organization who draws her strength and self-reliance from motherhood. Of this latter woman, or rather, of this force in woman, man always was and still is afraid, because it symbolizes the epitome of irrationality, the marvel of creation itself. This basic irrationality is associated with the unknown, indeed, finally is identical with the unseen, that is, with what is going on inside the woman. In this sense, woman's psychology as a whole can be designated as insideness, in contra-distinction to man's centrifugal outsideness. While she takes in, keeps and only coercively

[1] A variation of the familiar tale of Adam and Eve is to be found in an Armenian folk tale. In it, the heroine is a sort of combined Lilith-Eve, an immortal nymph willing to discard her immortality and meet death in order that she may experience creative love.

forced pushes out, the man scatters, wastes and creatively puts out. It is part of woman's mystery that it is all invisible, inside. Her real self is hidden, and she is hiding it! Man is her positive will, and yet he is inside her (like the child); she takes him in and yet depends on him. This identification permits a vicarious living through the other person (as *in* and *for* the child). She *is made* a woman by the man, but *becomes* a woman, in herself and in her own right through *motherhood* and the processes associated with it.

As far as psychology is concerned, we have stated the problem in the introductory chapters by claiming, besides a psychological difference of races, classes and individual types, an even more profound and universal difference in the psychology of man and woman. The different schools of psychology which, by the very fact of their existence, prove that man has not even succeeded in explaining all men as alike (equal), seem to agree at least in their attempt to explain woman as merely lacking in, or having qualities differing from, masculine characteristics. Indeed, the very name she was given, wo-man, epitomizes in its negative implication (no-man) this very attitude of rejection of her difference. What we find instead is an interpretation of woman in terms of masculine ideology fit for a type of modern woman built up on this masculinized psychology of the female. In this state of affairs we easily recognize the anticlimax of man's eternal striving for likeness springing from his ego-centric urge for self-perpetuation, only to end in the biological perversity of an ever-increasing assimilation of the different characteristics of the two sexes. This unfortunate confusion has not been helped by the contribution of modern woman to literature or even psychology, because she is as much under the spell of masculine psychology as is her male co-worker.

This same attitude of hers is borne out in her family-relationships where, as a daughter, she is apt to see in her father the personified principle of a creative God through whose will everything happens to her. Many women pass from that stage, though not without conflict or occasional rebellion, to the stage of motherhood, where everything is even more obviously happening to her. But whereas she can keep what she is given (for instance, the child without the man), the man has to have what he is given. Being more active by nature, the man is constantly driven to doing things, changing them, in order always to feel sure of being able to control them, because he cannot accept them even if they are man-made. In fact, sex itself, this very life-principle which man has bent to his own will, must be given him by woman. We are referring here to the fact that the girl has to be made into a woman by the man. This takes place on a purely physical plane in her initial intercourse and continues on an emotional and intellectual plane in the majority of cases. It is only natural that the woman's own personality should suffer from that biological predicament of hers, which usually comes in conflict with her individual self-development. After having become a woman, which however is not necessarily achieved by defloration and childbirth, she may be forced to develop her personality along masculine lines, which she is likely to do in any case if the woman in her has not been awakened at all.

In our civilization, this man-made influence is exercised first and foremost by the father, who, contrary to Freud's biological conception, does not awaken and foster the woman qualities in the little girl. On the contrary, in order to be accepted, that is, liked and loved by him (man), she takes on his masculine psychology, becomes like him, at best, his "pal." In this sense, the early relationship of the daughter to her father, is responsible for whatever masculine tendencies she may develop later in life. Especially since she cannot be a woman in relation to her father, her first becoming feminine, that is, liked by a man, is only possible on a masculine pattern, a paradox which lays the foundation for later neurosis. Against the fundamental violation of her woman-self, she rebels later by becoming a woman either against her father-pattern, thereby feeling herself to be "bad," (a sexual woman), or, when she stops fighting him, by identification with a feminine woman, leading to Lesbianism, i.e. becoming "good," like him.

Man's attitude towards woman and his conception of her have undergone decisive changes since he first accepted her difference so completely that he divorced his whole life from her. From this primitive acceptance of her difference he changed to the other extreme, a complete denial of it by an acceptance of her only in terms of likeness, that is, as sister, daughter, or eventually mother. Now, after having taken over her love-psychology with the Christian Agape, he again tries to achieve another likeness in wanting her to be masculine and encouraging this tendency in her.

The woman herself, on the other hand, has changed very little in her attitude throughout the ages; although it appears that she has always managed to live up to man's expectations of her. Those adaptations, however, are rather superficial, almost like fashions through which she has succeeded in attracting the man, thus overcoming his innate resistance towards sex and his tabu of woman. In this sense, the so-called "masculinity complex" of modern psychology appears to me merely another of those "fashions" which woman puts on to please the man in answer to his demand for likeness. Lately, some psychologists have proclaimed this to be the long-sought "psychology of woman" without realizing that this very thing happens in their consulting-rooms where woman acts up to their favoured theories. Others have gone "deeper" in explaining this "assimilation" of modern woman from the biological fact of bi-sexuality. But the masculine element in woman—and correspondingly, the feminine element in man—have always existed, without having had the effect of confusing the essential difference between man and woman. Plato's simile of the two halves meeting in sexual union is as little a realization of the bi-sexual principle in nature as are the numerous bi-sexual symbols of the primitives, who do not record the observation of a biological fact but express the ideological need in their immortality-religion of assuming a self-creative power in the double-individual.

Likewise the much-quoted customs of circumcision of the woman in primitive society are no proof for Freud's overrated "masculinity complex," that is, the woman's desire to be or become a man. She has always wanted and still wants first and foremost to be a woman, because this and this alone is her fundamental self and expresses her personality, no matter what else she may do or achieve. Those strange customs seem to signify an attempt to make the woman more feminine by removing any likeness she may have with the male. It is a crude ritualistic form of making her a woman, which is normally (biologically) achieved by defloration and most of all, by love. Therein, in my opinion, lies the most essential difference in the personality makeup of the two sexes. Whereas the man develops his social self through fatherhood and his personality through work, the woman has first to be made a woman—by the man; not only physically through defloration, but also emotionally by being loved and wanted, not temporarily but once and for all, that is, possessed and dominated. On the other hand, the woman's resistance to accepting the man is a natural physical one, the fear of pain, and not, as with the man, an ideological one concerning his need for immortality which the woman satisfies through her reproductive function in and with the child. That there is also an emotional resistance to submitting her personality is a matter of course, but this obstacle is normally overcome by her willingness to submit to the man whom she can respect and who loves her.

No wonder that Freud could explain human behaviour and the history of mankind from a patriarchal point of view; the world has been sexualized by man's interpretation of it, but the real psychology is man's need for interpretation of the world in his terms, on the one hand, and woman's nature freed from this superstructure of masculinization on the other. Hence, the masculinity-complex in woman, which Freud explained as a frustrated desire to be a man, represents only one result of this masculinization, that is, sexualization of woman in terms of man. The internalization of the woman, in receiving the seminal fluid, is totally different from the masculine orgasm in ejecting it, and inasmuch as man insists on her having an experience similar to his he is simply imposing his sex on her. The primitive custom of amputating the girl's clitoris at the time of maturity seems to have the meaning of making her more feminine by removing the source of masculine sex activity.

In this sense, one might almost say that the woman has no psychology at all, just as she has no language of her own. As far as we can see now, her real psychology, not the one furnished by man, consists of just that ability to take on any masculine ideology as a cloak for her real self. This being true not only for individual relationships but likewise for whole ages, indeed, for the woman type regardless of time and place, makes her psychology *irrational*; a contradiction in terms, for her nature remains incomprehensible to the man, who only sees in her what she becomes through him, hence, is justified in explaining it in terms of his own ideology. This, however, is only possible in rational terms of a man-made psychology, the aim of which is to explain rationally human nature, which at bottom is irrational.

This craving for rationality in man cannot be understood,

however, as a mere intellectual perversity; it rather finds its roots in his will-ful striving for control, which is another form of re-creating nature in terms of a planful and purposeful God. (God is not creation from fear but from will. It means, I, man, created the world! In my image!) While in the natural course of events the individual's life from birth to death, indeed, from his conception and its procreational antecedents to his own perpetuation, is a succession of happenings, in his rationalistic interpretation of life man rises beyond the passive life-principle to a creative, indeed, self-creative plan and purpose. With the woman's life, however, as it is governed by her biological and not her rational self, everything is still happening. From menstruation and the unavoidable course conception takes, through the period of pregnancy and childbirth to her relation to the child and man even her attitude towards any given civilization, all is colored by this passive, or rather, complacent acceptance of what comes to her. She is causal, he is dynamic, irrational; hence, had to make himself rational, just as he had to make himself creative, religious and social.

Herein is epitomized woman's sexual power as against her creative power, which is to say, the woman's strength lies in her sex, the man's in his creative will. Of this power of sex, man is afraid in himself and in woman, and this fear is quite different from his fear of man, which is social and rational. His fear of sex is really fear of the irrational, which he conceives of rationally as chaos, destruction, death. Hence, he fears the power of sex, which he has to control, as if it were the natural power of "chaos," which after all represents only life itself. With the difference, that life itself is not "chaotic," just irrational; our fear interpreting it as chaotic, from a rational point of view. This explains why the creative urge, being a will-ful channeling of those irrational forces, always is accompanied in man by destructive tendencies which put the fear of God into man's creativity. In order to avoid the much-feared "chaos" man has first to create chaos himself which he can only do by destruction. Thus he achieves what one might call his own will-ful irrationality, of which, however, he is more afraid than he could possibly be if he faced the natural chaos, which is his basic irrationality.

Woman, as the eternal bearer of the irrational element in human nature, for that reason always has been and still is "tabued," which in the original sense of the word means cursed and venerated, avoided and sought, feared and loved. As to her own fear, it is unlike man's fear—not fear of the irrational chaos, which is her very life-element, but fear of loss, of separation, which is bound up with child-birth and the care of the young, but carried over into her relation to the man whom she loves by taking him in, hence, is afraid of losing. This seems to be one and perhaps the deepest reason why she is and willingly makes herself so utterly dependent upon the man whose love she needs in order to maintain herself.

By the same token, she needs the man as a rational guide through this man-made world, which is totally foreign to her, no matter what the particular form of civilization, so long as it is a masculine one. She must feel in it not unlike Alice in Wonderland, strange and bewildered; for it is a world in the creation of which she did not partake and which she cannot possibly understand or live in without being protected by the male. Just as they speak two different languages, so the two sexes live in two different worlds linked like the motherland with her colonies by ties strong enough to keep the necessary cooperation between two independent entities, separated by yet uncharted seas. But just as she needs to be protected by him in this man-made civilization, so man needs to be protected by her from his own creation. In this sense, man has to operate like an increasingly perfected tool constantly adjusted and readjusted to the change of order brought about by himself, while woman, representing continuity underneath all the superficial, forced to keep pace with this unnatural movement, either becomes masculinized or, if she maintains her irrational self, stands out as a failure.

Man's psychology, that is to say, is constantly adapted to the changes brought about by his man-made civilization; hence, is better fit to cope directly with his environmental reality than woman, who merely follows in the wake of masculine civilization. His psychology is rational, while woman's psychology is irrational, and the child's psychology is still more irrational, that is, magical.

Whereas man develops his psychology to protect himself by control (will) woman takes on his psychology from an opposite motive, that is, to lose herself, to give herself to him. In this, the purely masculine ideology of his psychology is blocking her, just as much—although in a different way—as it does him in the living. From this results neurosis precipitated in woman by the blocking of her irrational self; in man, through expansion of the will-ful control blocking the natural life-force. Hence, the woman is much more extreme in her attitudes and reactions because she can only go the whole way: either totally accept herself as woman or completely resist it with a will-ful drive adopted from masculine psychology. Man, on the other hand, is much more partial in his reactions, being emotionally more individualistic. For woman is not only more irrational, but, by the same token, more collective by nature than man, who always remains a lone wolf and has to make himself social by law. Hence, his fears are social whereas woman's fears are biological; while man's only biological fear is the fear of sex, manifested as fear of woman, who in her turn is not afraid of sex but of man.

Here again we find this chapter of sexual psychology as full of paradoxes as any other area of human life. Man's biological function being incidental and temporal leads to his making his personality the absolute, eternal immortality-symbol; woman, on the contrary, finds her immortality in sexual procreation. In this sense, man's whole personality is built up ideologically, that is, is more abstract, while woman's personality, based as it is on a sound biological foundation, is quite concrete. Even man's conception of power, realistic as it seems, is an abstraction, i.e. his idea of controlled power, and not, as in the woman, a controlling power.

This fundamental biological difference of the male's wastefulness as against the female's preservation manifests itself in the whole range of their different attitudes towards life and towards man-made civilization. The question whether woman is fundamentally more giving than man can only be answered satisfactorily by our considering the dynamic principle operating, not only in the individual but equally in types and group-relationships. Just because she is so utterly conserving by nature woman appears to be so obviously giving. Her biological conservatism seems to account for her willingness to accept so readily the existing order of things, for prompted by her procreative instinct she has to preserve, no matter what. Man's behaviour, on the other hand, is dictated by his more selfish need for the preservation of his own ego, which lacks the continuity of woman's biological self. Hence, man is never satisfied with the existing order, which after all is his own creation, and has to keep changing it. True, in man's making of history woman always has been and still is instrumental, as borne out by the age-old slogan, "cherchez la femme." But I suspect that she has been permitted this rôle only because she so conveniently supplies the irrational element denied by man in the making and even more in the writing of history. Through her active participation in modern revolutionary movements, however, she grasps an opportunity to rebel with her irrational nature against this man-made civilization, though under the guidance and protection of man, who, however, is soon compelled to replace the revolutionary chaos of irrationality once more by the paradoxical Goddess of Reason.

Here again we find operating one of those many paradoxes inherent in human nature and defying all rational explanations of psychology. While woman is essentially conserving and preserving, and man's biological self expresses nature's wastefulness, man had to learn to be economic, hence, invented for himself his own economic principles primarily to check his natural wastefulness. The basic economic principle in nature is connected with procreation and aims at providing, if necessary, hoarding food supplies for the maintenance of the offspring. This natural law I see symbolized in the sequel to the Biblical story of the Fall, where man, after having accepted sex and with it procreation and death, is forced to provide and plan for food. Such provision, actually rooted in the maternal instinct of the female, has been taken over by man in his agricultural development, originally based, as we have shown, on his belief in his creative magic. Factually, anthropological research has furnished us with the information that in pre-historic times the woman attended to the work in the field (with a hack before the plough was invented), while man was hunting for meat or fighting for an easy spoil. Hence, to this day, man goes out to provide for a living, while the woman still feeds him, as she did not only in pre-historic times but still—with her own blood and milk in his early days of existence.

This different attitude towards food in man and woman—the one being potentially the eater, the other the cook—again points to a more giving nature in woman and a more taking desire in man. Although hunger, as the basic instinct for the preservation of the individual, has to be satisfied in man and woman alike, there are different ways of achieving it, depending on a fundamental difference in the attitude towards life. Again, the man being more greedy, that is, individualistic, in his satisfaction of hunger took over the task of providing food for his family as a personal responsibility, thus counteracting his economic selfishness. The woman, on the other hand, with her natural hoarding instinct, is not economic in the masculine sense of the word, as borne out by the criticism constantly brought against her, that she spends foolishly, that is, is not economical in the sense of the rational planning practised by man.

Here we are faced once more with a fundamental misunderstanding of language, based on a masculine interpretation of an essentially feminine quality. While woman is economic by nature, man has developed into an "economic type" to counteract his very nature, which is wasteful. No wonder, then, that in our present social crisis "economy" becomes wasteful and waste economical.[1] Such confusion results from having mixed up natural economics with man-made money economics, but this is basically a problem springing from the different attitude of the two sexes towards life. Once more in the course of history a great number of people are faced with the fear of starvation in the midst of plenty, that is, with the fear of extinction despite nature's wastefulness. Afraid of "waste," which is an essential part of life, we reject it as irrational only to have to become wasteful ourselves by dumping nature's product. This is done, presumably, to keep prices up; in reality, it only proves that it is impossible to control life by planning. The war-scare is another excuse to hoard, although more planfully, for approaching times of threatening destruction. In this connection, it is interesting to remember the old belief that as the aftermath of great wars there appears a compensatory increase, not only in the population but also in crops and breeds of domesticated animals.

[1] Hopkins, Henry. *Spending to Save,* N. Y., Norton, 1936.

Driven by his fear of extinction, man precipitates war against his fellowmen with the admitted or tacit slogan of nationalism—the conception that only one people has the right and the room to survive. In this sense, our modern wars, despite their ideological slogans, are not so much inspired by the need for imperialistic expansion as by the decadent fear of extinction. This fear I call decadent because notwithstanding all theories of fear in primitive man—it is self-created by man, who becomes afraid of his own power-ideology, which he has set up against the forces of nature in himself. Thus, the power of sex, feared by man above all, has been will-fully transformed by his population-policies into man-power, and this man-power, through commerce and labor-ideology finally becomes money-power. Just as industry, by means of economic theories, becomes an expression of this money-power, so modern wars—at least, since the time of Napoleon, the first modern dictator—have been fought to break the money-power through man-power, with the hope of restoring the dignity of the human individual. Similarly, classes and individuals are rebelling against this money-power with their man-power, as borne out by the labor warfare of strikes and definite transgressions of man-made law by rugged individualists who are marked as criminals when they attempt their rebellion single-handed.

On the other hand, the natural expression of man-power in work is basically not aimed at profit but at making a living, that is, the ability to survive, whereas the accumulation of profits, known as capitalism, is an outgrowth of the desire for lasting survival expressed in terms of a lasting fortune, which is still controlled by the "will" after death. Not only individuals successful in this enterprise have to learn that "you can't take it with you," but whole nations and empires perish through that ideology of money accumulation. The first financial collapse of that sort in the history of mankind was caused by capitalistic tendencies in the Roman Empire, a capitalism signifying the transition from the hoarding of foodstuffs to the hoarding of money with which to purchase it. England, though on her different industrial basis of productive capitalism, seems to be headed for a similar disaster, because she depends for her food supplies on foreign importation.

Since Marx, who anticipated the then-dormant dangers inherent in the capitalistic system, the world has embarked on another economic system, based on labor as well as on capital. And right now, particularly since the World War, our economics are changing again to the considering of the problem of unemployment as most important in our economic planning. The problem of unemployment, threatening the collapse of the world-wide economic system of international trade, has brought once more to our attention not only the financial but the moral and emotional value of labor and work for the individual. From time immemorial there has existed a natural division of individuals in their social function which contributed to, if it did not make up, the personality. The king, the priest, the magician, among the primitives, are outstanding examples of those types, representing as it were in their whole personality their social function. More complicated specializations in civilized societies have created more definite types of differentiation according to their profession: warriors, farmers, civil officers and so forth.

In mediaeval times, we find the different handicrafts and workmen organized in guilds, not so much for the purpose of profit gain as for the recognition of their personality-types as an accepted group by the community. A carpenter, a blacksmith, a baker or butcher represented a definite type of personality above and beyond their civic functions as members of a community, which in itself received its distinction in one way or another from other communities.

Thus, work became just as much a vital factor in the building up and maintaining of one's personality as did any religious, political or individual ideology. In this sense, man works primarily for his own self-respect and not for others or for profit. A disinclination or resistance to work indicates some fundamental lack in the personality, as is borne out by neurotic cases who not only feel unable to work but also unworthy of taking any money if they do work. This is not due to a feeling of inferiority, but usually only camouflages the deeper resistance to accepting the self, as a definite personality that is afraid to give in return lest it lose its autonomy. For the person who is working for the sake of his own satisfaction, the money he gets in return serves merely as fuel, that is, as a symbol of reward and recognition, in the last analysis, of acceptance by one's fellowmen.

In this taking to give something in return is epitomized a deeper biological process of emotional digestion, which in its satisfying effects contrasts sharply with the egocentric accumulation of one type of man and the destructive spending of the self in another. This digestive process of give and take is as necessary for the productive functioning of any given civilization as it is for the well-being and functioning of the individual in personal and social relationship. In relationship between the two sexes it manifests itself again paradoxically, in that the woman biologically taking in is emotionally giving, while the man basically spending has to take in. Since the woman is likely to develop a sense of guilt if she is too much the taking type and the man if he is too much spending, their mutual problem can only be solved by cooperation and complementary support.

Yet this process of emotional digestion is a constant one, since the integration of the self in either of the two sexes cannot be achieved once and for all, but is a continuous experience in which the will to control one's own self is just as strong as the desire to check the other. The individual who blocks one of those complementary functions in himself at the expense of the other never gains thereby but is always the loser. Keeping what he has, instead of letting the natural process of exchange take its course, does not make the personality stronger but rather fearful lest he lose it; and spending recklessly what he has makes the individual panicky for fear of destruction. Thus it usually happens that woman, whose natural strength lies in her sex, that is, the woman-self, puts it in her personality, whereas man, whose strength lies in his personality, has to confirm and assert it in sex.

Thus, modern woman's essential conflict is between her natural feminine self and her personality as manifested in her professional self, necessarily, though, in terms of masculine ideology. Although practically precipitated by the World War, the professional woman of our day suffers much less from the present economic crisis than from the age-old conflict between her genuine psychology and the masculine ideology imposed upon and taken on by her. This, borne out from the study of numerous neurotic cases, is proposed as a general explanation by such a distinguished writer as Virginia Woolf, who, in her recent book, *Three Guineas*, frankly admits that it was first and foremost the wish to escape from male domination that drove the "educated man's daughter" into professions opened to them by war-time necessity.

What Mrs. Woolf does not show, or know and say, however, is the other side of the picture, namely, that woman gladly had taken on this male domination on which she built up her own psychology, either to fit into man's ideology or in more recent times to take it over on to herself. That fact, however, does not invalidate her argument concerning the revolting woman, for rebellion is the more violent the more it is directed, not only against domination from without, but against one's own inner weakness in submitting willingly to it. This gradual liberation of woman from her own submissive will—the will not to will—was made possible by her adoption of the masculine ideology of willing. It started not more than about a century ago with Mary Wollstonecraft's *Vindication of the Rights of Woman* (1792). Interestingly enough, her declaration of independence was not so much the outgrowth of the crushing spirit of Puritanical commerce which practically ostracized the unmarried woman without means, as it was a personal reaction against a new domineering masculine ideology, that of Rousseau. This parlor-revolutionary "thinker," who had declared that a woman should never for a moment feel herself independent, remained himself all his life in utter dependence upon a woman, an obvious "mother-fixation" which later changed into a life-long masochistic relationship. It is again one of those paradoxes of human nature, precipitating world-historical events, that his political philosophy of independence, which inspired the French Revolution, should emerge from a man whose ideological rebellion sprang not from masculine strength but as a reaction against his feminine dependence.

Be that as it may, the boom of commerce in Puritanical England made of the virtuous woman another negotiable "good," while condemning the unmarried "spinster" as a social evil. In sharp contrast to such economic valuation of woman, Mary Wollstonecraft propounds a theory of the "leisure class" that seems quite modern in its classification of idle women with the idle rich, thus putting the unmarried woman and the bachelor type in one and the same class. Only a little more than one hundred years later, after the World War, the "rights of women" went into reverse. Women began to go "clinging vine." Having obtained nearly all the rights they had clamored for since the days of Mary Wollstonecraft, they began to look back with nostalgia to the age of privilege. And actually, at the present time, there is ample evidence of the continuation of the tendency.

Will people ever learn from such paradoxical developments that there is no other equality possible than the equal right of every individual to become and to be himself, which actually means to accept his own difference and have it accepted by others? The woman of today, however, finds herself in a difficult position. Man *likes* her ever so much like himself (being "like" means being "liked"), indeed, needs for his ego-support the likeness of the masculinized type, while his masculine self wants her to be a full-fledged woman, not only physically but also in her emotional submission and financial dependence.

As for herself, the woman is attracted to various professions not only by a desire for financial independence from an individual man (not men), but even more by the prospect of self-expression in work and social success resulting from it. But her very nature rebels not infrequently in unmistakable terms against any violation of her woman-self, resulting necessarily from the fact that her professional development in our civilization is only possible along the lines of masculine ideology. We do not need to refer to the well-known type of modern woman who, in spite of free love and all the sex she wants, remains dissatisfied and unhappy, in order to be convinced that it is much more than the physical side of the woman-self rebelling against frustration; it is the emotional and spiritual side craving for expression of the true woman-self in a masculine world which has no room or use for her. This deplorable state of affairs applies not only to the unmarried professional woman but likewise to the unhappily married woman with or without children—in other words, has become a universal problem of womankind.

Misinterpreted in terms of masculine ideology and herself caught in that very predicament, the woman can only express her personality—professionally or otherwise—in the thwarted form of neurotic symptoms which, though easily explained, cannot be "cured" by the further interpretation of a masculine psychology. All that is left to this modern type of woman is to act one rôle or the other as well as she can. She either acts the perfect woman which the man wants her to be, or, for the same reason or for her own sake, she is forced to act the independent masculine type. In neither case, is she her own self. Not infrequently this acting of a certain rôle becomes second nature and may be fairly successful, until such time as the unavoidable "breakdown" is due. In other cases, the woman-self takes refuge in lying and deception, which, however, actually may reveal her true self. This lying is really an attempt not only to be what the man wants but to find for herself a place in this man-made world which is actually foreign to her but in which she is only able to operate in the disguise of a rational being by borrowing man's psychology. In doing this, she does tell his "rational" truth, by means of her own irrational one.

At any rate, her desire to be wanted by the man to whom she wants to submit is the strongest factor in the building-up of the woman's personality, and in that sense she is made a woman through her mate, not merely physically but also characteriologically. Yet this individual development of the woman-love in relation to the man was made possible first by the Christian love-ideology, which actually formulated and thus made universally acceptable the woman-emotion of being wanted. At various times there have been different ideas, ideals and theologies influencing and often determining the personality build-up of the woman. Yet they have all one thing in common: they are man-made, hence, all aim at an assimilation to man's liking. In the woman, on the other hand, they all spring from one and the same source, namely, from the desire and need to be wanted, that is, loved. Needless to repeat, this kind of love is originally a moral conception, which only gradually, in our Western civilization, became associated with sex. It operates as a matter of course likewise in all educational and authoritative relationships, such as those between parents and child, teacher and pupil, between friends, and last but not least, in the mate-relationship of the two sexes.

Whatever the personal ideal, or the prevalent ideology may be, in the last analysis this striving for a personality is always determined by the desire to be good in the opinion of the other or the community. Here the urge for perfection of the self harmonizes with the need for completion in the other. While the ideal of perfect womanhood is to be wanted (loved), man is supposed to build his personality on the desire to want (will). His need to be wanted—for the support and justification of the Self—usually finds expression and satisfaction in worldly success, whereas the woman's positive will is converted into her desire to be wanted by the one whom she loves for it. The woman, particularly, whose whole being is centred in the surrendering emotion of the Agape depends so much more than the man on the complementary fulfilment through the man. Inasmuch as this is lacking, her need to be loved is distorted and thwarted in various ways which have been described psychologically in terms of neurosis. Wide and deepened experience in the field of psychotherapy has convinced me that the ultimate "cause" of most feminine neurosis is modern man, with his lack of masculine qualities and his inability to want his woman lovingly, instead of will-fully. In such a case, the woman may either become her own narcissistic admirer, who, herself will-ful, will only yield to the strong man whom she can respect and admire, or she will develop the opposite type of character who submits sexually to the male without surrendering her whole self to her loving nature. This type, termed in modern psychology, "masochistic," does not represent an exaggeration of her natural passivity but rather the frustrated expression of her need to surrender, applied in a masculine fashion to herself. This predicament of having to play forcibly the rôle of the dominating male to herself is borne out by the observation that most of those "masochistic" types, paradoxically enough, show definite "masculine" character traits. Their "masochism" is explained, not infrequently by themselves, either as a desire to please a sadistic man, if such be the case, or more generally as a means or at least a symbol of being molded and changed by the male. In spite of appearance, such self-willed submission to her own self has nothing of a sacrificial nature. If she is not wanted, that is, loved, she at least wants to be used or even abused, as long as the man needs that. Such pseudo-sacrificial attitude is nothing but a perverted expression of her biological self which, in any case, is to be used, that is, destroyed by nature through her procreative function.

Psychology Beyond the Self

OUR psychological age, inaugurated by Nietzsche and brought to a close by Freud, can be best understood in its cultural significance if we apply the viewpoints and methods of both these men simultaneously to the comprehension of its development. Especially will this be so if we apply Nietzsche's "Kulturpsycologie" as it emerged from the Franco-Prussian War, enriched by our analytical insight, to an understanding of the puzzling quarrels of the different schools of psychology. The very fact that psychoanalysis itself, in the midst of its individualistic enthusiasm, was suddenly confronted with the social and cultural problems precipitated by the World War justifies an examination into its background and its spiritual significance for our age. The torrential onrush of all those irrational forces on the fragile structure of Freud's highly speculative system was reflected in his first recognition of the problem of death (in an article little known and quite neglected by himself), and more so in his pessimistic treatise on *The Discontent of Civilization.*[1] This latter may well signify the logical conclusion of his life-work, for in it he finally admitted how important is the rôle aggression plays in human behavior; a conclusion Alfred Adler had arrived at, twenty years before, when he based his Individual Psychology on the aggressive urge and its manifestation in the will-to-power. Nietzsche already had declared the will-to-power to be the driving force of human behavior. But while Nietzsche's

[1] Civilization and Its Discontents. N. Y., 1930. Jonathan Cape & Harrison Smith.

philosophy affirmed this essential factor in human psychology positively, Freud, condemning it, drew the pessimistic conclusion that the whole of society is sick, or, more generally stated, that civilization seems to amount to a neurotic symptom on a grand scale.

We do not know to what extent Freud was aware of the significance of his statement that he had the whole of humanity as his neurotic patient. It implied, in the first place, an admission of futility with respect to individual psychotherapy, which, as a matter of fact, plays very little rôle in his later writings, and in which, in any case, he never had much confidence (he spoke of it as the white-washing of a negro) ; secondly, it betrayed—at least to the seeing eye—his messianic complex, for the illness of whole civilizations, formerly the domain of other therapeutic ideologies put forward by religious or secular leaders, could never be taken care of in a consultation room. As a matter of fact, Freud's psychological system, which was supposed to be the result of scientific empiricism, has been received and taken up as an ideology fought for and against with a zeal only comparable to that shown in religious wars. Just as he himself could so easily confess his agnosticism while he had created for himself a private religion, it seems that, even in his intellectual and rational achievements, he still had to express and assert his irrational needs by at least fighting for and about his rational ideas. In the third place, it should be added, Freud condemned all civilization, not on the ground of human unhappiness—which after all is man's lot on earth—but for its failure to follow his system of thought and reform. Be that as it may, not until the end of his therapeutic career did Freud permit himself to join his great predecessors in the philosophic appreciation of human psychology; that is, besides Schopenhauer, the two great diagnosticians of modern man's ills, Nietzsche and Ibsen. While Nietzsche, out of his creative suffering, projected his ideal of the superman as a means of cure, his contemporary Ibsen, with analytical precision, showed that with his heritage modern man is bound to fail through his guilt, which seems inseparably attached to any positive assertion of the will.

It is with his therapeutic attempt to remove the guilt by tracing it back "causally" to the individual's experience in childhood that Freud steps in. How presumptuous, and at the same time, naive, is this idea of simply removing human guilt by explaining it causally as "neurotic"! Such approach to the individual who seems inhibited by excessive guilt was not only a "therapeutic," but also an ideological one; he worked not only with the objective of helping the suffering individual but at the same time on the tacit basis of a reformer, assuming that civilization as he found it in his environment was on the whole right and that the individual who seems to be in the wrong has to learn to adjust to it. Brought up in the scientific ideology of the last century, Freud used an approach meant to explain human behavior reductively, that is, from the most primitive biological plan which science has revealed as the basis of all life. But the history of mankind shows that human life is characterized by a denial of that very foundation, as exemplified by the primitive's belief in spiritual immortality as against sexual mortality. Nietzsche, by approaching human problems culturally, saw more clearly for he recognized the moral conflict, both in the individual and in groups and nations, as the problem of problems. In this sense, Nietzsche appears as the first and only thinker who realized this problem and tried to liberate human psychology from its involvement with moral issues, which are foreign to it and only cloud the picture.

In blaming "Jewish-Christian morality," which, with his anti-Semitic master Schopenhauer, he throws into one and the same pot, Nietzsche overlooked the deep need in the human being for just that kind of morality; hence, his bizarre picture of the amoral superman, an anti-Christ only conceivable for a megalomaniac who considers himself a seer. Yet it cannot be accidental that the two systems which definitely aim at reforming the individual and society, those of Marx and Freud, should have been propagated by Jews. Marx, by denying his Jewish heritage, could project it onto the under-privileged class of the proletariat; Freud, by affirming Judaism, seems to have identified his suffering people with the inhibited and frustrated group of neurotics. Unfortunately, most patients whom he saw seemed to suffer from the conflict with that very morality which he held up to them as necessary for their adjustment. His moral code, moreover, as he translated it into psychological theory, put the emphasis on the Decalogue rather than on Christian ethics, which he quite naively derided in his *The Future of an Illusion*,[1] a book, in my opinion, betraying his unconscious doubt concerning the future of psychoanalysis as a modern religion, taken up temporarily by under-privileged neurotics.

In accordance with the primitive moral code of the Decalogue, Freud put the emphasis on external restrictions and deprivations for the guidance of individual behavior, that is to say, on punishment and reward, rather than on the inner voice of the individual's conscience as indicated in the Christian religion and elaborated in Kant's Protestant ethics. Such internal regulation of human behavior, as against the Freudian position, I emphasized in my first book,[2] where I assumed a self-inhibiting impulse inherent in the individual which creates protective limitations against the irrational self. The Decalogue itself, with its commands and threats, is but one of the evidences for such a conception, which thereby appears attributed to God, that is, is

[1] Horace Liveright and the Institute of Psycho-Analysis, N. Y., 1928.
[2] *Der Kunstler*, 1907.

inherent in human nature. This ethical aspect was later emphasized by Jung, of Zurich, the son of a minister, who, through his support, was instrumental in making the psychoanalytic movement internationally known and recognized. While Jung himself saw in the irrational unconscious chiefly the thread of the demonic as expressed in mythological symbolism, Freud, after having tried to rationalize the irrational, at least to his own satisfaction, attempted rather late some kind of internalization of it in his conception of the super-ego. But, like all later elaborations of his original materialistic concepts, this one, too, represents a compromise rather than a solution, in that the individual's conscience is again derived from external prohibition, especially that of the father whom Freud elevates into a figure of god-like power.

The overwhelming importance of the father, likewise a characteristic of Jewish tradition and mentality, represents the rational aspect of Freudian psychology, whereas the vital relationship to the mother is conceived of as merely an "infantile" fixation. Thus Freud could see in the Greek Oedipus-saga an exemplification of the fourth commandment of the Decalogue, and completely neglect its real significance as an enactment of man's heroic struggle against his human fate. Far from trying to enforce the fourth commandment, as Freud would have it, the Greek tragedy of King Oedipus is meant to teach a lesson to the presumptuous intellectualism of the first Western thinkers who sought to solve the riddle of human existence by philosophic speculation. The wise Oedipus, the clever solver of riddles, typifies the sophisticated intelligentsia of later Greece in their futile attempt at rationalizing the irrational, symbolized in the blind yet meaningful forces of fate, which in the end leave man as blind as his fate.

Nietzsche, in interpreting Oedipus' incest and parricide as manifestations of the superman's swerving from the course of nature by transgressing her laws, expresses the deeper experiential truth that "he who by his wisdom hurls nature into the abyss of annihilation, has also experienced in himself the dissolution of nature." This is the meaning of the old traditional wisdom that he who sees the truth must die, because the truth is not only a rational comprehension or interpretation of life but includes—must include if it be truth—its irrational forces, which are destroying the very instrument of the truth-seeker. It is at this point that the whole psycho-analytic movement appears in a deeper sense as a direct attack of man's over-rated intellectual self upon the irrational, an attempt which through man's fear of it was diverted into a rational explanation and a mechanistic conception of it. Only from such a self-inhibitory diversion of one extreme into the other is it intelligible that psychoanalysis could be claimed, on the one hand (for example, by Thomas Mann) as a romantic movement, while philosophically inclined vitalists in Germany criticized its over-rationalized mechanization. This simultaneous representation of the rational and irrational elements is one of the paradoxes inherent in psychoanalysis and makes intelligible the two reactions within the Freudian school, the theories of Jung and Adler, as exaggerations of its two aspects, the rational and irrational, which in the very beginning separated Freud from his master, Breuer.

Dr. Breuer, a practising physician in Vienna, many years Freud's senior, had experimented on hysterical patients with a psycho-therapeutic method based on hypnotic sleep. While Freud pursued those experiments and also investigated the phenomenon of hypnotic suggestion at Bernheim's clinic in Nancy, Breuer had an experience with one of his women patients which once and for all scared him off from the threatening forces of the irrational self as manifested in the therapeutic situation. This patient had seemingly fallen in love with Breuer and imagined having a child by him—a phantasy which Breuer treated as a pathological hallucination. Freud, in his cases, succeeded in explaining similar "irrational" manifestations as a repetition of past phantasies, particularly as experienced in childhood, thereby making them not only intelligible but acceptable to the patient as well as to himself. Whether or not this explanation in terms of "transference" was actually effective in individual cases is in this connection not so important as are the psychological and ideological conclusions which Freud derived from his interpretation.

First among these is the logical deduction that the bringing into consciousness of the unconscious must be the therapeutic agent; an assumption based on two presuppositions: one, that he did actually bring the unconscious into consciousness and not his interpretation of it which may have had no correlate in the patient; the other, that the emotional factor which he dismissed as "transference" was not itself the therapeutic agent or at least instrumental in effecting the change. It is easy to see, at any rate, how the fear of the unconscious, that is, of the life-force itself, from which we all seem to recoil, leads to an over-estimation of the rational mind, i.e. some kind of understanding which would calm the fear. What operates therapeutically is the promise and hope of some kind of intellectual control over the irrational forces; but to evaluate the intellectual interpretation itself as the therapeutic factor leads to the building up of a theory of psychology which is at best therapeutic, that is, consoling, but certainly not scientific, and least of all, constructive.

The therapeutic use of Freud's rational ideology may be justifiable, inasmuch as it helps the patient, but becomes destructive as a general philosophy of life into which it has developed. It is another paradox that Freud had to defend his therapy when he was accused of leading the individual to an uninhibited expression of his impulses. Although his psychology has been used to justify such behavior as "therapeutic," he himself was more right than he knew in denying any such purpose. For his psychology is born of the spirit of inhibited and inhibiting negation of life and as such does not lead to life. That it could nevertheless be interpreted that way finds its deeper explanation in a misunderstanding on the part of Freud himself. The patient's impulse-life manifesting itself verbally in the analytic situation was taken by Freud at its face value, that is, as a real desire for living on the patient's part, though it was only possible as a gesture in the artificially limited and inhibited relationship with the therapist. To put it bluntly, in one sentence which shakes the foundation of the whole Freudian system and of psychology in general, for that matter: Freud, without knowing it, interpreted the analytical situation in terms of his world-view and did not, as he thought, analyze the individual's unconscious objectively. Since he did not know the first and could not achieve the second, he really achieved neither of the two. His real achievement lies in the establishment of the analytical situation, an artificial relationship in which we can find epitomized the paradoxical workings of all the irrational forces in human nature, provided we do not insist on interpreting it in terms of a preconceived psychology as purely rational. As it is, Freud's causal interpretation of the analytic situation as repetition (chiefly in recollection) of the past—instead of an emphasis on it as a new experience in the present—amounts to a denial of all personal autonomy in favor of the strictest possible determinism, that is to say, to a negation of life itself. Such a detached attitude may be justified in the realm of pure science, that is, of theoretical psychology, but is certainly contrary to all therapeutic endeavors, which ought to aim towards life itself.

Here is shown the most fundamental, and at the same time, disastrous paradox of psychonalysis, which I pointed out, in 1922,[1] as the methodological confusion between theory and therapy and which I elaborated philosophically in terms of the distinction between *Truth and Reality*,[2] in 1930. The rationalistic slogan of Socrates that virtue can be taught and that self-knowledge is healing appears revived in Freud's therapeutic conviction that truth in and by itself is curative; one of those principles the opposite of which is just as true, is borne out by Ibsen's evaluation of what he calls the individual's life-lie. It is the climax of irony that the Greek Oedipus-saga, on the interpretation of which Freud based the justification of his truth-therapy, explains the tragic failure of the hero from just this same intellectual curiosity about the truth. Not unlike Ibsen's heroes, Oedipus, too, perishes as soon as he knows the truth about himself, revealed by the historical self-analysis of his past in true Freudian fashion.

But at least in his case this understanding follows real living, since the Greeks were still wise enough to let the hero first enjoy the happiness of his life-lie before the Gods destroy it at the end of his life through the truth. But just as much as the hero, so the frustrated neurotic of our day, wants to live, i.e. not merely to understand but also to express, his irrational self; whereas the rational type of the therapist, because he is fearful of life, can only understand. Thus, the analytic situation, representing essentially a human, and not a medical problem, was converted by Freud from an experience of deliverance, which the neurotic seeks from his ego and egocentricity, into a psychological comprehension of this ego by way of introspection. Historically, we can still follow the path along which this bending of the irrational self to the demands of the rational ego took place. From the beginning Freud's rational therapy of analysis had its roots in the hypnotic experiments of the

[1] *Development of Psychoanalysis* (with Ferezczi), N. Y., 1925.
[2] *Truth and Reality,* Alfred Knopf, N. Y., 1936.

French psychiatrists at the turn of the century; hence, its background, not only its material, is that mystical sphere of emotionalism which Freud tried to rationalize with his "unconscious thinking" without really explaining it thereby.

In this deeper sense, there really is no psychology of the neurotic as against normal psychology, but only a psychology of difference, that is to say, the neurotic's psychology is only pathological from the rational point of view prevalent in a given civilization. This difference in psychology is essentially a difference between experience and understanding, that is, between the acting and the thinking type, or between spontaneous living and intellectual control of it through will. Such a contrast of types seems to be historically epitomized in the psychology of the Jews as it developed from their totally different experience in their early history. Originally a number of nomadic tribes strongly united in their fight for existence, the Jewish type, as we know him, developed his typical characteristics in Babylonian exile. There a justification had to be found for the suffering of the race if they were to endure and survive it. The only way to achieve that was to accept for the time being their slavery as fate which God had meted out to them to test their strength in the faith, that is, in themselves. Hence, we have the conception of a collective guilt unique with the Jews, and by the same token their ideology of the people chosen by God for a special destiny which would materialize in an indefinite future. Thus the Jews became the first historians in the philosophic sense of the word, going beyond the mere recording of events to an interpretation of their experience from a supernatural point of view. That is to say, everything which happened to them had to have a deeper meaning predestined by Providence. From the unhappy experience imposed on them by fate they construed a conscious and planful making of history, which explains their zeal for reform. It was only in our days that Nietzsche, the admitted anti-Christ and the tacit anti-Jew, in one of his grandiose syntheses, challenged this attitude with the rhetorical question as to whether it is possible to make history consciously and purposefully, in a word, rationally.

Not only did the Jews in exile take on willingly what Nietzsche calls the "slave-morality" but they became, by the same token, the cultural slaves of the Egyptians. James Henry Breasted, the well-known archeologist, proved, beyond doubt, the case of the Jews as the parasites of Egyptian culture.[1] This living on borrowed culture is a typical phenomenon in the history of civilization; as a rule the victors take on the civilization of their victims, the conquered. From the numerous examples of that strange process we mention only the northern conquerors of the Greek peninsula in prehistoric times of the Ionic migration, and in our day the Germans who, to every seeing eye, propound the Jewish ideology of the chosen people. Strange as it is, this assimilation and spiritual utilization of a foreign civilization corresponds exactly to the assimilation of a foreign ideology by the average type and has its sequel in what we term vicarious living in personal relationship. The meaning of it seems to be a protection of one's own ego—or nation as the sum of egos—from direct living and spending of the self. Naturally, this trick is bound to fail, not merely because nature cannot be cheated, but because such an attempt is destructive, for in itself it denies the very essence of living. It has succeeded only with the Jew, who has survived all other nations and civilizations just by living permanently on borrowed cultures but not, like the victorious nations, making it his own. They perish through the guilt of conquest, plus the guilt of assuming the culture of the conquered. Thus the Jew, while externally accepting the foreign civilization he lives in and with and

[1] *The Dawn of Conscience,* Charles Scribner's Sons, N. Y., 1933.

by, lives on his real self, whereas the conquerors of other civilizations actually live on borrowed cultures—something which inevitably ends sooner or later in national bankruptcy.

From this symbolic life of the Jew in civilizations contrary to his personality makeup and foreign to his mentality, there follows, in spite of all the emphasis on difference as manifested in anti-Semitism, a mutual assimilation of characteristics fatal to both parties and above all to the general psychology emerging from this state of affairs—however much the fusion must be recognized as a necessary and unavoidable process. It seems to me that inasmuch as the Jew really takes on—not merely superficially assimilates—characteristics of his host he becomes, or at least appears, "neurotic" because they do not fit him; whereas likewise his host, inasmuch as he takes on characteristics of the Jew—because they seem to be useful—becomes neurotic on his part through an assimilation of foreign trends. We saw and learned to understand that same process working in the relationship between two individuals where the taking on too much of the characteristics of the other leads to confusion manifested in neurotic behavior. In the case of the Jew, however, this becomes a universal problem of mankind typical for any kind of minority differing sufficiently from the majority around it. Inasmuch as congenital or ideological difference is felt as inferiority, it may happen between members of one and the same race or civilization, or between members of different civilizations, regardless of whether one party is Jewish or not.

Thus Jewish influence in the world of ideas—like morality and psychology—become intelligible from the same contrast of character-type which explains anti-Semitism. The inhibiting force of human conscience springing from creative guilt, which manifests itself in modern times as moral illness as diagnosed by Nietzsche and Ibsen, was imposed on the Jews from without by their masters and accepted by them in their prohibitive moral code. Thus their negative and collective guilt results from a deprivation of life expressed in terms of fear of punishment and not, as with the genuine creator of culture, as a result of creative presumption. Hence, Freud's explanation of the sense of guilt, although true for the one type of inhibited living, is not true for the opposite type of creative living. For him, Freud's explanation may operate therapeutically but is not true to his psychology, which is the opposite. Yet Freud's ideology was accepted by the culturally creative type of our times, because for him the psychoanalytic ideology serves as a consolation for his creative conscience which is explained in terms of external intimidation, whereas in reality it springs from internal presumption.

In a word, degenerate man of Western civilization accepted the psychoanalytic ideology which was foreign to his genuine psychology as a convenient justification for his exhausted instincts inhibited by guilt; just as once before a desperate humanity had accepted Jewish morality in Christianity, as an ideology of deliverance. An important difference, though, is that Christianity signified a new interpretation, a revitalization of an outlived ideology in terms of the needs of the present; whereas psychoanalysis merely offers a consolation and justification of the existent type of man. We come here upon perhaps the strangest paradox of cultural symbiose, a state of affairs in which one type of people accepts the genuine psychology of another type—diametrically different from it—as a therapeutic ideology, and this therapeutic ideology is then proclaimed to be the general psychology of both types, indeed, of mankind, regardless of time and place.

From this it follows, as I have said, that Freud's whole doctrine of neurosis can be understood as a projection of the Jew's position in our present-day civilization; just as

Marx projected the fate of the suppressed Jew—from which he liberated himself—onto the under-privileged proletariat, the "slaves" of the capitalistic state. According to this conception, Freud could see in civilization only the suffering of the individual and not his positive assertion in creative achievement. Hence, he only knows the guilt resulting from frustration as the "cause" of human suffering which could be "therapeutically" alleviated by lessening external restrictions. But since the Jew's deprivation from participation in creative living was imposed from without and accepted by him as his psychology, it is not "neurotic" with him but the creative type of man (or nation), who himself erects these inner limitations in his own moral conscience, is bound to become neurotic in the course of this process. On the other hand, the Jew, while he assimilates this inner check from the creative type among whom he lives, may also become neurotic inasmuch as their ideology is foreign to him.

This discussion of the historic rôle of the Jew as the eternal carrier of the most ancient civilization, namely, the Babylonian, throughout the centuries does not imply any evaluation one way or another of his present or future fate in our world of discords. This much might be said, however: it does not seem to me a good omen that the Jew is forced through the new wave of persecution to create his own genuine civilization in his "promised land," which obviously is helpful only as long as it is promised and not realized. Fortunately for the survival of the Jew, his original desire to become like other people, that is, to have a land of his own with a state and a king, has been frustrated, for with the realization of it he is bound also to perish, as have all other civilizations for just that reason. One reason for his eternal persecution is to be found in that very privilege of a better chance for survival which the under-privileged seem to enjoy; biologically, too, as borne out by the disproportionate increase in population among the poorer classes. Notwithstanding Darwin and his ambiguous "survival of the fittest," the individual best adapted to his environment, hence, strongest, has not always the best chance for survival, even in the animal kingdom, because he is too highly specialized and in times of crisis is at a disadvantage as compared with the more adaptable, or rather, over-adaptable creature. Unless his "law" of the survival of the fittest is interpreted in reverse, that is, that the fittest is the one who survives, it is not only meaningless but misleading. Thus, anti-Semitism is not so much a racial hatred as it is a resentment of a certain type whose disadvantages turn out to be advantageous to the extent of providing a realistic basis of permanent survival, that is, real immortality.

Although the rôle of the Jew in human civilization epitomizes on a world-historic scale the psychological paradoxes of human nature and behavior, there is still another story of symbiotic assimilation much more profound in its basis and much more significant in its effect on human nature, because it does not concern the perpetuation of culture throughout the ages but the very core of life: the perpetuation of the human race as such. We are referring to the matter already discussed at length—the position of the woman in this man-made world, and her position as ascribed to her by man and accepted by her as an imposition from without. In this sense, woman's place in life and her psychology has often been compared to that of the Jew, inasmuch as she has been subjected throughout history to the treatment a slave is given, has been persecuted periodically as the scapegoat for all human evils (medieval witchcraft), in fact, was pictured as the "cause" of evil itself, a curse which the Jew took from her not only by becoming the scapegoat but by inventing the first psychology as an explanation of evil in the human being. This, incidentally, is another and in my opinion the deepest reason for the hatred of the Jew; for by pointing out the source of the evil in the human being himself—which he had to do in order to justify his punishment—he became a representative of the evil, indeed, he stood for evil itself.

This derogatory attitude towards the woman still echoes in Freud's conception of her whom he saw only as an "object" of masculine desire destined to satisfy man's sexual lust. His psychology of the woman as an emasculated male (castration-complex) bears witness to his egocentric conception of her as a no-man (wo-man), by which he merely followed traditional prejudice without arriving at a real psychology of the female. Only very late—in fact, towards the end of his psycho-therapeutic career—did he think it time to discover "female sexuality," that is, to separate the development of the little girl from that of the little boy. His reluctance to do so was only gradually overcome by theoretical disagreement with some of his followers, especially women, and can be understood from the fact that such an admission of difference would invalidate his fundamental conception, the Oedipus-complex. For only reluctantly, and for that matter purely theoretically, did Freud assign to his all-important father-figure the second place and acknowledge the predominant rôle of the mother for the girl's development, a shift of emphasis which I had initiated several years before.[1]

Freud's conception of the woman is not only derived from masculine psychology but more especially from the definite patriarchal attitude of Old Testament tradition. Scientifically, this means that even the man is not conceived of by him psychologically as the male—in spite of the overrating of the libidinal drive—but as the *father* or prospective father or prospective son; that is, in man's procreative rôle in the biological scheme of the species. Here, again,

[1] Especially in the *Trauma of Birth,* 1924, and *Genetic Psychology,* 1927.

we meet the Old Testament emphasis on procreation as the only means of immortality for a culturally frustrated people. His conception of the woman is not of an independent individual in her own right but as an instrument for man's procreative ideology. In this sense, woman's procreative nature was not accepted as such but put into the service of man's need for biological immortality, which he could achieve in no other way. Hence, the strict sexual tabus among the Jews, not prohibiting sex as such, in fact, rather encouraging it, but, contrary to the exogamic tabu of the primitives, condemning intercourse with women outside the Jewish clan. Consequently, incestuous relationships, which were made impossible among primitives, abound in the Old Testament; hence, Freud's realistic conception of the incest problem which was an ideological one in Antiquity and became a moral issue in modern times.

Thus, Freud's conception of the woman appears to be the outgrowth of the patriarchal attitude in the Old Testament, but with it he has fallen victim to the same confusion as did some of his forerunners in the psychology of the sexes, as for example, Schopenhauer, Nietzsche and Freud's contemporary Weininger, who drew a definite parallel between the psychology of the Jew and the woman. As little as there is a real psychology of the woman in the Freudian system, so one would seek there in vain for a psychology of the Jew, who after all must have a specific psychology different from the non-Jew. In an attempt to solve this paradoxical phenomenon, I have come to the conclusion that the specific Jewish psychology, expressed in Freudian doctrine as a general psychology, is projected in toto upon the woman, who therefore is depicted as enslaved, inferior, castrated, whereas in the psychology of the male the masculine qualities appear exaggerated to the point of caricature in a libidinal superman. Since woman, in the course of history, actually has suffered from the very beginning a fate similar to that of the Jew, namely, suppression, slavery, confinement and subsequent persecution, one might say that the psychology which the Jew took on as a result of his early fate was essentially a feminine one. What Freud attempted unconsciously in his ideology therefore was the projection of those feminine characteristics of the Jew upon the woman, thereby achieving a kind of therapeutic self-healing for the Jewish race.

This gigantic projection of the Jew's inferiority complex on the woman in order to save the crumbling ideology of the strong Old Testament father-ideal was naturally bound to fail. The first and immediate reaction came from Adler who threw the inferiority right back to the man where it belongs, but at the same time fell short of seeing the woman's striving for a personality and psychology of her own other than in terms of a "masculine protest" against her feminine rôle. Woman is at least biologically superior to the male, and could only be conceived of as "castrated" from a masculine inferiority which is rooted in man's fear of woman. This aspect of the sexual psychology was emphasized by Jung, who, at the same time, sensed in Freud's theories a racial psychology which only led him to offset it by another racial psychology of his own.

The cultural implications of this psychological confusion and diffusion are manifold and important. Parallel to the projection of masculine inferiority onto the woman runs Freud's interpretation of creative expression as "neurotic," as seen from the point of view of the frustrated type, who is either deprived of expression or has to deny it in himself. This interpretive criss-crossing leads to a general leveling of all human psychology to the common denominator of a neurotic world-view, according to which almost every manifestation of human thought and behavior has been labeled "pathological" or "abnormal," except the psychology itself which is claimed as an unfailing standard. This standard is easily recognized as the rational self, in its most subtle guise, as the own ego's self-revelation for the purpose of controlling the irrational self. Thus, in psychological terminology, the consciously controlled self from his rational point of view labels all irrational manifestations as "neurotic." Hence, the term has been used, or rather, misused, in our present day as a convenient label by which to designate everything with which we do not agree, or of which we disapprove. In this sense, rationalistic psychology was only an outgrowth of the mentality of our age which is, or rather, was up to recently so highly rationalized that the irrational had only the neurotic form of expression. But to attempt to cure this result of rationalism by more rationality is just as contradictory as a war to end wars, or an effort to strengthen a weakening democracy by more democracy.

The only remedy is an acceptance of the fundamental irrationality of the human being and life in general, an acceptance which means not merely a recognition or even admittance of our basic "primitivity," in the sophisticated vein oi our typical intellectuals, but a real allowance for its dynamic functioning in human behavior, which would not be lifelike without it. When such a constructive and dynamic expression of the irrational together with the rational life is not permitted, it breaks through in violent distortions which manifest themselves individually as neurosis and culturally as various forms of revolutionary movements which succeed *because* they are irrational and not in spite of it.

Even if a more harmonious medium is struck temporarily by any given civilization, it seems to challenge the irrational by introducing a foreign element into its dynamic functioning. Thus I understand the need for a complementary psychology as we find it operating on every plane of life:

from the individual conception of the Double, manifested in what we termed "twin-relationship" to the acceptance of the exceptional psychology of the deviate by the masses, to the world-wide process of the diffusion of cultures in which one civilization reacts necessarily upon the other. The ego needs the Thou in order to become a Self, be it on the individual plane of human relationship or on the social plane of a foreign group-ideology, or on the broadest basis of one civilization needing another one for its development and maintenance. The tragic element in this process is that the ego needs a Thou to build up an assertive self with and against this Thou.

Just as in individual therapy this complementary Thou is only partly assimilated, while partly reciprocated, so all inspirational ideologies as well as cultural diffusions are in the last analysis therapeutic, that is, serve the purposes of strengthening a self—be it personal, social or national —by borrowed support from the opposite type, whether directly as borrowed strength or indirectly as strengthening the assertive forces by stimulating them antagonistically. In this sense, we do not have to carry the personality build-up beyond the psychology of the individual by showing the real stuff it is made of because we find it to be by its very nature beyond the individual. The psychology of the Self is to be found in the Other, be that Other the individual Thou, or the inspirational ideology of the leader, or the symbiotic diffusion of another civilization. Inasmuch as this symbiotic twinship operates as mutually complementary it is therapeutic, that is, strengthening, although at best on borrowed strength which can last only temporarily. But inasmuch as the two opposing personalities or ideologies or civilizations assert their difference, it is bound to produce violent reactions of a revolutionary nature in personal relationships and of social crises on a bigger scale, which are then condemned as neurotic by the rational self. Granted an acceptance of the fundamental irrationality of the human being and life in general with allowance for its dynamic functioning in human behaviour, we have the basis for the emergence of everything of which mankind is capable in personal and social capacity for betterment.

A CATALOG OF SELECTED

DOVER BOOKS

IN ALL FIELDS OF INTEREST

STICKLEY CRAFTSMAN FURNITURE CATALOGS, Gustav Stickley and L. & J. G. Stickley. Beautiful, functional furniture in two authentic catalogs from 1910. 594 illustrations, including 277 photos, show settles, rockers, armchairs, reclining chairs, bookcases, desks, tables. 183pp. 6½ × 9¼. 23838-5 Pa. $8.95

AMERICAN LOCOMOTIVES IN HISTORIC PHOTOGRAPHS: 1858 to 1949, Ron Ziel (ed.). A rare collection of 126 meticulously detailed official photographs, called "builder portraits," of American locomotives that majestically chronicle the rise of steam locomotive power in America. Introduction. Detailed captions. xi + 129pp. 9 × 12. 27393-8 Pa. $12.95

AMERICA'S LIGHTHOUSES: An Illustrated History, Francis Ross Holland, Jr. Delightfully written, profusely illustrated fact-filled survey of over 200 American lighthouses since 1716. History, anecdotes, technological advances, more. 240pp. 8 × 10¾. 25576-X Pa. $11.95

TOWARDS A NEW ARCHITECTURE, Le Corbusier. Pioneering manifesto by founder of "International School." Technical and aesthetic theories, views of industry, economics, relation of form to function, "mass-production split" and much more. Profusely illustrated. 320pp. 6⅛ × 9¼. (USO) 25023-7 Pa. $8.95

HOW THE OTHER HALF LIVES, Jacob Riis. Famous journalistic record, exposing poverty and degradation of New York slums around 1900, by major social reformer. 100 striking and influential photographs. 233pp. 10 × 7⅞.
22012-5 Pa $10.95

FRUIT KEY AND TWIG KEY TO TREES AND SHRUBS, William M. Harlow. One of the handiest and most widely used identification aids. Fruit key covers 120 deciduous and evergreen species; twig key 160 deciduous species. Easily used. Over 300 photographs. 126pp. 5⅜ × 8½. 20511-8 Pa. $3.95

COMMON BIRD SONGS, Dr. Donald J. Borror. Songs of 60 most common U.S. birds: robins, sparrows, cardinals, bluejays, finches, more—arranged in order of increasing complexity. Up to 9 variations of songs of each species.
Cassette and manual 99911-4 $8.95

ORCHIDS AS HOUSE PLANTS, Rebecca Tyson Northen. Grow cattleyas and many other kinds of orchids—in a window, in a case, or under artificial light. 63 illustrations. 148pp. 5⅜ × 8½. 23261-1 Pa. $3.95

MONSTER MAZES, Dave Phillips. Masterful mazes at four levels of difficulty. Avoid deadly perils and evil creatures to find magical treasures. Solutions for all 32 exciting illustrated puzzles. 48pp. 8¼ × 11. 26005-4 Pa. $2.95

MOZART'S DON GIOVANNI (DOVER OPERA LIBRETTO SERIES), Wolfgang Amadeus Mozart. Introduced and translated by Ellen H. Bleiler. Standard Italian libretto, with complete English translation. Convenient and thoroughly portable—an ideal companion for reading along with a recording or the performance itself. Introduction. List of characters. Plot summary. 121pp. 5¼ × 8½.
24944-1 Pa. $2.95

TECHNICAL MANUAL AND DICTIONARY OF CLASSICAL BALLET, Gail Grant. Defines, explains, comments on steps, movements, poses and concepts. 15-page pictorial section. Basic book for student, viewer. 127pp. 5⅜ × 8½.
21843-0 Pa. $3.95

BRASS INSTRUMENTS: Their History and Development, Anthony Baines. Authoritative, updated survey of the evolution of trumpets, trombones, bugles, cornets, French horns, tubas and other brass wind instruments. Over 140 illustrations and 48 music examples. Corrected and updated by author. New preface. Bibliography. 320pp. 5⅜ × 8½. 27574-4 Pa. $9.95

HOLLYWOOD GLAMOR PORTRAITS, John Kobal (ed.). 145 photos from 1926–49. Harlow, Gable, Bogart, Bacall; 94 stars in all. Full background on photographers, technical aspects. 160pp. 8⅜ × 11¼. 23352-9 Pa. $9.95

MAX AND MORITZ, Wilhelm Busch. Great humor classic in both German and English. Also 10 other works: "Cat and Mouse," "Plisch and Plumm," etc. 216pp. 5⅜ × 8½. 20181-3 Pa. $5.95

THE RAVEN AND OTHER FAVORITE POEMS, Edgar Allan Poe. Over 40 of the author's most memorable poems: "The Bells," "Ulalume," "Israfel," "To Helen," "The Conqueror Worm," "Eldorado," "Annabel Lee," many more. Alphabetic lists of titles and first lines. 64pp. 5³⁄₁₆ × 8¼. 26685-0 Pa. $1.00

SEVEN SCIENCE FICTION NOVELS, H. G. Wells. The standard collection of the great novels. Complete, unabridged. First Men in the Moon, Island of Dr. Moreau, War of the Worlds, Food of the Gods, Invisible Man, Time Machine, In the Days of the Comet. Total of 1,015pp. 5⅜ × 8½. (USO) 20264-X Clothbd. $29.95

AMULETS AND SUPERSTITIONS, E. A. Wallis Budge. Comprehensive discourse on origin, powers of amulets in many ancient cultures: Arab, Persian, Babylonian, Assyrian, Egyptian, Gnostic, Hebrew, Phoenician, Syriac, etc. Covers cross, swastika, crucifix, seals, rings, stones, etc. 584pp. 5⅜ × 8½. 23573-4 Pa. $12.95

RUSSIAN STORIES/PYCCKNE PACCKA3bl: A Dual-Language Book, edited by Gleb Struve. Twelve tales by such masters as Chekhov, Tolstoy, Dostoevsky, Pushkin, others. Excellent word-for-word English translations on facing pages, plus teaching and study aids, Russian/English vocabulary, biographical/critical introductions, more. 416pp. 5⅜ × 8½. 26244-8 Pa. $8.95

PHILADELPHIA THEN AND NOW: 60 Sites Photographed in the Past and Present, Kenneth Finkel and Susan Oyama. Rare photographs of City Hall, Logan Square, Independence Hall, Betsy Ross House, other landmarks juxtaposed with contemporary views. Captures changing face of historic city. Introduction. Captions. 128pp. 8¼ × 11. 25790-8 Pa. $9.95

AIA ARCHITECTURAL GUIDE TO NASSAU AND SUFFOLK COUNTIES, LONG ISLAND, The American Institute of Architects, Long Island Chapter, and the Society for the Preservation of Long Island Antiquities. Comprehensive, well-researched and generously illustrated volume brings to life over three centuries of Long Island's great architectural heritage. More than 240 photographs with authoritative, extensively detailed captions. 176pp. 8¼ × 11. 26946-9 Pa. $14.95

NORTH AMERICAN INDIAN LIFE: Customs and Traditions of 23 Tribes, Elsie Clews Parsons (ed.). 27 fictionalized essays by noted anthropologists examine religion, customs, government, additional facets of life among the Winnebago, Crow, Zuni, Eskimo, other tribes. 480pp. 6⅛ × 9¼. 27377-6 Pa. $10.95

FRANK LLOYD WRIGHT'S HOLLYHOCK HOUSE, Donald Hoffmann. Lavishly illustrated, carefully documented study of one of Wright's most controversial residential designs. Over 120 photographs, floor plans, elevations, etc. Detailed perceptive text by noted Wright scholar. Index. 128pp. 9¼ × 10¾.
27133-1 Pa. $11.95

THE MALE AND FEMALE FIGURE IN MOTION: 60 Classic Photographic Sequences, Eadweard Muybridge. 60 true-action photographs of men and women walking, running, climbing, bending, turning, etc., reproduced from rare 19th-century masterpiece. vi + 121pp. 9 × 12. 24745-7 Pa. $10.95

1001 QUESTIONS ANSWERED ABOUT THE SEASHORE, N. J. Berrill and Jacquelyn Berrill. Queries answered about dolphins, sea snails, sponges, starfish, fishes, shore birds, many others. Covers appearance, breeding, growth, feeding, much more. 305pp. 5¼ × 8¼. 23366-9 Pa. $7.95

GUIDE TO OWL WATCHING IN NORTH AMERICA, Donald S. Heintzelman. Superb guide offers complete data and descriptions of 19 species: barn owl, screech owl, snowy owl, many more. Expert coverage of owl-watching equipment, conservation, migrations and invasions, etc. Guide to observing sites. 84 illustrations. xiii + 193pp. 5⅜ × 8½. 27344-X Pa. $7.95

MEDICINAL AND OTHER USES OF NORTH AMERICAN PLANTS: A Historical Survey with Special Reference to the Eastern Indian Tribes, Charlotte Erichsen-Brown. Chronological historical citations document 500 years of usage of plants, trees, shrubs native to eastern Canada, northeastern U.S. Also complete identifying information. 343 illustrations. 544pp. 6½ × 9¼. 25951-X Pa. $12.95

STORYBOOK MAZES, Dave Phillips. 23 stories and mazes on two-page spreads: Wizard of Oz, Treasure Island, Robin Hood, etc. Solutions. 64pp. 8¼ × 11.
23628-5 Pa. $2.95

NEGRO FOLK MUSIC, U.S.A., Harold Courlander. Noted folklorist's scholarly yet readable analysis of rich and varied musical tradition. Includes authentic versions of over 40 folk songs. Valuable bibliography and discography. xi + 324pp. 5⅜ × 8½. 27350-4 Pa. $7.95

MOVIE-STAR PORTRAITS OF THE FORTIES, John Kobal (ed.). 163 glamor, studio photos of 106 stars of the 1940s: Rita Hayworth, Ava Gardner, Marlon Brando, Clark Gable, many more. 176pp. 8⅜ × 11¼. 23546-7 Pa. $10.95

BENCHLEY LOST AND FOUND, Robert Benchley. Finest humor from early 30s, about pet peeves, child psychologists, post office and others. Mostly unavailable elsewhere. 73 illustrations by Peter Arno and others. 183pp. 5⅜ × 8½.
22410-4 Pa. $5.95

YEKL and THE IMPORTED BRIDEGROOM AND OTHER STORIES OF YIDDISH NEW YORK, Abraham Cahan. Film Hester Street based on Yekl (1896). Novel, other stories among first about Jewish immigrants on N.Y.'s East Side. 240pp. 5⅜ × 8½. 22427-9 Pa. $5.95

SELECTED POEMS, Walt Whitman. Generous sampling from *Leaves of Grass*. Twenty-four poems include "I Hear America Singing," "Song of the Open Road," "I Sing the Body Electric," "When Lilacs Last in the Dooryard Bloom'd," "O Captain! My Captain!"—all reprinted from an authoritative edition. Lists of titles and first lines. 128pp. 5³⁄₁₆ × 8¼. 26878-0 Pa. $1.00

THE BEST TALES OF HOFFMANN, E. T. A. Hoffmann. 10 of Hoffmann's most important stories: "Nutcracker and the King of Mice," "The Golden Flowerpot," etc. 458pp. 5⅜ × 8½. 21793-0 Pa. $8.95

FROM FETISH TO GOD IN ANCIENT EGYPT, E. A. Wallis Budge. Rich detailed survey of Egyptian conception of "God" and gods, magic, cult of animals, Osiris, more. Also, superb English translations of hymns and legends. 240 illustrations. 545pp. 5⅜ × 8½. 25803-3 Pa. $11.95

FRENCH STORIES/CONTES FRANÇAIS: A Dual-Language Book, Wallace Fowlie. Ten stories by French masters, Voltaire to Camus: "Micromegas" by Voltaire; "The Atheist's Mass" by Balzac; "Minuet" by de Maupassant; "The Guest" by Camus, six more. Excellent English translations on facing pages. Also French-English vocabulary list, exercises, more. 352pp. 5⅜ × 8½. 26443-2 Pa. $8.95

CHICAGO AT THE TURN OF THE CENTURY IN PHOTOGRAPHS: 122 Historic Views from the Collections of the Chicago Historical Society, Larry A. Viskochil. Rare large-format prints offer detailed views of City Hall, State Street, the Loop, Hull House, Union Station, many other landmarks, circa 1904–1913. Introduction. Captions. Maps. 144pp. 9⅜ × 12¼. 24656-6 Pa. $12.95

OLD BROOKLYN IN EARLY PHOTOGRAPHS, 1865–1929, William Lee Younger. Luna Park, Gravesend race track, construction of Grand Army Plaza, moving of Hotel Brighton, etc. 157 previously unpublished photographs. 165pp. 8⅞ × 11¾. 23587-4 Pa. $12.95

THE MYTHS OF THE NORTH AMERICAN INDIANS, Lewis Spence. Rich anthology of the myths and legends of the Algonquins, Iroquois, Pawnees and Sioux, prefaced by an extensive historical and ethnological commentary. 36 illustrations. 480pp. 5⅜ × 8½. 25967-6 Pa. $8.95

AN ENCYCLOPEDIA OF BATTLES: Accounts of Over 1,560 Battles from 1479 B.C. to the Present, David Eggenberger. Essential details of every major battle in recorded history from the first battle of Megiddo in 1479 B.C. to Grenada in 1984. List of Battle Maps. New Appendix covering the years 1967–1984. Index. 99 illustrations. 544pp. 6½ × 9¼. 24913-1 Pa. $14.95

SAILING ALONE AROUND THE WORLD, Captain Joshua Slocum. First man to sail around the world, alone, in small boat. One of great feats of seamanship told in delightful manner. 67 illustrations. 294pp. 5⅜ × 8½. 20326-3 Pa. $5.95

ANARCHISM AND OTHER ESSAYS, Emma Goldman. Powerful, penetrating, prophetic essays on direct action, role of minorities, prison reform, puritan hypocrisy, violence, etc. 271pp. 5⅜ × 8½. 22484-8 Pa. $5.95

MYTHS OF THE HINDUS AND BUDDHISTS, Ananda K. Coomaraswamy and Sister Nivedita. Great stories of the epics; deeds of Krishna, Shiva, taken from puranas, Vedas, folk tales; etc. 32 illustrations. 400pp. 5⅜ × 8½. 21759-0 Pa. $9.95

BEYOND PSYCHOLOGY, Otto Rank. Fear of death, desire of immortality, nature of sexuality, social organization, creativity, according to Rankian system. 291pp. 5⅜ × 8½. 20485-5 Pa. $7.95

A THEOLOGICO-POLITICAL TREATISE, Benedict Spinoza. Also contains unfinished Political Treatise. Great classic on religious liberty, theory of government on common consent. R. Elwes translation. Total of 421pp. 5⅜ × 8½. 20249-6 Pa. $7.95

MY BONDAGE AND MY FREEDOM, Frederick Douglass. Born a slave, Douglass became outspoken force in antislavery movement. The best of Douglass' autobiographies. Graphic description of slave life. 464pp. 5⅜ × 8½. 22457-0 Pa. $8.95

FOLLOWING THE EQUATOR: A Journey Around the World, Mark Twain. Fascinating humorous account of 1897 voyage to Hawaii, Australia, India, New Zealand, etc. Ironic, bemused reports on peoples, customs, climate, flora and fauna, politics, much more. 197 illustrations. 720pp. 5⅜ × 8½. 26113-1 Pa. $15.95

THE PEOPLE CALLED SHAKERS, Edward D. Andrews. Definitive study of Shakers: origins, beliefs, practices, dances, social organization, furniture and crafts, etc. 33 illustrations. 351pp. 5⅜ × 8½. 21081-2 Pa. $7.95

THE MYTHS OF GREECE AND ROME, H. A. Guerber. A classic of mythology, generously illustrated, long prized for its simple, graphic, accurate retelling of the principal myths of Greece and Rome, and for its commentary on their origins and significance. With 64 illustrations by Michelangelo, Raphael, Titian, Rubens, Canova, Bernini and others. 480pp. 5⅜ × 8½. 27584-1 Pa. $9.95

PSYCHOLOGY OF MUSIC, Carl E. Seashore. Classic work discusses music as a medium from psychological viewpoint. Clear treatment of physical acoustics, auditory apparatus, sound perception, development of musical skills, nature of musical feeling, host of other topics. 88 figures. 408pp. 5⅜ × 8½. 21851-1 Pa. $9.95

THE PHILOSOPHY OF HISTORY, Georg W. Hegel. Great classic of Western thought develops concept that history is not chance but rational process, the evolution of freedom. 457pp. 5⅜ × 8½. 20112-0 Pa. $8.95

THE BOOK OF TEA, Kakuzo Okakura. Minor classic of the Orient: entertaining, charming explanation, interpretation of traditional Japanese culture in terms of tea ceremony. 94pp. 5⅜ × 8½. 20070-1 Pa. $2.95

LIFE IN ANCIENT EGYPT, Adolf Erman. Fullest, most thorough, detailed older account with much not in more recent books, domestic life, religion, magic, medicine, commerce, much more. Many illustrations reproduce tomb paintings, carvings, hieroglyphs, etc. 597pp. 5⅜ × 8½. 22632-8 Pa. $9.95

SUNDIALS, Their Theory and Construction, Albert Waugh. Far and away the best, most thorough coverage of ideas, mathematics concerned, types, construction, adjusting anywhere. Simple, nontechnical treatment allows even children to build several of these dials. Over 100 illustrations. 230pp. 5⅜ × 8½. 22947-5 Pa. $5.95

DYNAMICS OF FLUIDS IN POROUS MEDIA, Jacob Bear. For advanced students of ground water hydrology, soil mechanics and physics, drainage and irrigation engineering, and more. 335 illustrations. Exercises, with answers. 784pp. 6⅛ × 9¼. 65675-6 Pa. $19.95

SONGS OF EXPERIENCE: Facsimile Reproduction with 26 Plates in Full Color, William Blake. 26 full-color plates from a rare 1826 edition. Includes "The Tyger," "London," "Holy Thursday," and other poems. Printed text of poems. 48pp. 5¼ × 7. 24636-1 Pa. $3.95

OLD-TIME VIGNETTES IN FULL COLOR, Carol Belanger Grafton (ed.). Over 390 charming, often sentimental illustrations, selected from archives of Victorian graphics—pretty women posing, children playing, food, flowers, kittens and puppies, smiling cherubs, birds and butterflies, much more. All copyright-free. 48pp. 9¼ × 12¼. 27269-9 Pa. $5.95

PERSPECTIVE FOR ARTISTS, Rex Vicat Cole. Depth, perspective of sky and sea, shadows, much more, not usually covered. 391 diagrams, 81 reproductions of drawings and paintings. 279pp. 5⅜ × 8½. 22487-2 Pa. $6.95

DRAWING THE LIVING FIGURE, Joseph Sheppard. Innovative approach to artistic anatomy focuses on specifics of surface anatomy, rather than muscles and bones. Over 170 drawings of live models in front, back and side views, and in widely varying poses. Accompanying diagrams. 177 illustrations. Introduction. Index. 144pp. 8⅜ × 11¼. 26723-7 Pa. $7.95

GOTHIC AND OLD ENGLISH ALPHABETS: 100 Complete Fonts, Dan X. Solo. Add power, elegance to posters, signs, other graphics with 100 stunning copyright-free alphabets: Blackstone, Dolbey, Germania, 97 more—including many lower-case, numerals, punctuation marks. 104pp. 8⅛ × 11. 24695-7 Pa. $7.95

HOW TO DO BEADWORK, Mary White. Fundamental book on craft from simple projects to five-bead chains and woven works. 106 illustrations. 142pp. 5⅜ × 8. 20697-1 Pa. $4.95

THE BOOK OF WOOD CARVING, Charles Marshall Sayers. Finest book for beginners discusses fundamentals and offers 34 designs. "Absolutely first rate . . . well thought out and well executed."—E. J. Tangerman. 118pp. 7¾ × 10⅝. 23654-4 Pa. $5.95

ILLUSTRATED CATALOG OF CIVIL WAR MILITARY GOODS: Union Army Weapons, Insignia, Uniform Accessories, and Other Equipment, Schuyler, Hartley, and Graham. Rare, profusely illustrated 1846 catalog includes Union Army uniform and dress regulations, arms and ammunition, coats, insignia, flags, swords, rifles, etc. 226 illustrations. 160pp. 9 × 12. 24939-5 Pa. $10.95

WOMEN'S FASHIONS OF THE EARLY 1900s: An Unabridged Republication of "New York Fashions, 1909," National Cloak & Suit Co. Rare catalog of mail-order fashions documents women's and children's clothing styles shortly after the turn of the century. Captions offer full descriptions, prices. Invaluable resource for fashion, costume historians. Approximately 725 illustrations. 128pp. 8⅜ × 11¼. 27276-1 Pa. $10.95

THE 1912 AND 1915 GUSTAV STICKLEY FURNITURE CATALOGS, Gustav Stickley. With over 200 detailed illustrations and descriptions, these two catalogs are essential reading and reference materials and identification guides for Stickley furniture. Captions cite materials, dimensions and prices. 112pp. 6½ × 9¼. 26676-1 Pa. $9.95

EARLY AMERICAN LOCOMOTIVES, John H. White, Jr. Finest locomotive engravings from early 19th century: historical (1804–74), main-line (after 1870), special, foreign, etc. 147 plates. 142pp. 11⅜ × 8¼. 22772-3 Pa. $8.95

THE TALL SHIPS OF TODAY IN PHOTOGRAPHS, Frank O. Braynard. Lavishly illustrated tribute to nearly 100 majestic contemporary sailing vessels: Amerigo Vespucci, Clearwater, Constitution, Eagle, Mayflower, Sea Cloud, Victory, many more. Authoritative captions provide statistics, background on each ship. 190 black-and-white photographs and illustrations. Introduction. 128pp. 8⅞ × 11¾. 27163-3 Pa. $12.95

EARLY NINETEENTH-CENTURY CRAFTS AND TRADES, Peter Stockham (ed.). Extremely rare 1807 volume describes to youngsters the crafts and trades of the day: brickmaker, weaver, dressmaker, bookbinder, ropemaker, saddler, many more. Quaint prose, charming illustrations for each craft. 20 black-and-white line illustrations. 192pp. 4⅜ × 6. 27293-1 Pa. $4.95

VICTORIAN FASHIONS AND COSTUMES FROM HARPER'S BAZAR, 1867–1898, Stella Blum (ed.). Day costumes, evening wear, sports clothes, shoes, hats, other accessories in over 1,000 detailed engravings. 320pp. 9⅜ × 12¼. 22990-4 Pa. $13.95

GUSTAV STICKLEY, THE CRAFTSMAN, Mary Ann Smith. Superb study surveys broad scope of Stickley's achievement, especially in architecture. Design philosophy, rise and fall of the Craftsman empire, descriptions and floor plans for many Craftsman houses, more. 86 black-and-white halftones. 31 line illustrations. Introduction. 208pp. 6½ × 9¼. 27210-9 Pa. $9.95

THE LONG ISLAND RAIL ROAD IN EARLY PHOTOGRAPHS, Ron Ziel. Over 220 rare photos, informative text document origin (1844) and development of rail service on Long Island. Vintage views of early trains, locomotives, stations, passengers, crews, much more. Captions. 8⅞ × 11¾. 26301-0 Pa. $13.95

THE BOOK OF OLD SHIPS: From Egyptian Galleys to Clipper Ships, Henry B. Culver. Superb, authoritative history of sailing vessels, with 80 magnificent line illustrations. Galley, bark, caravel, longship, whaler, many more. Detailed, informative text on each vessel by noted naval historian. Introduction. 256pp. 5⅜ × 8½. 27332-6 Pa. $6.95

TEN BOOKS ON ARCHITECTURE, Vitruvius. The most important book ever written on architecture. Early Roman aesthetics, technology, classical orders, site selection, all other aspects. Morgan translation. 331pp. 5⅜ × 8½. 20645-9 Pa. $8.95

THE HUMAN FIGURE IN MOTION, Eadweard Muybridge. More than 4,500 stopped-action photos, in action series, showing undraped men, women, children jumping, lying down, throwing, sitting, wrestling, carrying, etc. 390pp. 7⅞ × 10⅝. 20204-6 Clothbd. $24.95

TREES OF THE EASTERN AND CENTRAL UNITED STATES AND CANADA, William M. Harlow. Best one-volume guide to 140 trees. Full descriptions, woodlore, range, etc. Over 600 illustrations. Handy size. 288pp. 4½ × 6⅜. 20395-6 Pa. $5.95

SONGS OF WESTERN BIRDS, Dr. Donald J. Borror. Complete song and call repertoire of 60 western species, including flycatchers, juncoes, cactus wrens, many more—includes fully illustrated booklet. Cassette and manual 99913-0 $8.95

GROWING AND USING HERBS AND SPICES, Milo Miloradovich. Versatile handbook provides all the information needed for cultivation and use of all the herbs and spices available in North America. 4 illustrations. Index. Glossary. 236pp. 5⅜ × 8½. 25058-X Pa. $5.95

BIG BOOK OF MAZES AND LABYRINTHS, Walter Shepherd. 50 mazes and labyrinths in all—classical, solid, ripple, and more—in one great volume. Perfect inexpensive puzzler for clever youngsters. Full solutions. 112pp. 8⅛ × 11. 22951-3 Pa. $3.95

PIANO TUNING, J. Cree Fischer. Clearest, best book for beginner, amateur. Simple repairs, raising dropped notes, tuning by easy method of flattened fifths. No previous skills needed. 4 illustrations. 201pp. 5⅜ × 8½. 23267-0 Pa. $5.95

A SOURCE BOOK IN THEATRICAL HISTORY, A. M. Nagler. Contemporary observers on acting, directing, make-up, costuming, stage props, machinery, scene design, from Ancient Greece to Chekhov. 611pp. 5⅜ × 8½. 20515-0 Pa. $11.95

THE COMPLETE NONSENSE OF EDWARD LEAR, Edward Lear. All nonsense limericks, zany alphabets, Owl and Pussycat, songs, nonsense botany, etc., illustrated by Lear. Total of 320pp. 5⅜ × 8½. (USO) 20167-8 Pa. $5.95

VICTORIAN PARLOUR POETRY: An Annotated Anthology, Michael R. Turner. 117 gems by Longfellow, Tennyson, Browning, many lesser-known poets. "The Village Blacksmith," "Curfew Must Not Ring Tonight," "Only a Baby Small," dozens more, often difficult to find elsewhere. Index of poets, titles, first lines. xxiii + 325pp. 5⅜ × 8¼. 27044-0 Pa. $8.95

DUBLINERS, James Joyce. Fifteen stories offer vivid, tightly focused observations of the lives of Dublin's poorer classes. At least one, "The Dead," is considered a masterpiece. Reprinted complete and unabridged from standard edition. 160pp. 5³⁄₁₆ × 8¼. 26870-5 Pa. $1.00

THE HAUNTED MONASTERY and THE CHINESE MAZE MURDERS, Robert van Gulik. Two full novels by van Gulik, set in 7th-century China, continue adventures of Judge Dee and his companions. An evil Taoist monastery, seemingly supernatural events; overgrown topiary maze hides strange crimes. 27 illustrations. 328pp. 5⅜ × 8½. 23502-5 Pa. $7.95

THE BOOK OF THE SACRED MAGIC OF ABRAMELIN THE MAGE, translated by S. MacGregor Mathers. Medieval manuscript of ceremonial magic. Basic document in Aleister Crowley, Golden Dawn groups. 268pp. 5⅜ × 8½. 23211-5 Pa. $7.95

NEW RUSSIAN-ENGLISH AND ENGLISH-RUSSIAN DICTIONARY, M. A. O'Brien. This is a remarkably handy Russian dictionary, containing a surprising amount of information, including over 70,000 entries. 366pp. 4½ × 6⅛. 20208-9 Pa. $8.95

HISTORIC HOMES OF THE AMERICAN PRESIDENTS, Second, Revised Edition, Irvin Haas. A traveler's guide to American Presidential homes, most open to the public, depicting and describing homes occupied by every American President from George Washington to George Bush. With visiting hours, admission charges, travel routes. 175 photographs. Index. 160pp. 8¼ × 11. 26751-2 Pa. $10.95

NEW YORK IN THE FORTIES, Andreas Feininger. 162 brilliant photographs by the well-known photographer, formerly with *Life* magazine. Commuters, shoppers, Times Square at night, much else from city at its peak. Captions by John von Hartz. 181pp. 9¼ × 10¾. 23585-8 Pa. $12.95

INDIAN SIGN LANGUAGE, William Tomkins. Over 525 signs developed by Sioux and other tribes. Written instructions and diagrams. Also 290 pictographs. 111pp. 6⅛ × 9¼. 22029-X Pa. $3.50